W9-BXN-157

EVALUATION IN EDUCATION

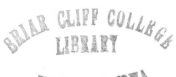
BRIAR CLIFF COLLEGE
LIBRARY
SIOUX CITY, IOWA

EVALUATION IN EDUCATION

Foundations of Competency Assessment and Program Review

RICHARD M. WOLF

PRAEGER PUBLISHERS
Praeger Special Studies

New York   •   London   •   Sydney   •   Toronto

Library of Congress Cataloging in Publication Data

Wolf, Richard M
  Evaluation in education.

  Includes bibliographies and index.
  1. Educational accountability. 2. Education--Aims
and objectives. 3. Educational research--Methodology.
I. Title.
LB2806.W7264   370'.1'8   78-25743
ISBN 0-03-049116-0

LB 2823

LB
2823
·W 64

PRAEGER PUBLISHERS, PRAEGER SPECIAL STUDIES
383 Madison Avenue, New York, N.Y., 10017, U.S.A.

Published in the United States of America in 1979
by Praeger Publishers,
A Division of Holt, Rinehart and Winston, CBS Inc.

9 038 987654321

© 1979 by Richard M. Wolf

All rights reserved

Printed in the United States of America

4493306

To
Marie

PREFACE

The field of educational evaluation is a relative newcomer to education. Before 1965 there was very little work done and correspondingly little thought in this field. The evaluation requirement in the Elementary and Secondary Education Act of 1965, coupled with accountability demands on educational institutions, has resulted in a great deal of evaluation activity. A large number of federally funded educational programs must be formally evaluated annually. The same is true for many state and local programs. While a great deal of activity goes on under the heading of evaluation, relatively few people are trained to do such work. There is also, alas, a widespread lack of agreement about what evaluation is and how evaluation studies should be conducted.

There have been some efforts to remedy this situation. A number of people have developed models for evaluation. Unfortunately, each model is somewhat different from the others, and confusion abounds. Some of the work is rather idiosyncratic and jargon-laden. A second effort to help evaluation workers has been the production of edited books. These contain either original papers or reprints of previously published material. Often there is no unified point of view in such works, and one paper sometimes contradicts another. The reader is generally not able to draw much guidance and direction from such works.

This book attempts to furnish evaluation workers with a comprehensive, coherent, and integrated view of educational evaluation. It is intended to be highly practical, yet based on sound theory. Accordingly, there is a fair amount of "how to" in the book, along with a theoretical base for such practice. A number of major ideas about educational evaluation that have proved their worth have been pulled together and incorporated into a comprehensive framework for evaluation. Chapter 2 presents the result of this effort and is one of the distinguishing features of the book. Chapter 1 contains general introductory material and, in addition, distinguishes evaluation from research and measurement.

Drafts of the entire book have been used with several groups of students and practitioners. It is my feeling that only as evaluation workers come to recognize the distinctive features of educational evaluation can the field fully develop and begin to realize its potential to contribute to the improvement of the educational enterprise. The eleven remaining chapters of the book seek to develop the basic ideas set forth in the first two chapters. There is liberal use of examples and an emphasis on adapting and using basic ideas in a variety of situations. My hope is that both students and practicing evaluation workers will find the approach offered here to be helpful.

It is impossible to acknowledge all the people who have contributed to my thinking about educational evaluation. Benjamin Bloom and Ralph Tyler were early and important influences on my thinking, and I am especially grateful to them. Emmy Hookham of UNESCO prevailed on me in 1973 to write a monograph on evaluation. This assignment caused me to begin to crystallize my thinking about evaluation and attempt to organize it in a coherent fashion. W.L. Renwick, Director of General Education for New Zealand, made it possible for me to spend a semester in New Zealand as a Fulbright Lecturer where I was able to develop, refine, and test out many of the ideas that appear here. During that time I had the opportunity to work with Dr. C.E. Beeby of New Zealand Council for Educational Research, whose influence on my thinking and this book will be most evident. Finally, I want to thank Prof. Neville Postlethwaite of Hamburg University and Dr. Margery Bernstein of the Mamaroneck, N.Y., Public Schools. They are members of my old guard who, on numerous occasions, have prodded me to clarify my thinking by their thoughtful reactions and wise counsel. In addition, they have both read the draft manuscript and furnished numerous suggestions. Any errors or misstatements that remain are solely my responsibility.

Richard M. Wolf
New York

CONTENTS

LIST OF TABLES AND FIGURES

EVALUATION IN EDUCATION

1

THE NATURE OF
EDUCATIONAL EVALUATION

INTRODUCTION

Any work that sets out to deal with a relatively new aspect of education is obliged to furnish the reader with a definition, description, and discussion of that aspect. This is particularly true of the burgeoning field of educational evaluation in which there is considerable confusion. This confusion stems partly from the fact that many of the techniques and procedures used in evaluating educational enterprises are rather technical, and educators are often not knowledgeable about such matters. A more basic reason for the confusion, however, is that different authors have different notions of what educational evaluation is or should be. These dissimilar views often stem from the training and background of the writers, the particular professional concerns with different aspects of the educational process, and even from specific subject-matter concerns. One result is that a reader unfamiliar with the field is all too often exposed to written works that not only differ but are even contradictory. Such writings are not just expressions of honest differences about what evaluation is about and how it should be carried out. They are reflections of a deeper confusion which attends the development of a relatively new field of inquiry.

One goal of this book is to reduce the confusion about what evaluation is and is not, how it should be organized and carried out, how the results of evaluation studies should be reported, and how they can be used. It is not the intention, however, to shield the reader from honest differences that exist within the field. These can and should be exposed and discussed. However, it is not considered necessary or even desirable to deal with a number of highly idiosyncratic viewpoints regarding educational evaluation. Rather, the emphasis here is on the presentation of a conceptualization of educational evaluation that attempts to be comprehensive, coherent, sensible, and practical. It combines features emphasized by a number of writers in the field but attempts to weld them into a unified view of educational evaluation. It sometimes sacrifices the private concerns of writers when it is felt that these interfere with basic ideas of evaluation. The critical reader can deal with the subtleties, complexities, and differences that exist at the frontiers of evaluation, once the basic ideas are learned.

TOWARD A DEFINITION OF EVALUATION

There are several definitions of educational evaluation. They differ in level of abstraction and often reflect the specific concerns of the person who formulated them. At the most general level, evaluation has been defined as "the assessment of merit" (Popham 1975). This definition, unfortunately, does not help very much since it is left to the reader to determine what is meant by the terms "assessment" and "merit." A somewhat more elaborate definition is provided by L. J. Cronbach who defines evaluation as "[the] collection and use of information to make decisions about an educational program" (Cronbach 1963). By "educational program" Cronbach means anything ranging from a set of instructional materials and activities, distributed on a national level, to the educational experiences of a single learner.* The context of Cronbach's remarks, however, is the curricula that were developed in the late fifties and early sixties, which were intended to upgrade quality of instruction and learning in various subject-matter areas. Cronbach's concern was with the tryout and modification of the new courses that emerged from various study groups and educational laboratories. It was his belief that only by extensive information-gathering activities in actual classroom situations would it be possible to determine where and how the programs were succeeding and failing, so that modifications could be made on as sound a basis as possible. Cronbach's article suggests various kinds of

---

*The term *learner* will be used throughout this book rather than *student*. The reason for this is that *learner* is a broader term and can encompass students, teachers, administrators, and even parents and community members; in short, any one that is the intended beneficiary of an educational treatment. The focus of evaluation is, in most cases, on educational programs intended for students, but the use of the broader term *learner* should alert the reader to wider areas in which evaluation can be carried out. While the focus of this book is clearly on education, the ideas presented are applicable to evaluation of programs in a variety of fields in the helping professions such as psychology, social work, etc. Readers interested in the evaluation of programs in fields other than education can benefit from an examination of the ideas presented here but will need to apply them to their own area of concern or consult one of the suggested additional readings supplied at the end of each chapter.

information that could be sought in an evaluation enterprise and how these could be analyzed and used in decision making for the purposes of course improvement. His article goes on to discuss a number of other issues in evaluation, some of which will be taken up later.

It is Cronbach's definition of evaluation which is of interest here. In it are two elements. The first—"the collection and use of information"—puts equal emphasis on collection and use of information. The idea is that decisions are to be made on the basis of information, not on impressions or beliefs about how an educational program is supposed to function. In his article, Cronbach clearly states the kind of information he has in mind. He is primarily interested in information relating to learner performance. Specifically, Cronbach wants to find out what changes a course or curriculum produces in learners; what kinds of questions learners can answer after having studied a particular subject for a period of time, what kinds of problems they can solve, what kinds of issues they can deal with. This kind of information, Cronbach asserts, should provide the basis for sound decision making. The second element of Cronbach's definition—"to make decisions"—denotes an action orientation. Evaluation, accordingly, should lead to action, as opposed to conclusions not acted on. While he does not say so specifically, evaluation activity that does not contribute to the decision-making process is a waste of time and money. Evaluation, Cronbach asserts, must contribute to the decision-making process, notably to course improvement, if it is to have any justification in education.

This definition of evaluation, emphasizing the collection and use of information about learner performance for purposes of making sound decisions about educational programs, is a distinct improvement on the "assessment of merit" definition; but it still does not go far enough in saying what evaluation is. A more extended definition, supplied by C. E. Beeby, describes evaluation as "the systematic collection and interpretation of evidence, leading, as part of the process, to a judgment of value with a view to action" (Beeby 1975). There are four key elements to this definition. First, the use of the term "systematic" implies that what information is needed will be defined with some degree of precision and that efforts to secure such information will be planful. This does not mean that only information which can be gathered through the use of standard tests and other related measures will be obtained. Information gathered by means of observational procedures, questionnaires, and other self-report measures can also contribute to an evaluation enterprise. The important qualification is that whatever kind of information is gathered, it should be acquired in a systematic way. This does not exclude, a priori, any kind of information.

The second element in Beeby's definition, "interpretation of evidence," introduces a critical consideration sometimes overlooked in evaluation. The mere collection of evidence does not by itself constitute evaluation work. Yet uninterpreted evidence is often presented to indicate the presence (or absence) of quality in an educational venture. High dropout rates, for example, are frequently cited as indications of the failure of voluntary educational programs. Doubtless, high dropout rates are indicators of failure in many cases, but not all. There may be very good reasons why people drop out of educational programs. Personal problems, acceptance into higher level educational programs, and landing a good job are reasons for dropping out which may in no way reflect on the program. In some cases, dropping out of an educational program may indicate that a program has been successful. For example, a few years ago, the director of a community college program training people for positions in the computer field observed that almost two-thirds of each entering class failed to complete the two-year program. On closer examination it was found that the great majority of "drop outs" had left the program at the end of the first year to take well paying jobs in the computer department of various companies (usually ones they had worked in while receiving their training). The personnel officers and supervisors of these companies felt that the one year of training was not only more than adequate for entry- and second-level positions but provided the foundation on which to acquire the additional specialized knowledge and skill required for further advancement. Under such circumstances, a two-thirds dropout rate before program completion was no indication of a program failure or deficiency. Clearly, information gathered in connection with the evaluation of an educational program must be interpreted with great care. If the evaluator cannot make such interpretations himself, he must enlist the aid of others who can; otherwise, his information can seriously mislead. In the above example, the problem of interpretation was rather simple. Dropout statistics are easily gathered, and one can have some confidence in the numbers. More complex situations arise when one uses various tests, scales, or observational and self-report devices such as questionnaires and opinionnaires. In these situations the interpretation of evaluative information can be extremely difficult. Unfortunately, the interpretation of information has too often been neglected. Specific mention of it in a definition is welcome since it focuses attention on this critical aspect of the evaluation process.

The third element of Beeby's definition—"judgment of value"—takes evaluation far beyond the level of mere description of what is happening in an educational enterprise. It casts the evaluation worker, or the group of persons responsible for conducting the evaluation, in a role that not only permits but requires that judgments about the worth of an educational endeavor be made. Evaluation not only involves gathering and interpreting information about how well an educational program is succeeding in reaching its goals, but judgments about the goals themselves. It involves questions about how well a program is helping to meet larger educational and social goals. Given Beeby's definition, an evaluation worker who does not make—or if, for political or other reasons, an openly harsh judgment is inexpedient, does not strongly imply—a judgment of value is not, in the full sense of the term, an evaluation worker. Whoever does make such a judgment, after the systematic groundwork has been laid, is completing an evaluation.

Lest the reader get the mistaken impression that the evaluation worker has some kind of special power in education, a distinction needs to be made between two kinds of judgment. The first is the judgment of value on the program, curriculum, or institution being evaluated. This is the type described above which is clearly within the scope of the evaluation worker's professional function. The second kind of judgment is taken in light of the first and, along with other relevant factors, is the decision on future policy and action. It is clearly in the domain of administrators, governing boards, and other policy makers. If these decision makers make both kinds of judgments, they are taking over an essential part of the professional evaluation function. This is to be avoided.

An illustration may be given. Several years ago this writer was involved in the evaluation of a program for disadvantaged junior high-school students that was held on Saturday mornings at a local school. Expectations with regard to student performance were more than fulfilled. There was a high degree of enthusiasm among students and teachers, parents were pleased that their children were constructively occupied. The program, while voluntary, was heavily and consistently attended. All in all, it was highly successful, and the evaluation report clearly communicated this. The most difficult task that one faced in preparing the evaluation report was suggesting ways in which the program could be improved.

Unfortunately, the program was terminated at the end of the year. The reason given was that the program was too expensive. Opening a public school on Saturday morning required additional outlays for heating and light, custodial salaries, as well as for an administrator, required for legal reasons. When these additional costs and, one suspects, inconveniences were taken into account, it was decided that the program (although highly successful) could no longer be justified. The situation, however, was one in which the evaluation workers fulfilled their professional function and the administrators fulfilled theirs. The fact that the decision about future policy was inconsistent with the judgment of the value of the program must be accepted as one of those unhappy situations in which extraneous factors had a determining influence on future action.

It is also possible—although somewhat less likely—that a decision will be made to retain a marginally effective program. It may be that the political or public-relations value of a program is deemed important enough to continue it despite low effectiveness. It is also possible that funds are available to operate a program of marginal quality which would not be available for other more worthwhile endeavors. It is the decision maker's job to determine whether to fund it or not. The point remains: the evaluation workers, or those charged with the evaluation of a program, will render a judgment of value; it is the responsibility of decision makers to decide on future policy and action. Each has their area of responsibility, and each must be respected within their domain. This point must be understood at the outset. If it is not, there is danger that evaluation workers may become frustrated or cynical when they learn that policy decisions have been made contrary to what results of their evaluation would suggest.

The last element of Beeby's definition—"with a view to action"— introduces the distinction between an undertaking that results in a judgment of value with no specific reference to action and one that is deliberately undertaken for the sake of future action. The same distinction is made by Cronbach and Suppes although the terms "conclusion-oriented" and "decision-oriented" are used (1969). Educational evaluation is clearly decision-oriented. It is intended to lead to better policies and practices in education. If this intention is in any way lacking, evaluation probably should be dispensed with. Evaluators can use their time to better advantage.

So far no mention has been made about what kinds of actions might be undertaken as the result of an evaluation study. The range is considerable. A conscious decision to make no changes at all could result from a carefully conducted evaluation study; or a decision to abolish a program altogether could be made. Between these extremes, modifications in content, organization and time allocation could occur, as well as decisions about additions, deletions, and revisions in instructional materials, learning activities, and criteria for staff selection. Such decisions come under the general heading of course improvement and are discussed in some detail by Cronbach (1963). M. Scriven uses the term "formative evaluation" to characterize many of these kinds of decisions (1967). In contrast, decisions about which of several alternative programs to select for adoption or whether to retain or eliminate a particular program are "summative" in nature, to use Scriven's terminology. Scriven's distinction between formative and summative evaluation has achieved a fair measure of popular acceptance. The basic point is that evaluation studies are undertaken with the intention that some action will take place as a result.

DIFFERENCES BETWEEN EVALUATION, MEASUREMENT, AND RESEARCH

Beeby's definition of evaluation goes some distance towards specifying what evaluation is. However, in order to function effectively, a definition must not only say what something is; it should also say what it is not. This is particularly important in regard to evaluation. Three activities that are related to evaluation are measurement, research, and learner appraisal. Evaluation shares some similarities with each. The differences, however, are considerable and need to be examined so that evaluation can be brought more sharply into focus.

Evaluation and Measurement

Measurement is the act or process of measuring. It is essentially an amoral process in that there is no value placed on what is being measured. Measurements of physical properties of objects such as length and mass do not imply that they have value; they are simply attributes of interest. Similarly, in the behavioral sciences, measurement of psychological characteristics such as knowledge, neuroticism, attitudes toward various phenomena, problem-solving, and mechanical reasoning does not in itself confer value on these characteristics.

In evaluation, quite the opposite is the case. The major attributes studied are chosen precisely because they represent educational values. Objectives are educational values. They define what we seek to develop in learners as a result of exposing them to a set of educational experiences. They can include achievements, attitudes toward what is learned, self-esteem, and a host of other prized outcomes. Such outcomes are not merely of interest; they are educational values. Thus, while evaluation and measurement specialists often engage in similar acts, such as systematically gathering information about learner performance, there is a fundamental difference between the two in the value that is placed on what is being measured.

A second important distinction between evaluation and measurement inheres in the object of attention of each. By tradition and history, measurement in education is undertaken for the purpose of making comparisons between individuals with regard to some characteristic. For example, two learners may be compared with regard to their reading comprehension. This is accomplished by administering the same reading comprehension test to the two learners and seeing how many questions each has answered correctly. Since they have been given the same test, a basis for comparison exists. This is the traditional measurement approach. In evaluation, on the other hand, it is often neither necessary nor even desirable to make such comparisons between individual learners. What is of interest is the effectiveness of a program. In such a situation, there is no requirement that the learners be presented with the same test. In fact, under some circumstances, it may be prudent to have them answer entirely different sets of questions. The resulting information can then be combined with that obtained from other learners and summarized in order to describe the performance for an entire group. Such a procedure introduces efficiencies into the process of information gathering and will be discussed in more detail later. The point to be made here is that evaluation and measurement are typically directed towards different ends: evaluation toward describing effects of *treatments*; measurement toward description and comparison of *individuals*. In evaluation, it is not necessary that different learners respond to the same questions or tasks.

Closely related to the notion of measurement is learner appraisal. Appraising the proficiencies of learners for purposes of diagnosis, classification, marking and grading is usually considered the prerogative of those charged with the instructional function; typically, teachers. The introduction of systematic evaluation procedures has been viewed in some cases as an intrusion on this traditional teacher function. Nothing could be further from the truth. Evaluation is directed toward judging the worth of a total program and, sometimes, for judging the effectiveness of a program for particular groups of learners. It is not an external testing program that is intended to supplant teacher responsibility for learner appraisal. In fact, it is—more often than not—simply not possible to do so. For example, if in the course of evaluating a program, it is decided to have different groups of learners answer different sets of questions, the resulting evaluative information will contribute absolutely nothing to the process of learner appraisal. Measurements of individual learner proficiencies will still have to be made to fulfill the appraisal function. Thus, teachers need not fear that systematic evaluation of educational programs will intrude on the appraisal role of their professional teaching function. Quite the opposite may occur. (Teachers wishing to use evaluative information to assist them in appraising learner performance may find themselves frustrated when they learn that evaluative information does not help them in this regard).

Evaluation and Research

Evaluation and research share a number of common characteristics. There are some notable differences, however. Research, typically, aims at producing new knowledge which may have no specific reference to any practical decision, while evaluation is deliberately undertaken as a guide to action. This distinction is highlighted in the last phrase of Beeby's definition of evaluation—"with a view to action." Any distinction based on motivation is obviously fragile, and one operation can shade into another; but in practice there is usually a marked difference in content, presentation, and often method between research, inspired by scholarly interest or an academic requirement, and an investigation undertaken with a definite practical problem in mind. To be sure, scholarly research has often led to highly practical payoffs—the work of atomic physicists in the 1930's is a dramatic case in point. A basic difference in motivation, however, remains.

A more basic distinction between evaluation and research lies in the *generalizability* of results that each type of activity produces. Research is concerned with the production of knowledge that is as generalizable as possible. For example, a research worker may undertake an investigetion to determine the relationship between student aspiration and achievement. The study will be designed and carried out in such a way as to insure results that are as generalizable as possible. They will obtain over a wide geographic area, apply to a broad range of ages, and be as true in several years as now. Generalizability of results is critical in research. Little or no interest may attach to knowledge that is specific to a particular sample of individuals, in a single location, studied at a particular point in time. In fact, if a researcher's results can not be duplicated elsewhere, they are apt to be dismissed. In their now famous chapter on designs for research in teaching, D. T. Campbell and J. Stanley drew attention to the notion of generalizability, when they discussed threats to the integrity of various designs under two broad headings—internal validity and external validity (1963). External validity was *their* term for generalizability.

Evaluation, in contrast, seeks to produce knowledge specific to a particular setting. Evaluators, concerned with the evaluation of a reading improvement program for third graders in a single school or school district, will direct their efforts toward ascertaining the effectiveness of the program in that locality. The resulting evaluative information should have high local relevance for teachers and administrators in that school district. The results may have no scientific relevance for any other school in any other locality; well-intentioned educators, interested in such a program, will have to determine its effectiveness elsewhere in a separate enterprise.

The fact that evaluation does not produce generalizable knowledge has produced an interesting phenomenon in the United States and elsewhere. Scholarly journals typically report results of research studies. Such journals rarely, if ever, publish the results of evaluation studies. The justification for such a policy is that evaluation studies rarely produce knowledge that is sufficiently general in nature to warrant widespread dissemination. Thus, typical practice is for an evaluation enterprise to produce a few copies of a report for local consumption. Educators in other localities may often fail to learn of successful programs that are going on elsewhere, unless they meet with persons from those places at conferences and professional meetings.

Another important distinction between evaluation and research lies in the area of method. In research there are fairly well developed canons, principles, procedures, and techniques for the conduct of studies, which have been explicated in various works (Kerlinger 1975, Kaplan 1964; Campbell and Stanley 1966). These methods serve to insure the production of dependable and generalizable knowledge. While the methods of research frequently serve as a guide to evaluation endeavors, there are a number of occasions when such methods are neither necessary nor practicable. Evaluation is not research, and the methods of the latter do not need to dictate the activities of the former. This issue will be taken up in detail in chapter 9.

Some writers assert that any evaluative effort must rigorously employ the methods of experimental research and that anything less is apt to be a waste of time and money. This is an extreme position. While research methods are often useful in planning evaluation studies, they should not be worn as a straitjacket. Meaningful evaluative activity can be carried on that does not follow a research model. For example, a program intended to train people in a particular set of skills, e.g., welding, could be undertaken with a single select group of learners and their proficiency ascertained at the conclusion of the training program. Such an enterprise would violate most, if not all, of the precepts of scientific research, e.g., lack of randomization, absence of a control group, etc. However, it could yield highly pertinent evaluative information that could be used for a variety of purposes. An inability to follow research prescriptions for the design and conduct of studies need not be fatal for evaluation work. There are occasions when departures from a strict research orientation are necessary and appropriate. The important point is that substantial and important work can be done in evaluation that does not require the use of formal research methods. One must, of course, be extremely careful. A number of specific considerations in the design and conduct of evaluation studies will be presented in chapter 9.

* * * * * *

The above discussion was intended to introduce the reader to the concept of educational evaluation. Definitions of educational evaluation were presented and discussed, and evaluation was briefly contrasted with measurement and research. But definition and contrast can only go so far. In a way, the remainder of this book is an elaborate attempt to convey to the reader the nature of educational evaluation, and what it entails. Before proceeding to a more systematic and detailed examination, some background material needs to be given so that the reader may see educational evaluation in a larger context.

THE ROLE OF EVALUATION IN THE EDUCATIONAL PROCESS

The prominence given to educational evaluation can be traced to the mid-sixties. The United States Congress passed the Elementary and Secondary Education Act of 1965 (ESEA) which provided massive amounts of funds for the improvement of educational programs. This was by far the most ambitious piece of educational legislation ever passed by the federal government and provided considerable amounts of money for local education agencies and universities. The ESEA also contained a requirement that programs funded under Titles I and III of the Act be evaluated annually and that reports of the evaluation be forwarded to the federal government. Failure to comply with this requirement could result in a loss of funding for programs. Since considerable monies were involved, the requirement to evaluate federally funded programs was to be taken seriously. The fact that many, if not most, local education agencies had little idea of how to go about evaluating their programs did not receive adequate consideration. Certainly, the educational community was ill-prepared to undertake such a massive amount of evaluation work. There was considerable scurrying around in the early years of the ESEA, and many of the evaluation efforts were poor. Nonetheless, the intent of Congress was clear. If the monies being considered for investment in education were to have any chance of significantly improving the enterprise, then it was important to keep track of how they were being spent and what *kinds* of results were being obtained.

It was unfortunate that what came to be known as the "evaluation requirement" was introduced in the way that it was. Still, it seems unlikely that the need to evaluate the worth of educational programs would have been taken so seriously or so quickly without such a spur. One unfortunate aspect of the requirement to evaluate arose from the fact that evaluation, initially, was viewed by many as an activity engaged in to satisfy an external funding agency, i.e., the federal government, rather than as an integral part of the educational enterprise. It was also unfortunate that only externally funded programs were, in fact, evaluated. Resources were often not available for evaluating conventional programs.

The view that developed in the mid- and late-sixties regarding the evaluation requirement was, to say the least, lamentable. It was also in marked contrast to the outlook that evaluation was an integral part of the educational process, which had been developing since the late 1920s and early 1930s, principally under the advocacy of Ralph Tyler. Briefly, Tyler's rationale postulated three major elements in the educational process: objectives, learning experiences, and appraisal procedures.* Since objec-

---

*Tyler originally used the term *evaluation* to denote those procedures used to appraise learner progress toward the attainment of objectives. He saw such procedures as being critical for furnishing information about the extent to which objectives were being attained and about the appropriateness and efficacy of the learning experiences. In this book, the term *evaluation* is used in an even broader way. It includes not only Tyler's views but procedures tives will be treated in detail in chapter 3, it is only necessary to mention here that *objectives* refer to ones intentions for an educational endeavor. They represent the desired, or valued performances or behaviors that individuals in a program are intended to develop. An educational program's purposes may range from having learners (whatever their age or other characteristics) acquire a narrowly specified set of skills to reorganization of an entire life style. The nature of the objectives is not significant at this point. What is important is that an educational program be undertaken with some intentions in mind and that these intentions refer to desired changes in the learners served by the program.

The term *learning experiences* refers to those activities and experiences that learners undergo in order to acquire the desired behaviors. For example, if a program in nutrition education is concerned with learners acquiring information about the importance of including various food groups in a diet, the learning experiences designed to help students acquire this information might include reading, lecture, audio-visual presentations, and the like. *Learning experiences* is a broad term that includes both individual and group activities carried on within an educational institution at the instigation of educators for the sake of attaining the objectives of the program. Thus, if a teacher requires that learners visit a museum to view a particular exhibit, this would be classified as a learning experience, provided it is intended to help attain a particular objective. Correspondingly, homework assignments, individual projects, and term papers—completed outside of school—would also be classed as learning experiences. According to Tyler, learner appraisal in the educational process is critical because it is concerned with ascertaining the extent to which the objectives of the program have been met. For a representation of the educational process as formulated by Tyler see Figure 1.1.

The representation is a dynamic one as signified by the two directional arrows, linking each element with each of the others. Beginning with objectives—the arrow pointing to learning experiences—indicates that objectives serve as a guide for the selection or creation of learning experiences. For example, if a geometry course is supposed to develop deductive thinking abilities in learners, then learning experiences that require work with other than geometry content, such as newspaper editorials, advertisements, and the like, will have to be included in the program. Other examples could easily be cited. The central point is that the nature of one's objectives will be an important determiner of the learning experiences that constitute the operational program. The

---

used in making judgments about the overall merit of an educational enterprise. Judgments of overall merit involve considerations of the worth of the objectives being pursued, their costs, and some measure of their acceptance by learners, teachers, and community.

FIGURE 1.1

Representation of Educational Process

Objectives

Learning
Experiences

Learner
Appraisal

Source: Adapted from R. Tyler, ed., *Educational Evaluation: New Roles, New Means.* Yearbook of the National Society for the Study of Education. Chicago: University of Chicago Press, 1969.

arrow—pointing from objectives to learner appraisal—indicates that the primary (some would maintain the exclusive) focus of appraisal is on gathering evidence as to the extent to which the objectives of a program have been attained. Just as the objectives provide specifications for the establishment of learning experiences, they also furnish specifications for learner appraisal. To return to the previous example, a program that seeks to have students develop and use deductive thinking in life-situations might require, in its appraisal of learning, evidence regarding student proficiency to apply deductive principles to the analysis of a variety of material outside the realm of geometry.

The two arrows stemming from objectives in Figure 1.1 are easily explained. The meaning of the other arrows is less apparent but no less important. The arrow pointing from learning experiences to learner appraisal is indicative of the fact that learning experiences can provide exemplars for the development of appraisal tasks. The activities that students engage in during the learning phase of a program should furnish ideas for appraisal situations. In fact, there must be a fundamental consistency between learning experiences and appraisal tasks for learners. If there isn't, something is amiss in the program. This is not to say that learning experiences and appraisal tasks must be identical. Appraisal tasks should contain an element of novelty for the learner. This novelty may appear in the content of the evaluation task, the form of it, or both. If there is no element of novelty, one does not have an educational program but, rather, a training program where learning experiences are designed to develop relatively narrow behaviors in the learner, and appraisal procedures are expected to ascertain only whether the narrow set of behaviors have been acquired. Education, on the other hand, involves the acquisition of fairly broad *classes* of behaviors. Thus, the arrow pointing from learning experiences to learner appraisal indicates that learning experiences furnish ideas and suggestions for learner appraisal; but there should not be an overspecification of appraisal procedures.

The two arrows pointing from learner appraisal to objectives and to learning experiences are especially important. In the case of the former, the arrow signifies that appraisal procedures should furnish information about the extent to which the objectives are being attained. This is an important function of learner appraisal. In addition, appraisal information can furnish valuable information that may result in the modification of some objectives and the elimination of others. Particular objectives may have been included as a result of noble intentions on the part of a group of educators, but appraisal activities may yield information that indicates the goals were not attained. This should cause the educators to reconsider the objectives. Should the objectives be modified or perhaps eliminated? Are the objectives realistic for the group of learners served by the program? Are the resources necessary for achieving the objectives available? Such questions will, of course, have to be answered within the context of a particular situatiòn. In raising these questions here, we seek to illustrate how the results of appraisal activities can provide information pertinent to the review of objectives.

The arrow pointing from learner appraisal to learning experiences is suggestive of two important notions. First, just as appraisal activities can furnish information as to which objectives are being successfully attained and which are not, learner appraisal can also provide information bearing on which learning experiences appear to be working well and which ones are not. In any educational enterprise there will be a variety of learning experiences. It is unreasonable to expect that all will be equally effective. Appraisal procedures can furnish information as to which learning experiences are succeeding, which ones may be in need of modification, and which ones should, perhaps, be eliminated. This is the notion of formative evaluation described by M. Scriven (1967) and discussed in some detail by Cronbach (1963). A second important idea suggested by the arrow pointing from appraisal to learning experiences is that tasks, exercises, and problems, developed by evaluation specialists, may be suggestive of new learning experiences. The incorporation of novel and imaginative appraisal materials into the learning phase of a program has, on occasion, contributed significantly to the improvement of learning. Of course, the appropriation of such materials for the improvement of the quality of the learning experiences renders the materials unusable for appraisal purposes. However, this is usually considered a small price to pay for the improvement of the quality of the learning experiences.

The last arrow, which points from learning experiences to objectives, denotes that learning activities can result in encounters involving teachers, learners, and learning materials which can suggest new objectives. Alert and sensitive teachers can identify potentially important new objectives. A teacher, for example, may be conducting a discussion with a group of learners and, as happens, the discussion will take a turn in an unexpected direction. The teacher may allow the discussion to follow this new course with considerable benefit to all. Such a development may lead the teacher to ask that specific provisions be made to insure such benefits by incorporating one or more new objectives into the program. If one does not make formal provision for such activities, then they may not occur in the future—the basic limitation of incidental learning being that if it is not formally provided for, it may not take place. For this reason the arrow—pointing from learning experiences to objectives—has been included.

The above characterization of the educational process is attributed to Tyler (1950); its roots can be seen in his earlier work (1934). The important point to note is that Tyler saw evaluation as central to the educational process and not as an appendage—to be carried out merely to satisfy the demands of an outside funding agency. All serious writers about evaluation share Tyler's basic view about the critical role evaluation has to play in the educational process, although there is considerable variance as to how this role should be fulfilled. Unfortunately, the view about the centrality of evaluation in the educational process is neither universally shared by educational practitioners nor, when it is held, necessarily applied. For example, a number of writers in the field of curriculum development exhort practitioners to engage in the systematic evaluation of educational programs but furnish little guidance as to how this function should be carried out. Even practitioners will often give lip service to the importance of evaluation but will do little or nothing about it.

While Tyler's view of education and the role of evaluation in the educational process has been of enormous value to persons in curriculum development as well as to those in educational evaluation, it provides only a foundation for current evaluation thought and practice. Technical developments in the methods of evaluation, measurement, research, decision theory, information sciences, and other related areas, as well as new demands for educational planning, have resulted in additions and modifications to Tyler's basic views. In the next chapter, an attempt will be made to present some of these ideas within a framework for educational evaluation.

SUMMARY

This chapter sought to introduce the reader to the concept of evaluation and to describe it in some detail. An important feature of a definition is not only to say what something *is* but also what it *is not*. Accordingly, evaluation was contrasted with two related activities, measurement (including learner appraisal) and research, and some basic differences were noted. The chapter also presented a summary of a view of the educational process that placed evaluation squarely in that process. Attention was given to the role of evaluation by relating evaluation to two other key elements in the educational process: objectives and learning experiences.

REFERENCES

Beeby, C.E. June 1975. "The Meaning of Evaluation." Paper delivered at Evaluation Conference, Department of Education, Wellington, New Zealand.

Campbell, D.T. and Stanley, J. 1963. "Experimental and Quasi-experimental Designs for Research on Teaching." *Handbook of Research on Teaching*, edited by N.L. Gage, pp. 171–246. Chicago: Rand McNally.

———. 1966. *Experimental and Quasi-Experimental Designs for Research on Teaching.* Chicago: Rand McNally.

Cronbach, L.J. 1963. "Course Improvement through Evaluation." *Teachers College Record* 64: 672–683.

Cronbach, L. and Snow, R. 1977. *Aptitudes and Instructional Methods.* New York: Irvington Publishers.

Cronbach, L.J. and Suppes, P. (eds.). 1969. *Research for Tomorrow's Schools: Disciplined Inquiry for Education.* New York: MacMillan.

Kaplan, A. 1964. *The Conduct of Inquiry.* San Francisco: Chandler.

Kerlinger, F. 1973. *Foundations of Behavioral Research.* 3rd ed. New York: Holt, Rinehart and Winston.

Popham, W.J. 1975. *Educational Evaluation.* Englewood Cliffs, N.J.: Prentice-Hall.

Scriven, M. 1967. "The Methodology of Evaluation." In *Curriculum Evaluation*, Edited by R.E. Stahe. AERA Monograph Series on Evaluation, no. 1. Chicago: Rand McNally.

Tyler, R. 1934. *Constructing Achievement Tests.* Columbus, Ohio: Ohio State University.

———. 1950. *Basic Principles of Curriculum and Instruction.* Chicago: University of Chicago Press.

ADDITIONAL READINGS

Apple, M., Sulkoviak, M. and Lufler, H. (eds.). 1974. *Educational Evaluation: Analysis and Responsibility.* Berkeley: McCutchan.

Borich, G. 1974. *Evaluating Educational Programs and Products.* Englewood Cliffs, N.J.: Educational Technology Publications.

Furst, E. 1958. *Constructing Evaluation Instruments.* New York: Longmans Green.

Smith, E. and Tyler, R. 1943. *Appraising and Recording Student Progress.* New York: Harper.

Struenig, E. and Guttentag, M. 1975. *Handbook of Evaluation Research*, vols. 1 and 2. Beverley Hills: Sage Publications.

Suchman, E. 1967. *Evaluative Research.* New York: Russell Sage Foundation.

Tyler, R. (ed.). 1969. *Educational Evaluation: New Roles, New Means.* Yearbook of the National Society for the Study of Education. Chicago: University of Chicago Press.

Walberg, H. (ed.). 1974. *Evaluating Educational Performance.* Berkeley: McCutchan Publications.

2

A FRAMEWORK FOR EVALUATION

INTRODUCTION

The purpose of this chapter is to present a clear, coherent, and comprehensive view of educational evaluation. In addition, it is intended to be sensible and practical. Since evaluation work so often involves teachers, administrators, lay boards, consumers, and community members in the planning, execution, or reporting of results, it is important that the general form of an evaluation study be understood, appear reasonable, and can be carried out in a real-life situation with all of the attendant problems of a natural setting.

The formulation of a view of evaluation that meets the above requirements is no easy task. It is not that there are no guides to help one. On the contrary, there are at least eight classes of models and, counting conservatively, twenty specific models of educational evaluation (Stake 1975, p. 33). It is not within the purview of this book to attempt to describe and compare all or even some of the models here; that would probably be more confusing than enlightening. Fortunately, descriptions and comparisons of a number of these models already exist and the interested reader is referred to those sources (Worthen and Sanders 1973; Popham 1974; Stake 1975).

While discussion of various evaluation models is beyond the scope of this book, some of the ways in which they differ can be noted in order to assist in formulating a view of evaluation which attempts to transcend, take account of, and, in some way, accommodate these differences. One way in which evaluation models differ is in terms of what is considered to be the major purposes of educational evaluation. One group of writers, perhaps best exemplified by Cronbach (1963), sees improvement of instructional programs as the chief aim of evaluation. Educational programs are developed, tried out, modified, tried out again, and eventually, accepted for adoption on a broad scale. Whether one holds a linear view of the process of research, development, and dissemination, characteristic of much of the curriculum development work of the early and mid-sixties, or some alternate view of the process of improvement of education, is not critical here. Evaluation in any case is seen as supplying the information that will lead to improvement of the instructional endeavor. Evaluative information provides feedback to curriculum workers, teachers, and administrators so that intelligent decisions regarding program improvement can be made. Such a feedback and quality control role for evaluation, if carefully planned and carried out, is supposed to doom every curriculum development enterprise to succeed!

In contrast with this view is the position that evaluation efforts should be directed toward formal, experimental comparative studies. In such instances evaluation efforts are directed at producing educational analogues of environmental-impact reports. Just as an environmental-impact report estimates the likely effects of a particular planned project, educational evaluation in such cases should be able to inform educators and community of the likely effects of adopting a particular educational program. The methods used to arrive at such estimates center around planned, comparative studies. In well-conducted research studies, it should be possible to conclude that one program out-performs another (or fails to) in terms of various criteria, usually some collection of measures of student performance. Advocates of such a role for educational evaluation are often concerned with overall judgments about educational programs based on a comparison with one or more alternative programs.

The difference in views of the major purposes to be served by evaluation, presented above, has been drawn as sharply as possible. In reality, there is general acknowledgment of the validity of alternative purposes to be served by educational evaluation by writers holding different views. Unfortunately, the acknowledgment is often not translated into a modification of one's model so as to accommodate alternative viewpoints. This is not to say that a particular purpose for educational evaluation is, necessarily, wrong. In many instances it may be correct and highly appropriate. The point is that most models of evaluation are generally limited in terms of the purposes envisaged for educational evaluation, each tending to emphasize a limited set of purposes.

A second basis for distinguishing among various approaches to evaluation is the training and background of the proponents of those approaches. Although evaluation work has been going on for a long time, it has only attained prominence in recent years. Consequently, many workers in the "new" field received their training in more conventional disciplines. Each area of training, whether it be curriculum development, educational psychology, measurement and statistics or whatever, has its own major theoretical concerns, methodological emphases, and outlook. The models proposed by evaluation workers often reflect their scholarly orientation even though there is often some attempt to accommodate their views to the realities and demands of real-world evaluation situations. Sometimes such effort succeeds reasonably well; sometimes they do not. For example, some writers received extensive training in the methods of behavioral research. Such writers are often strong advocates of formal experimental studies for evaluating educational endeavors. The procedures of experimental research, while ideally suited for laboratory studies in which the experimenter can exercise almost total control over all relevant conditions (including breeding several generations of laboratory animals in order to have just the right strain of animal), can hardly be applied to actual educational settings where the evaluation worker, typically, exercises an extremely limited degree of control. Yet, some writers seriously suggest that such tightly controlled studies not only are desirable but are the only permissible ones. Fortunately, there are very few such advocates. The point is, however, that by training or background, people bring particular views, concerns, or emphases to the field of evaluation from other disciplines. Sometimes this can be of benefit to the field of evaluation when it raises new issues and problems. To the novice, however, such divergence can be a source of confusion because it suggests an absence of a basic structure to the field.

A third and somewhat related distinguishing characteristic among the various approaches to educational evaluation stems from the nature of the subject or discipline that is the focus of evaluation efforts. Specialists in subject-matter areas in which evaluative work is contemplated or already underway can be counted on to have something to say about what should be evaluated and how this should be done. Differences among specialists from various fields often reflect basic differences in orientation as to the nature of the subject and what can be gained from studying it. In art education, for example, a writer such as E. Eisner (1977) presents a view of his subject (and a list of claimed benefits for studying it) that is vastly different from that held by such writers as E.G. Begle (1963) and M. Beberman (1958) in mathematics education. The differences cannot be lightly dismissed. They are genuine and reflect basically different orientations arising out of the nature of the subjects. Any comprehensive view of evaluation must seek to accommodate them.

A fourth distinguishing characteristic in approaches to evaluation stems from the emphasis that each accords to different parts of the evaluation process. Such differences in emphasis can stem from a variety of sources; their origin is not of concern. The emphasis accorded a particular aspect of the evaluation process can serve as the basis for an entire approach to evaluation. For example, workers with a background in or disposition toward administration may view decision making as the key element in the evaluation process and develop a scheme for educational evaluation in which decision making is crucial. Others with a concern for precision and careful measurement will advocate an approach in which precise specification of learner behavior and the development of instruments to ascertain this becomes the overriding concern of evaluative activity. Likewise, individuals concerned with social cohesion may devote considerable effort to studying how programs function, and how individuals relate to one another within the program and to others outside the program. There are any number of points of emphasis that can be adopted in an evaluation enterprise. Such points can become not only the focal point for evaluation work but, in extreme cases, the almost exclusive concern. Imbalance like this is, of course, to be avoided.

A FRAMEWORK FOR EVALUATION

In formulating a framework, a conscious effort has been made to accommodate a variety of viewpoints about educational evaluation. Obviously the framework cannot be all-inclusive; some approaches are mutually exclusive and contradictory. When the purposes of evaluation differ, different parts of the framework will receive different emphasis. The framework presented here should not be regarded as a model. While various writers have proposed different models of evaluation, what is presented here does not claim to be a model. It is hoped that it will be helpful to the reader in *thinking* about educational evaluation and will be useful in *planning* and *conducting* evaluation studies.

Comprehensive evaluation of educational treatments, whether they be units of instruction, courses, programs, or entire institutions, requires the collection of five major classes of information. Each class of information is necessary although not sufficient for evaluation of an educational enterprise. In setting forth these five major divisions, it is recognized that some may be of little or no interest in a particular evaluation-undertaking. What is being avoided is the possibility of neglecting any important class of information for determining the worth of a program. Thus, the framework allows for errors of commission—for example, collecting information that will have little bearing on the determination of the merit of a program—while avoiding errors of omission: failing to gather information that may be important. Two reasons for this position may be given. One, if a particular class of information turns out to be unimportant, it can simply be disregarded. Two, if it is known in advance that a particular class of information will have little bearing on the outcome of the evaluation, it simply need not be gathered. This does not reflect on the framework *per se* but only on the inappropriateness of a part of it in a particular situation. On the other hand, failure to gather information about particular relevant aspects of an education venture indicates a faulty evaluation effort; this should be avoided.

Initial Status of Learners

The first class of information relates to the initial status of learners. It is important to know two things about the learners at the time they enter the program: who they are, and how proficient they are with regard to what they are supposed to learn. The first sub-class of information—who are the learners?— is descriptive in nature and is usually easily obtained. Routinely one wants to know the age, sex, previous educational background, and other status and experimental variables that might be useful in describing or characterizing the learners. Strictly speaking, such information is not evaluative. It should be helpful in charting whether the learner population is changing, thus suggesting that modifications to the program may be needed. The second sub-class of information—how proficient the learners are with regard to what they are supposed to learn—is more central to the evaluation. Learning is generally defined as a change in behavior or proficiency. If learning is to be demonstrated, it is necessary to gather evidence of at least two moments: (1) at the beginning of a set of learning experiences; and (2) at some later time. Gathering evidence about the initial proficiencies of learners furnishes the necessary baseline information for estimating, however crudely, the extent to which learning occurs during the period from start to finish. (Determining whether the learning occurred as a direct result of the program or was due to other factors is an issue that will be dealt with in chapters 9 and 10.) A related reason for determining the initial proficiency-level of learners stems from the fact that some educational enterprises may seriously underestimate initial, learner status with regard to what is to be learned. Consequently, considerable resources may be wasted in teaching learners already proficient. Mere end-of-program evidence gathering would lead one to the erroneous conclusion of program effectiveness when what had actually happened was that already developed proficiencies had been maintained.

It is important that a determination of the initial level of proficiencies of learners be undertaken before an educational enterprise gets seriously underway. Only then can one be sure that the learners are assessed independently of the effects of the program. Studying learners *after* they have had some period of instruction makes it impossible to determine what the learners were like before instruction began. While the point seems self-evident, it has been violated so often in recent years that several methodologists have published articles in professional journals about this to sensitize workers in the field.

The one instance in which gathering data about the initial proficiencies of learners could be omitted is when what is to be learned is so specialized in nature one can reasonably presume that the initial status of learners is virtually nil. Examples where such a presumption could be reasonably made would include entry-level educational programs in computer programming, welding, and cytotechnology. Outside such specialized fields however, it is worth the relatively small investment of time, energy, and expense to ascertain the initial status of learner proficiency.

To determine the initial status of learners can be a large order. If complete information about every variable of interest were obtained for every learner, several hours at the very least—more likely several days—of information-gathering would have to be used. This would, in effect, curtail the amount of time available for instruction.

Since any evaluation scheme must be practical, it is worth digressing to comment on how relevant information can be gathered with a minimum of intrusion on instructional time. (Details regarding these procedures will be given in chapters 5, 9, and 10.) First, much of the background information that is useful in describing a group of learners can be located in existing records, thus eliminating the need for gathering the information directly from learners during instructional time. Second, it is not necessary to require *all* learners to respond to a full set of instruments. A sample, chosen so as to be representative of all learners enrolled in a program, curriculum, or institution, can be studied to furnish information that will characterize the total group. Third, a combination of sampling of individuals and a sampling of questions, items, and tasks that probe the proficiencies, abilities, and even affective outcomes an educational enterprise seeks to develop, can be undertaken. This dual sampling, which will be discussed at length in chapter 10, is referred to as *multiple matrix sampling* and lends itself particularly well for use in evaluation studies. One of its chief advantages is efficiency. Economies of 75–80 percent in the time required for information gathering are commonplace with multiple matrix sampling—with no great loss in the precision and quality of the information obtained. In practical terms, this means that it should be possible to obtain virtually all the information that one needs about the initial status of learners in no more than 30–40 minutes.

Learner Performance After A Period of Instruction

The second major class of information required in evaluation studies relates to learner proficiency and status *after* a period of instruction. The basic notion here is that educational ventures are intended to bring about changes in learners. Hence, it is critical to determine whether the learners have changed in the desired ways. Changes could include increased knowledge, ability to solve various classes of problems, ability to deal with various kinds of issues in a field, proficiencies in certain kinds of skills, changes in attitudes, interests and preferences, etc. The changes sought will depend on the nature of the program, the age- and ability-levels of the learners and a host of other factors. Whatever changes a program, curriculum, or institution seeks to effect in learners must be examined to determine whether they have occurred and to what extent. The only way this can be done is through a study of learner performance. Whether the particular changes in learner behavior can be attributed to the effects of the educational experiences is, however, another matter (to be dealt with in detail in chapter 9). Before such a determination can be made, however, it should be ascertained whether learners indeed have learned what they were expected to.

The notion that information about what has been learned should be obtained after a period of instruction has often been interpreted to mean that learners must be examined at the end of a program or course. This is not correct. *When* information should be gathered is a function of the purposes of those who will be the major consumers of the evaluation. The developer of a program, for example, might be keenly interested in finding out how effective particular units of instruction are in bringing about particular changes in learners—e.g., increased knowledge, ability to solve certain kinds of problems—and also in the effectiveness of specific lessons. Such information may enable the developer to detect flaws in the program and make appropriate modifications. The same program developer might be relatively uninterested in learner performance at the end of the program. Moreover, summative information may be at such a general level as to be virtually useless in helping him detect where the program is working, and where it is not. Someone else, on the other hand, who is considering the adoption of a program, may have little interest about how learners are performing at various points in the program; his interest lies in the field status of the learners. That is, have they learned what was expected by the conclusion of the program? A positive answer could lead to a decision to adopt the program; a negative one, to possible rejection. Different persons will approach an evaluation enterprise with different questions, and such differences should be reflected in decisions concerning what information should be gathered and when it should be gathered.

The above distinction closely parallels the one between formative and summative evaluation noted earlier. It is not, however, the only distinction that can be made. What is important is that a schedule of information-gathering with regard to learner performance is consistent with the purposes for undertaking the evaluation and that the phrase "after a period of instruction" is not restricted to end-of-course information gathering.

There are two kinds of learner-performance information to be gathered after a period of instruction. First, one is interested in the particular abilities, skills, affective outcomes, and the like that are intended to result from a set of organized educational experiences. (The technical term for such outcomes is "objectives" and will be discussed in some detail in the next chapter.) Collecting information regarding achievement of the objectives of an educational venture is vital. The aim in gathering such information is to ascertain as fully as possible what objectives are being attained and to what extent. Evaluation work should furnish information with regard to each and every educational objective for an educational enterprise.

The second kind of information about learner performance that should be gathered is less well known and not universally accepted. It involves learner proficiency with regard to outcomes *not* formally included in the stated objectives of the program. Because of the somewhat special nature of such outcomes, they are not included here. They will be presented below in the fifth class of information (Supplemental Information). Incidental outcomes are mentioned here solely because they complement the learner-performance information gathered with regard to stated program objectives.

Execution of Treatment

The third class of information to be collected in an evaluation study centers on the educational treatment being dispensed, whether it is a course, program, curriculum or an entire institutional setting. At the very least, one needs to know whether the treatment was carried out. If so, to what extent? Did the treatment get started on time? Were the personnel and materials necessary for the program available from the outset or, as has been the case in a number of externally funded programs, did materials and supplies arrive shortly before the termination of the program? Questions regarding the implementation of the intended program may seem trivial but are, in fact, critical. Often it is simply assumed that an intended program occurred on schedule and in the way it was intended. This assumption is open to question but, more importantly, to study. Any responsible evaluation enterprise must determine whether and how an educational program was carried out.

Information about the execution of a program should not only meet the minimal requirement of determining whether a program has been carried out as intended; it should also furnish some descriptive information about the program in operation. Such information can often be used to identify deficiencies in the program as well as possible explanations for success. The collection of information about the program in operation will rely heavily on the regular use of observational procedures and—in some cases—on the use of narrative descriptive material. Who actually gathers such information is a matter that can be decided locally. Evaluation workers, supervisors, or other administrative personnel can share in the performance of this critical function. Maintenance of logs or diaries by teachers in the program could contribute to meeting informational needs in this area. Even participant-observer instruments, along the lines developed by Pace and Stern (1958), where individuals are asked to report on particular practices and features of an environment, could be useful.

Failure to determine the extent to which a designed program was not fully implemented opens evaluation studies to serious criticism. One of the classic educational studies in the United States, the Eight Year Study of the Progressive Educational Association, suffered from this fatal flaw—the thirty schools in the experimental group did not, in fact, modify their programs sufficiently from those of traditional schools as to constitute an experimental treatment. More recently, some observers have noted one possible explanation as to why evaluations of early Head-start Programs failed to show any effects: their failure to get started on time, secure the necessary qualified personnel, obtain adequate materials and supplies, and operate with any clear set of plans. It is hoped that educational programs, developed to meet particular needs, will not be subject to the criticism Shaw leveled in a different context when he observed that the main problem with Christianity was that it had never been tried.

Costs

The fourth major class of information is costs. Unfortunately, costs have not received adequate attention in evaluation work. Why this is so is not clear. Perhaps early educational evaluation efforts were directed toward ascertaining the efficacy of competing instructional treatments that had equal price tags. In such cases, cost considerations were not a major concern. Today, however, the range of available treatments—in the form of units of instruction, courses, programs, curricula, and instructional systems—have widely varying costs. These need to be reckoned so that administrators and educational planners, as well as evaluation workers, can make intelligent judgments about educational treatments. Not only must direct costs be reckoned—for example, the cost of adoption—but indirect costs as well. Costs of in-service training for teachers who are to use a new program, for example, must be determined if a realistic estimate of the cost of the new program is to be obtained. An evaluation specialist, whose training and experience may be in measurement, research methodology, or curriculum development, may not be able to perform the necessary cost estimation. If he cannot, then he needs to find someone who can. An evaluation making no reference to costs is rarely of practical value, however interesting it may be academically. The educational administrator, probably, already has a fair idea of what can be accomplished if money were no object. The real problem for the administrator is to make wise decisions when cost *is* a factor.

Information about costs should be considered as early as possible in the evaluation of educational programs. (One recognizes, of course, that cost information may need to be modified as time passes.) Careful cost estimation can lead to better planning and more intelligent decision making when laudable but costly programs are considered for trial, let alone adoption. Traditionally, evaluation workers have neglected the entire issue, leaving administrators to worry about such mundane matters. This has been unfortunate. An evaluation worker's professional function involves gathering *all* relevant information about an educational enterprise. Costs are certainly relevant and, in some cases, may be a critical consideration in judging the worth of an educational venture.

Supplemental Information

The fifth class involves supplemental information about the effects of a program, curriculum, or institution and is composed of three subclasses. The first includes the reactions, opinions, and impressions of learners, teachers, and others associated with the enterprise being evaluated. They could be administrators, parents, other community members, even prospective employers. The purpose of gathering such information is to find out how an educational treatment is viewed by various groups. Such information is no substitute for more direct information about what is actually being learned, but it can play a critical role in evaluating the overall worth of a program in a larger institutional context. There have been occasions when programs, instituted by well-intentioned educators, have succeeded fairly well in achieving their objectives, and at a reasonable cost. However, controversy about such programs—inside or outside the institution—have led to their termination. One can cite as examples the installation of programs of sex education in schools in highly conservative communities or the adoption of textbooks that were considered to contain offensive material by sizable segments of a community.

Supplemental information—in the form of views and reactions of groups connected with an educational venture—can be highly instructive in a number of ways. It can (1) provide information about how a program is being perceived by various groups; (2) help formulate information campaigns, if there is a serious discontinuity between what is actually taking place in a program and what is perceived to be taking place; and (3) alert evaluation workers and administrators about the need for additional information as to why a particular program is being viewed in a certain way by one or more groups. Such information may also prevent evaluation workers from developing what Scriven (1972) has described as a kind of tunnel vision which sometimes develops from restricting evaluation efforts to determine how well program objectives have been achieved. For example, attaining a limited set of objectives in a sex education program for elementary school students, at the cost of a sizable amount of local support and conflict between school and community, might be simply too steep a price to pay.

Information about the views and reactions of various groups connected with an educational enterprise can be gathered fairly easily through the use of questionnaires and interview techniques. The value of gathering such information should not be underestimated. Neither should it be overestimated. There have been a number of evaluation efforts that have relied solely on the collection of the views and reactions of individuals and groups having some connection to a program. Educational evaluation should not be confused with opinion polling. It is important to find out how well an educational venture is succeeding in terms of what it set out to accomplish. This requires the collection of information about learner performance outlined in the first two classes of information. *In addition*, supplemental information about how a program is being received by various groups is important to an overall evaluation of its worth.

The instances cited above, where supplemental information in the form of views and reactions of various groups were extreme, do occur; admittedly, the frequency is low. Generally, reactions to educational programs tend to be on the mild side with a tendency on the part of the public to view new programs in a somewhat favorable light—especially if they have been fairly well thought through and reasonably well-presented. If reactions to educational programs are fairly mild, ranging, for example, from acquiescence to some positive support, little further attention need be accorded such information. However, one is not apt to know in advance what the views and reactions of various parties are likely to be. Consequently, it is necessary to consciously find them out.

The second sub-class of supplemental information involves learner performances not specified in the objectives of the program. Developers of educational programs, courses, and curricula are improving in their ability to specify what should be learned as a result of exposure to instruction, and the responsibility for assessing learner performance with regard to specified objectives is now generally accepted. However, it is also reasonable to inquire how well *broader* goals of education are being served by a particular program. "An ideal evaluation" Cronbach points out (1963, pp. 121–122):

> would include measures of all the types of proficiency that might reasonably be desired in the area in questions, not just the selected

outcomes to which this curriculum directs substantial attention. If you wish only to know how well a curriculum is achieving *its* objectives, you fit the test to the curriculum; but if you wish to know how well the curriculum is serving the national interest, you measure all outcomes that might be worth striving for. One of the new mathematics courses may disavow any attempt to teach numerical trigonometry, and indeed, might discard nearly all computational work. It is still perfectly reasonable to ask how well graduates of the course can compute and can solve right triangles. Even if the course developers went so far as to contend that computational skill is no proper objective of secondary instruction, they will encounter educators and laymen who do not share this view. If it can be shown that students who come through the new course are fairly proficient in computation despite the lack of direct teaching, the doubters will be re-assured. If not, the evidence makes clear how much is being sacrificed. Similarly, when the biologists offer alternative courses emphasizing microbiology and ecology, it is fair to ask how well the graduate of one course can understand issues treated in the other. Ideal evaluation in mathematics will collect evidence on all the abilities toward which a mathematics course might reasonably aim; likewise in biology, English or any other subject.

Cronbach's view is not universally accepted. Some writers assert that any attempt to test for outcomes not intended by the program developers is imposing inappropriate and unfair criteria on the program. There is always a danger of being unfair. Present also is the highly practical problem of deciding what kinds of learner-performance information, not specified in the objectives, should be obtained. It would seem that *some* information along these lines should be gathered. The examples cited by Cronbach above furnish some useful guides about the kind of additional information program developers should obtain. It is important that supplemental information about learner performance, when obtained, be analyzed and reported separately from information bearing directly on the *intended* outcomes of a program. Any evaluation effort must not only be done fairly but appear to be done fairly. The inclusion of information about learner competencies, not intended as part of an instructional program, must be handled delicately. Separate treatment and reporting of such information is a minimal prerequisite of fairness.

While Cronbach maintains that an ideal evaluation effort would gather evidence about learner performance on all outcomes an educational enterprise might reasonably aim at, in practice the amount of supplemental performance information will necessarily be limited. Unless a program is heavily funded and has the requisite staff to develop evidence-gathering measures for the whole range of supplemental performance information desired, it is unrealistic to expect that very much can be done. Some efforts, albeit modest ones, can be made. It would be best to use the bulk of available resources to obtain learner-performance information with regard to intended outcomes and to supplement this with some additional measures. Don't dilute the evaluation effort by trying to measure everything and end up doing a mediocre or even poor job. This is a matter of planning and strategy. One can always expect that the resources available for evaluation will be limited. This is not a tragedy. Failure to use available resources effectively, however, can lead to undesired results. It is recommended that the major use of available resources be devoted to obtaining the most relevant information about learner performance. This would entail examining how much has been learned with regard to the intended outcomes; some provision can (and should) be made with regard to other learner-performance outcomes that might result from the kind of program being evaluated.

The third sub-class of supplemental information has to do with the side effects of educational programs, courses, and curricula. Admittedly, this is not an easy matter. Just as pharmaceutical researchers have long known that drugs can have effects on patients other than the ones intended, educators are realizing that their undertakings can have side effects too. Sometimes such unintended effects can be beneficial, e.g., when a program designed to improve reading skills of learners not only improves reading proficiency but increases self-esteem. Negative side-effects may also occur: in a rigorous academic high-school physics course students may learn a great deal of physics but their interest in learning more physics in college may be markedly reduced and, in many cases, extinguished.

While one can cite side effects of educational programs at length, prescriptions about what to look for and how to detect them are hard to give. Evaluation workers must first recognize that side effects can occur in any educational program. Evaluation workers must strive to be as alert and as sensitive as possible about what is happening to learners as they move through a set of educational experiences. This means attending not only to learner performance in relation to stated objectives, but to any general class of behaviors, including interests and attitudes, that may be developing. This is not an easy task, but if the evaluation workers can maintain a level of receptivity about behaviors, not directly specified by the objectives of a program, there is a fair chance that such behaviors will be discerned when they appear.

Another way of detecting the side effects of educational programs is through the use of follow-up procedures. Following up learners into the next level of education or into their first year of employment can furnish clues. In the example cited above about the rigorous high-school physics course, the critical information about the negative effect of the program on interest in learning more physics came from a follow-up study. (It was found that students who had taken the innovative physics course were taking additional physics courses in college at less than one-half the rate of comparable students who had taken a conventional high school physics course.) However, it is not likely that formal follow-up studies will yield such clear-cut results. Moreover, formal follow-up studies often require more resources than are available at most institutions. Even when such resources are plentiful, it is not usually clear how they should be put to use. The detection of unintended effects is an elusive business. Rather than attempt to conduct formal follow-up studies, it is usually better to employ rather loosely structured procedures. Open-ended questionnaires and interviews with teachers at the next level in the educational ladder, with employers of graduates as well as with graduates themselves, could furnish clues about side effects of programs that could then be studied more systematically. It is also possible that the first sub-class of supplemental information—views and reactions of various groups connected with a program—could provide clues about program side effects. Whatever strategy is employed to detect them, it should probably be somewhat loosely structured and informal.

* * * * * * * * *

The framework for evaluation presented above specifies the major classes of information required for a comprehensive evaluation of an educational enterprise. Detailed procedures for the collection of each class of information are presented in subsequent chapters along with discussions about the analysis and interpretation of evaluative information and the synthesis of results into judgments of worth. Before such complex undertakings can be initiated however, it is critical that the necessary information is obtained. The framework presented in this chapter is an *agenda* for information gathering.

There are three major features that underly the framework which should be made explicit. First, at the core of the framework is the notion that learner performance is the major basis for evaluation of educational courses, programs, and curricula. That is, educational ventures are set up to bring about certain changes in learner performance. How well they succeed in doing so is considered essential for evaluating their worth. This is the reason for inclusion of the first two classes of information. A second major feature of the framework is that learner performance is a necessary although not sufficient condition for the evaluation of educational treatments. How effectively the program was carried out; how much the program costs, as well as what people think of the program; and what unintended effects of the program has; all are considered vital to a comprehensive evaluation. This is somewhat of an expansion over a number of previous attempts to deal with the evaluation function. Lest this expansion be considered too burdensome for effective evaluation because of the ever present fact of limited resources, it should be noted that *conventional* evaluation efforts usually waste a good deal of time and money. A number of specific and detailed suggestions will be made later on as to how a *comprehensive* evaluation effort can be planned and carried out without any increase in resources allocated to evaluation.

The third major feature underlying the framework is the idea that evaluation is central to the educational process. This view was presented in chapter 1 when evaluation was related to objectives and learning experiences. It is a notion that has been endorsed by educators for a long time. Unfortunately, it has been practiced far less than it has been preached. By specifying the involvement of evaluation workers in the execution of the intended program, in the reckoning of costs and the collection of a range of supplemental information, the evaluation function will become more closely allied with the educational process. No longer can the evaluation worker be one who is only present at the start of a program, when the objectives are presented, and at the conclusion of a program, when the data are gathered; rather he or she will have a continuing role to play throughout the course of an educational venture. This centrality of the evaluation role is perhaps the most noteworthy feature of the framework.

The expanded and more central role of evaluation in the educational process will lead not only to higher-quality evaluation work but to more useful evaluation information. It would seem likely, for example, that the distinction between formative and summative evaluation that has held sway for a number of years might be considerably diminished, if evaluation were an ongoing operation rather than an episodic one. While the prospect of a continuing role for evaluation that is central to the educational process has a number of attractive features, it is not without risks. One of the oft-observed phenomena is the general mistrust that program developers and teachers have of evaluation workers. Such suspicion is, of course, understandable. Evaluation workers are often seen as threats to the continued existence of programs because of the judgmental function associated with evaluation. Certainly, as long as evaluation workers have little contact with the programs they are supposed to be evaluating, there are good grounds for such suspicion and distrust. Closer touch between evaluation workers, program personnel, and the programs being evaluated is needed if the evaluation specialist is to fulfill his professional function. Increased contact can serve to ameliorate the traditional suspicion and distrust directed at evaluation workers by increasing the amount and kinds of information which the evaluation worker is not only exposed to but needs to systematically gather in order to fulfill his professional function properly.

Evaluation workers, on the other hand, tend to be wary about increased contacts with program developers, teachers, and the ongoing program itself. Such caution is based on a belief that their objectivity as evaluation workers will somehow be compromised by closer contact with program personnel. This is a real concern, and evaluation workers must be prepared to deal with it. Some ideas about how to deal with it will be presented in chapters 11–13. The point to note here is that while limited contact with a program, course, or curriculum may preserve the detachment of the evaluation worker, it will deprive him of a considerable body of information he requires in order to perform the evaluation function. Much of the information specified in the framework will demand that the evaluation workers be in close, continuing contact with personnel connected with the enterprise he is supposed to be evaluating. There is no way to avoid it.

SUMMARY

In this chapter, a framework for educational evaluation was presented. The framework is composed of five major classes of information judged necessary for a comprehensive evaluation of an educational enterprise. They are (1) initial status of learners, (2) learner performance after a period of instruction, (3) execution of the treatment, (4) costs, and (5) supplemental information. The latter class has three sub classes: opinions and reactions of various groups connected with the enterprise, supplemental learnings, and side effects.

Each class of information is considered necessary for a total evaluation effort. The amount of resources devoted to the collection of each class of information may vary considerably however, depending on the purposes for which the evaluation is undertaken. If the major purpose of an evaluation is to determine whether to adopt a particular program or not, one pattern of resource allocation may be adopted; if the chief purpose is improvement of an existing program, another strategy may be followed. In each case, however, attention needs to be given to each of the major classes of information.

REFERENCES

Beberman, M. 1958. *An Emerging Program of Secondary School Mathematics.* Cambridge, Mass.: Harvard University Press.

Begle, E.G. 1963. "The Reform of Mathematics Education in the United States." In *Mathematical Education in the Americas,* edited by H. Fehr. New York: Bureau of Publications, Teachers College, Columbia University.

Cronbach, L.J. 1963. "Course Improvement through Evaluation." *Teachers College Record* 64: 672–683.

Eisner, E. 1977. "On the Uses of Educational Connoisseurship and Criticism for Evaluating Classroom Life." *Teachers College Record* 3: 345–358.

Pace, C.R. and Stern, G. 1958. "An Approach to the Measurement of Psychological Characteristics of College Environments." *Journal of Educational Psychology* 49: 269–277.

Popham, W.J. 1975. *Educational Evaluation.* Englewood Cliffs, N.J.: Prentice-Hall.

Scriven, M. 1972. "Prose and Cons About Goal-Free Evaluation." *Evaluation Comment* 3.

Stake, R.E. 1975. "Program Evaluation, Particularly Responsive Evaluation." *Occasional Paper Series* 5. Kalamazoo: The Evaluation Center, Western Michigan University.

Worthen, B.R. and Sanders, J.R. 1973. *Educational Evaluation: Theory and Practice.* Worthington, Ohio: Charles A. Jones.

3

EDUCATIONAL OBJECTIVES

Much has been written on the subject of educational objectives in the past twenty years. Some of it has been highly personalistic, fetishistic, idiosyncratic; some, pure nonsense. There remain today disagreements over what educational objectives are and controversy over how they should be expressed. The purpose of this chapter is to define and describe educational objectives, noting areas of disagreement among specialists, tracing where educational objectives come from, and—finally— addressing the issue of how educational objectives should be expressed. Throughout the chapter an attempt will be made to present a balanced and sensible view of educational objectives, remarking areas where problems remain and identifying points of contention.

We may begin by stating what educational objectives are and describing the critical aspects of such statements. An educational objective is a statement of a desired change in the behavior of a learner. There are several elements in this definition. First, an objective is a statement about a learner. It is *not* a statement about what the teacher does or will do. Nor is it a statement about the activities in which a learner is expected to engage. Thus the following expressions "to provide a range of reading materials for students," and "to teach division of fractions" do not qualify as statements of educational objectives since they are not statements about learners; the implied subject in both statements is the teacher. Whatever other deficiences may be noted about the statements above, their failure to be about learners (rather than teachers) renders them unacceptable as statements of educational objectives.

A second element in the definition of an educational objective is that it is a statement about a *desired* change in the learner. The term "desired" indicates that the particular behavior the learner is expected to develop is prized; it is valued. Educators are interested not in just any changes in learners coming about as a result of a planned set of learning experiences: they look for particular changes. The word "desired" indicates that certain changes in learners are considered important and other kinds are not. It is simply not possible to study every conceivable change that might occur in learners as a result of a set of educational experiences. Educational objectives represent the outcomes of a process of valuation and, consequently, certain kinds of learner behaviors will be given highest priority. In other words, educational objectives are values.

The third element in our definition is "change." Learning denotes a change in the behavior of an individual. In fact, this is the common definition of learning. If a group of learners already exhibit a set of desired behaviors *before* they undergo a set of educational experiences, then it is foolish to accord these behaviors the status of objectives. For example, if students in a nutrition education program can correctly distinguish protein-rich foods from foods that are not, then it is unnecessary to make this an objective of the program. It would not only be a waste of time but might delude educators into thinking they were accomplishing something positive when, in fact, they were merely certifying a proficiency the learners already possessed. Educational programs, curricula, and institutions are intended to help learners acquire new sets of behaviors, not affirm things they already know and can do.

The last element in the definition is "behavior." This is an often troublesome term since it has been subject to such an array of interpretations that one is obliged to specify how it is to be used in any situation. In this book, behavior will be used to denote what an individual says or does. Learner behavior can range from a response given to a specific question such as "What is the name of the capital of Idaho?" to the organization and expression of a set of ideas in written or oral form. It would include not only the ability to reproduce acquired information but to apply principles in novel situations, carry out various kinds of analyses, and exhibit particular response tendencies in various situations, such as approaches to dealing with certain classes of phenomena and generating novel products. In short, anything that the learner might say or do is an example of a behavior.

The definition is purposely broad. It does, however, exclude certain *internal* states of individuals. For example, the term "understands" would not, of itself, be considered behavioral; since it does not require any "saying" or "doing" on the part of the learner. For this reason some writers would exclude such terms as "understands," "knows," "comprehends," etc. from the language of educational objectives: they are not behavioral in nature. Besides not meeting the definitional requirement of behavior, terms that are descriptive of internal states of learners present formidable problems in evidence gathering. How, such writers ask, is one to ascertain whether a learner understands something? What is meant by the term "understands"?

No doubt these are troublesome questions and evaluation work would be less complex and difficult if nonbehavioral terms were routinely excluded from the language of educational objectives. There are, however, three reasons for not doing this. First, terms such as "understands," "knows," etc. have long been a part of the vocabulary of educators, and unilaterally to exclude them seems unwise. While evaluators may be dubious about the ability of teachers to assess learner understanding, teachers often are confident of their ability to do so. It would seem more productive to investigate such contentions than to exclude them on an priori basis. Second, teachers often have in mind certain kinds of behavior, however imperfectly formulated, when they use terms referring to internal states. It would appear to be more productive for teacher and evaluator to clarify what is *meant* by such terms than abandon them entirely. Very likely teachers do have in mind a particular set of behaviors when they use terms such as "understands." Since one of the initial tasks in evaluating an educational enterprise is to obtain a fairly clear set of statements of educational objectives, evaluators would be advised to employ all avenues of approach to this task. Accepting teacher nomenclature, however imprecise and nonbehavioral that may be, as a point of departure could prove productive. A decision initially to accept the terms used by program developers and teachers and explore their meaning in a particular situation is, thus, not only an acknowledgement of their equal professional role but the first step towards a clarification of those intentions. This is one service that evaluators can furnish teachers that will be of immediate and sometimes considerable benefit.

A third reason for accepting nonbehavioral terms is that they often serve as concise and useful summarizations for a set of behaviors a teacher wishes to develop in learners. A problem frequently encountered in expressing educational objectives is that statements of objectives become lengthy and wordy. If a fairly full expression of objectives becomes too cumbersome, teachers will likely pay it little attention. Whatever can be done to express educational objectives as succinctly as possible is usually well worth the effort, since it increases the likelihood that teachers will attend to them. Thus, the use of terms such as "understands," "knows," etc., may serve as useful summarizations for elaborated sets of behaviors. This can be satisfying for both teacher and evaluator. Consider the list of behaviors (shown in Table 3.1) that could clarify "understanding." In given situations teachers might endorse several, most, or all of them as constituting proficiencies they have in mind when using the term "understanding." An evaluator, although perhaps disinclined to use the term, is still in a position to proceed with developing ways of determining whether students have attained specific proficiencies.

TABLE 3.1

Outline of Proficiencies Indicating Understanding

1. States concepts, ideas in own words.
2. Recognizes whether there are sufficient data to solve a problem.
3. Recognizes relevancy of data for a particular problem.
4. Identifies errors in procedure and structure.
5. Given situation, identifies applicable principle.
6. Given a principle, identifies situation using it.
7. Makes reasonable inferences from data.
8. Given set of data, predicts outcomes.
9. Predicts consequences if errors or changes in procedures occur.
10. Detects similarities and differences, and relationships.
11. Given outcome, reconstructs data to support it.
12. Generalizes or classifies.
13. Identifies underlying principles or causes of several events.
14. Organizes ideas, objects, events, etc., into new patterns.
15. Gives novel examples.

Source: Compiled by the author.

SOURCES OF EDUCATIONAL OBJECTIVES

The definition presented earlier and described in some detail can only be considered as an opening volley in any discussion of educational objectives. Before proceeding to the ways in which educational objectives can be formulated and expressed, let us briefly consider how educational objectives came into being. An examination of the bases for the development of educational objectives will provide a base for dealing with them.

The three major sources for educational objectives are (1) the needs of the learner; (2) the needs of the society; and (3) the material to be learned. Careful investigation into the nature of the learners can help identify learner needs which an educational program might meet. For example, in an area where persons find it difficult to organize themselves to study, an educational program may attempt to ameliorate this problem through systematic instruction and guidance. Investigators in a number of fields of human development seek to identify various kinds of individual needs. The general aim of such work is to describe the status of a group of learners with respect to a characteristic, or set of characteristics, and compare this with what the best-of-present knowledge and theory would indicate is a desirable state of affairs. Any gap would then indicate a need that exists for a given group of learners. An attempt to formalize this process and so make it usable by educators and community members—at a local level—has resulted in the development of various needs-assessment procedures and instruments. Possible areas in which needs might be identified for learners at the junior high-school level (for example) could include (1) health; (2) immediate social relationships, including life in the family and with friends and acquaintances; (3) sociocivic relationships, including civic life, the school, and the community; (4) consumer aspects of life; (5) occupational life; and (6) recreation. These categories are only suggestive of broad areas within which needs could be identified. Needs of the learner, once identified, could furnish one basis for the formulation of educational objectives.

The second source for educational objectives relates to the needs of the society. It has been well described by Tyler (1950, p. 11).

> The effort to derive objectives from studies of contemporary life largely grew out of the difficulty of accomplishing all that was laid upon the schools with the greatly increased knowledge which developed after the advent of science and Industrial Revolution. Prior to this time the body of material that was considered academically respectable was sufficiently small so that there was little problem in selecting the elements of most important from cultural heritage. With the tremendous increase in knowledge accelerating with each generation after the advent of science, the schools found it no longer possible to include in their program all that was accepted by scholars. Increasingly the question was raised as to the contemporary significance of particular items of knowledge or particular skills and abilities.

An educational institution simply cannot teach everything; one must choose. One basis for selection lies in the needs of contemporary society. Need here refers to a competency that the individual will require in order to function effectively, productively, and satisfyingly as a citizen in society. Identifying such needs is somewhat hazardous because society is constantly changing. Too close a focus on the transitory needs of a society could lead to developing educational programs that provide individuals with outdated skills and proficiencies. For example, establishing a program to train people to perform tasks that will soon be automated is not only economically wasteful but constitutes a grave disservice to the learners who go through such a program. The identification of societal needs must be based on a careful analysis of the kinds of competencies likely to be in high demand for some time to come. Such competencies may include being able to gather and analyze information so as to make intelligent choices as consumers, being able to get along with others in a work situation, and so forth. Identifying societal needs is not restricted to vocational requirements; it can include a broad range of skills and abilities required for effective functioning in contemporary society.

The third source for educational objectives comes from the nature of the material to be learned. Specialists in subject-matters have much to contribute. While structure, methods of investigation, principles, and information in a discipline will serve *in part* as determiners of what is to be taught in a particular subject, subject-matter experts should be consulted at length about which aspects of a subject to include in an educational program. A note of caution should be added. The educator's concern with teaching a subject matter to a group of learners is not the same as the specialist's. In fact, the two concerns can diverge considerably. An educator is primarily interested in identifying and organizing those aspects of a subject judged relevant for learners of a particular age, ability-level, having specific sets of needs and interests. Subject-matter specialists, however, tend to be concerned with the training of specialists in their areas. They may see little difference between the general educational needs of learners and the special educational needs of future specialists. Those charged with the development of educational programs should make sure that the expertise of subject-matter specialists is used wisely in educational planning. A lax stance by program developers regarding this can result in educational programs that fail to meet either the needs of the learners or the needs of the larger society.

Curriculum development in the United States—from the launching of the first Soviet sputnik in 1957 until the mid 1960s—can be interpreted historically as a period when subject-matter specialists dominated the process of curriculum development. From various fields, they produced educational programs that were highly effective in training budding physicists, chemists, etc. The programs, unfortunately, were not as effective in meeting the educational needs of the broad group of learners served by the schools. Certainly, educational planners will need to make use of all the expertise they can get in fashioning sound educational programs. However, the decision-making function can neither be delegated away nor wrested from them by any single group, whether specialists in subject-matters, manpower experts, psychologists, human development specialists, or whatever. The planners of educational programs must maintain control over their endeavors.

The needs of the learner, the needs of society, and the nature of study materials, while the three major *sources* for educational aims, do not constitute educational objectives in their own right. Before a learner need, societal need, or any part of a subject can achieve the status of educational objective, it must undergo a valuation process; that is, it must be judged important and desirable by some group of educators. Thus, perceived deficiencies in the writing abilities of young people do not in themselves define a set of educational objectives with regard to writing; they are only suggestive. Only when a group of educators consciously decides that writing proficiency is a matter of importance for an institution to develop will writing proficiency achieve the status of an objective. Such *conscious* decision elevates a need to an objective.

In formulating educational objectives, the process by which a need or an aspect of subject is invested with value may be deliberate or casual; it must take place, however. It is frequently extremely complex: there often are inherent conflicts between the needs of the learner, the needs of society, and the nature of the subject to be learned. The conflict between proponents of general education and those who advocate the kind of specialized education that equips learners with marketable competencies reflects a continuing debate regarding the basic mission of an educational institution. In one case, the basic educational mission is viewed in terms of meeting a set of identified learner needs; in the other, it is seen in terms of meeting a set of societal requirements. When formulating a set of objectives for an educational program, choices have to be made; and such choices are usually among competing alternatives from each of the three sources of educational objectives.

Deciding what will achieve the status of an objective involves a philosophy of education. It may not be clearly and explicitly formulated (and often is not), but in one way or another choices get made, and needs or aspects of a subject are elevated to objectives. A philosophy of education serves, as it were, to screen or filter a variety of often competing needs and subject-aspects, letting through as objectives only what is considered educationally worthwhile.

A second screen for filtering information about learner needs, societal needs, and the nature of the subject material to be learned is a psychology of learning. Educators may recognize a set of needs, wish to meet them through an instructional program, but decide not to do so because the likelihood of succeeding is too small. The reason for such a decision may be that the age or ability of a group of learners is simply too low to give much assurance of success. For example, the decision not to adopt a highly rigorous physics program could be based (quite realistically) on the fact that high-school students could not handle the material. Some of the questions that may be asked with regard to contemplated objectives according to E. Furst (1958, p. 45) are:

To what extent is growth toward the objective a function of general maturation or general intelligence as contrasted with instruction?

Can the objective be reasonably attained at a given level of maturity?

At what levels of maturity are particular objectives best attained?

How much growth can be expected of different kinds of learners with respect to a set of objectives?

Does the attainment of one objective facilitate attainment of other objectives?

What is the retention value of different kinds of outcomes? Are some
more lasting than others?

There are no complete or definitive answers to these questions. Yet
they must be addressed and answered, in some degree, if educational
planning is to embody any realism. Research exists which can be of use in
obtaining partial answers. The collective experience of teachers—with
particular kinds of learners—is another important guide in formulating
tentative answers to the questions; thus, contemplated objectives can be
subject to at least some reality testing.

In sum, educational objectives originate as a result of a deliberate
process, which begins with a consideration of learner needs, the needs of
society, and the nature of the subject matter to be learned. These three
sources of educational aims are intended to answer the question—What
needs to be done? A philosophy of education and the psychology of
learning serve to answer the questions of what *should* be done and what
can be done. Ideally, the process by which educational objectives are
formulated is a conscious and rational one. This does not mean that it is
antiseptic. Differences in value orientations, political realities, economic
considerations; all influence the process of formulation and selection of
objectives. In reality, things are not usually particularly tidy. Nevertheless, some set of educational objectives, no matter how crudely stated,
emerges from the planning process.

EXPRESSING EDUCATIONAL OBJECTIVES

While there is general agreement about where educational objectives
come from, considerable disagreement exists about how educational
objectives should be expressed. Ignoring those writers who despair about
ever expressing educational intentions in written form, a wide range of
views remains about how objectives should be expressed. At one extreme
are writers who prescribe precise, detailed statements about each proficiency learners should develop as a result of exposure to an educational
treatment. Such statements, these writers argue, should contain four
essential elements. They should (1) be about the learner; (2) refer to an
observable behavior; (3) specify the conditions under which the behavior
is to occur; and (4) state the standard for judging what is an acceptable
level of behavior. In sum, the objectives of a program would be expressed
by a string of such statements, each containing the four essential elements
listed above. At the other extreme stand those writers who think a short,
discursive statement that tries to convey the intent of an educational
course, program, or curriculum institution will suffice, and that considerable autonomy should be left to the judgment of professionals charged
with carrying out the treatment. There are, of course, a number of
intermediate positions.

Historically, evaluation specialists have advocated that statements of educational objectives (1) refer to learners rather than to teachers, learning activities, or aspects of subject matter; and (2) be expressed as clearly as possible. The reason for the first is quite simple. Since learner performance is widely accepted as a major basis for educational evaluation, the expression of educational intentions, in a form that focuses on the learner, is considered not merely desirable but critical. In addition, the clearer the expression is, the easier it becomes to determine whether learners have attained the stated objectives. If educational objectives did *not* focus on the learner and the expression of educational intentions was not made precise, the task of evaluating an institution, a curriculum, or program course would become exceedingly difficult, if not impossible.

Educators have generally accepted these views. In spite of frequent failure in execution, both educators and evaluation specialists remain committed to stating objectives in terms of learners and to achieving maximum clarity. One of the first tasks in evaluating an educational enterprise is for educator and evaluation specialist to work out together an adequate expression of the objectives of a program in a manner satisfying to both.

Once the criteria of focus on the learner and clarity of expression are agreed upon, some evaluation specialists have urged greater specificity in the expression of objectives. The reason for this is again fairly obvious. The more specific educational objectives are, the easier it will be to determine whether learners have attained them. However, new problems arose. First, in striving to achieve greater specificity in expression, the number of objectives began to multiply at an alarming rate. For example, where a dozen or so general and reasonably clear objectives had previously sufficed to express the intentions for a tenth-grade English course, attempts to spell out learner proficiencies in specific terms resulted in as many as 1,084 specific objectives! Clearly, such a list of objectives is unacceptable as well as unrealistic. No teacher can attend to so extended a list, provide learning experiences designed to attain each of the 1,084 listed objectives, and monitor student progress towards their attainment. Even an evaluator would be hard pressed to gather evidence with respect to all objectives.

Second, by trying to achieve greater specificity in expressing objectives, generalized proficiencies were fragmented into a series of highly specific and discrete behaviors that threatened to destroy the integrity of the generalized proficiency. For example, developmental reading programs at the elementary and junior high-school level have long held the development of reading comprehension as a major objective. To break this up into a number of highly specific and discrete behaviors manifestly undermines the notion of reading comprehension as a generalized ability. Consequently many educators have been reluctant to strive for the degree of specificity that some evaluation specialists have urged. This does not mean that educators cannot illustrate in specific terms what is meant by a general objective: they are often quite expert at doing so. On the contrary, a number of educators refuse to define certain objectives in too specific terms because they believe that doing so would destroy the integrity of such objectives.

The issue of the level of specificity in statements of educational objectives is far from being resolved. Faced with fundamental differences regarding the problem, one possible course of action is to express educational objectives in a general, clear form; then, where desirable, list specific objectives for component behaviors of the general objectives. When it is felt that breaking down a general objective into specific statements is undesirable, illustrative behaviors should be sought.

One frequently voiced dissatisfaction with statements of educational objectives, both general and specific, is that they fail to say anything about the basic structure, intentions, or framework of an educational enterprise. For example, two mathematics courses for the same grade level might have very similar statements of objectives, but one may adopt an approach that emphasizes conceptual development, while the other stresses application of principles to practical problems. In the opinion of many educators, statements about objectives, no matter how carefully constructed, are simply not capable of conveying anything about the flavor of a course, program, or curriculum. The absence of such information is not only distressing to educators; it is often a loss for evaluation specialists as well. Evaluation workers need all the information they can get in order to perform their professional function. The failure to obtain basic information about the educator's intents can pose serious problems for an evaluation enterprise.

The discussion suggests that educational intentions need expression on at least three levels. First, a short, discursive exposition (less than five pages) is required to communicate the basic intentions of an educational enterprise—its orientation, framework, and broad goals. Second, a set of clear, general statements of objectives should be given to describe the major areas in which changes in learner-performance are being sought. For a single course that runs for a semester or a year, a list of, perhaps, six to fifteen general statements should be adequate to characterize its intentions; a program or curriculum running for several years would have somewhat more. The purpose of such a set of statements is to describe in general terms what is included in the enterprise and, by implication, what is excluded as well; this should serve as a convenient summarization of goals to direct teacher and learner efforts. Third, a set of clear and specific objectives is needed to give further meaning to each general objective where this is possible. Where it is not, illustrative proficiencies for each general objective should be supplied. The term "specific objectives" used here is similar to N. Gronlund's term "specific learning outcomes" (1976,

p. 30) and is generally related to R.F. Mager's and W.J. Popham's term "instructional objectives," although there are some basic differences (Mager 1962 and Popham 1975). It is important that *all three* kinds of statements be obtained in order to express as fully as possible the intentions of an educational enterprise. Each type serves a particular purpose not to be met by either of the other two kinds.

Lest the reader think that preparing three different kinds of statements creates an unreasonable burden, it should be pointed out that our intention is just the opposite. Educators and even evaluation specialists will encounter considerable difficulty in trying to express adequately a set of educational intentions with a set of statements at a *single* level of abstraction. In trying to decide how general or specific a statement of an educational objective should be, the educator and the evaluation worker run a risk, on one hand, of being too general and omitting important, detailed material; on the other, of producing unwieldy strings of specific and detailed statements that will closely resemble a laundry list. By stating objectives at *several* levels, such difficulties may be avoided. The opportunity for a full expression of a set of educational intentions may now be realized.

These statements, of course, must be arranged in a logical and clear relationship. Unfortunately, no formula for constructing the three interlocking sets now exists. One need not, for example, begin with an expository statement, then proceed to the general and specific objectives, although that is one procedure and certainly logical. One can just as well start with a set of general objectives and proceed in both directions. The only requirement is that a clear relationship among the three sets of statements be maintained.

There are different requirements for formulating each kind of statement. The least restrictive of these applies to the general expository statement: an educator is free to express the basic intent of an educational venture in a discursive form. This may include the basic orientation, organizational framework, content coverage, and general expectations with regard to learner performance. Descriptive material of some of the learning experiences might even be given to convey some of the flavor of the venture. While one would place few restrictions on the development of such an expository statement, its purpose as a descriptive rather than promotional document must remain central at all times. It is a necessary although not sufficient expression of educational intentions.

GENERAL OBJECTIVES

Developing a set of general objectives is a more demanding business than preparing an expository statement. A general objective is a unitary statement, describing a learner state after exposure to an educational treatment. While some writers argue that such statements should refer to observable behaviors in learners, it is not considered essential. General objectives can refer to internal states in the learner—as indicated by use of the terms such as "knows," "understands," and "comprehends"— provided these terms are clarified either in an accompanying set of specific objectives, or in a set of illustrative examples, defining more precisely the nature of the proficiency that is intended. In formulating a set of general objectives, several guiding principles are useful.

1. Objectives should be stated in terms of the learner and not in terms of teacher purposes or learning experiences. This point, made earlier, becomes increasingly important as one moves from an expository statement to a listing of outcomes. An objective expressed as "Participates in group discussions" would be considered unacceptable, since it refers to a learning experience rather than to what a student should show as a result of such an experience. Why does a teacher want learners to participate in group discussions? Perhaps a teacher wants learners to participate in group discussions so they can effectively present their points of view, adjust their positions on the basis of evidence or soundly presented argument, and, with other learners, reach sound and reasonable conclusions. If these are the benefits the teacher seeks from "participation," then they should be stated as the goals. Mere participation in an activity is not an acceptable objective.

2. Statements of objectives should begin with a verb, denoting the desired learner behavior or state. This format tends to assure that the focus of the objective will be on the learner and what he is or does. It should not be a recital of subject-matter to be learned. To illustrate, the statement "A set is a well-defined collection of objects or elements" is about subject-matter to be learned. "Knows the meaning of basic terms in mathematics" is a statement of an objective.

3. Objectives should be stated in terms that have uniform meanings. Unfortunately, language used in expressing educational intentions is often vague. Terms such as "good citizenship," "conceptual ability," "critical thinking," and "appreciates" are highly ambiguous. They can mean very different things to different people. Furthermore, deciding what would constitute admissible evidence of "appreciation," "critical thinking," and "good citizenship" is itself a formidable problem. Such problems can be elimiated by avoiding the use of ambiguous terms. When used, it is the responsibility of the educator, with whatever assistance he can get from the evaluation specialist, to define them with precision, clarity, and specificity, in a set of specific objectives.

4. Objectives should be unitary statements. For example, the objective "Knows basic principles of balancing chemical equations and can apply them in the solution of problems" refers to two processes. The first

refers to a knowledge state in the learner; the second to an ability to use the principles in the solution of novel problems. If both of these are important, then each should be accorded the status of an objective.

5. Objectives should be stated at an appropriate level of generality. Their statement should be expressed at a level general enough to be further defined in a set of specific objectives. Thus "Knows the meaning of basic mathematical terms" would be an acceptable statement of a general objective since it could be defined further in a series of specific objectives. Listing the specific terms to be learned—such as "set," "subset," "intersection of sets," "union of sets," etc.—in a set of general objectives would be inappropriate; it would be too cumbersome to work with. It would also convey an impression that the course or program was atomistic in nature, and this might be untrue. On the other hand, an objective such as "Knows mathematics" is stated far too broadly to serve any useful purpose.

6. Objectives should be related to the learning experiences provided. This point was made earlier in characterizing the educational process (see chapter 1). Put simply, it is unrealistic to expect learners to achieve objectives when little or no opportunity is provided to attain them. In a biology course, where the learning experiences consisted of having read printed material, attended lectures, and carried out explicitly-formulated experiments in a laboratory, it would not only be unrealistic but highly unfair to expect students to write short, learned essays on biological topics at the end of the course. No opportunity to develop the ability was provided. Either the objective or the learning experiences needs to be modified.

7. Objectives should be realistic in terms of the time available for instruction, the characteristics of the learners, and the present state of knowledge. An illustration of an unrealistic objective would be "Understands the causes of alcoholism," since no one as yet knows the causes of alcoholism. Similarly, an objective for a group of seventh-graders which reads "Understand the use of nonliteral statements in literature" would probably be unrealistic because the maturity level of the learners, and the limited time available for instruction in a general course in English.

SPECIFIC OBJECTIVES

General objectives are the competencies that learners are supposed to acquire after undergoing a set of learning experiences. Since these objectives are stated in general terms, further elaboration is usually necessary. This is done by listing specific objectives. Usually, each general objective needs to be followed by more specific and detailed statements that define the particular learner performances that would constitute the achievement of a general objective. If a learner approached a teacher and asked, "What do I have to say or do to persuade you that I have achieved a particular general objective?" the answers to such a question—in clear and specific form—would constitute a set of specific objectives for a general objective.

Most general objectives require elaboration in a set of specific objectives in order to convey fully a set of educational intentions. The behaviors described in Table 3.1 (to indicate understanding) provide one example of a set of specific objectives. It isn't necessary that all possible behaviors be listed. What is needed is a set of clear and specific behaviors that could be considered representative of a general objective, and which one is willing to accept in evidence of attainment of the objective. Thus it might be possible to analyze a general objective into five or six specific behaviors which, taken together, would constitute a reasonably full explication of a general objective. There is usually no point in trying to generate lengthy and exhaustive lists of specific objectives for each general objective. In the first place, it is unlikely that the proficiency represented in each specific objective will receive separate attention in instruction. Second, it is equally unlikely that an attempt will be made to test for each and every proficiency. Third, long lists of specific objectives are extremely cumbersome for teachers to work with. Hence, they are apt to be ignored. Finally, an attempt to define exhaustively a general objective may give the erroneous impression that a general objective is nothing but the sum of discrete proficiencies, rather than a generalized proficiency. Too detailed an analysis of a general objective may undermine the wholeness and, consequently, the integrity of the objectives.

One example of such overanalysis is in the area of reading comprehension where attempts have been made to break this competency into a number of different abilities. Some of the specific skills that have been noted are ability to follow directions; identify direct details; draw inferences from written material; find antecedents of words and phrases; identify motives of characters; and identify the writer's purpose. The above analysis may be helpful in suggesting instructional emphases and specific test questions. Still, it does convey the impression that reading comprehension is made up of many separate skills, which is not true. Reading comprehension is a fairly generalized ability that manifests itself fairly uniformly through a variety of specific abilities as shown by Thorndike and others. Attempts to analyze reading comprehension—or any other general objective that is unitary in nature—into a number of specific skills can undermine the integrity of the general objective.

SUMMARY

One of the contributions that an evaluation worker can make to the educational process is in helping program developers and teachers clarify their educational intentions. It is neither necessary nor realistic for an evaluation specialist to expect that a well-formulated set of objectives already exists for the course, program, or curriculum he is called upon to evaluate. One of the first orders of business for the evaluation worker is to determine how the objectives of an enterprise are expressed, if expressed at all, and then work with program developers and teachers to clarify them. The development of the expository statement of the intentions of the enterprise might be undertaken first. Such an exercise should provide necessary background information about the enterprise—its orientation and direction. The formulation of a set of general objectives would then follow. Here the evaluator can assist the program developer and teachers by helping them formulate objectives in as clear a way as possible. Guidelines for formulating general objectives given in this chapter should be of assistance in the task. Last, the evaluator can help program developers and teachers define the general objectives in terms of the more specific learning outcomes that constitute the specific objectives. What are the things learners must say or do to convince program developers and teachers they have achieved each general objective? This is the key to defining specific objectives. The evaluator can help fashion such answers into clear, specific, behaviorally oriented statements of learner performance. The assistance an evaluator can provide in each of these tasks should not only enable program developers and teachers to clarify their educational intentions; it should furnish them with the basic specifications for evaluating an educational enterprise—in terms of the changes it produces in the learners it serves.

REFERENCES

Furst, E. 1958. *Constructing Evaluation Instruments.* New York: Longmans Green.

Gronlund, N. 1976. *Measurement and Evaluation in Teaching,* 3rd. ed. New York: Macmillan.

Mager, R.F. 1962. *Preparing Educational Objectives.* Belmont, Cal.: Fearon Publications.

Popham, W.J. 1975. *Educational Evaluation.* Englewood Cliffs, N.J.: Prentice-Hall.

Thorndike, R. 1973–74. "Reading as Reasoning." *Reading Research Quarterly* 9, no. 2: 135–147.

Tyler, R. 1950. *Basic Principles of Curriculum and Instruction.* Chicago: University of Chicago Press.

ADDITIONAL READINGS

Bloom, B. (ed.). 1956. *Taxonomy of Educational Objectives: Handbook I, The Cognitive Domain.* New York: Longmans Green.

Bloom, B., Hastings, T. and Madaus, G. (eds.). 1971. *Handbook of Formative and Summative Evaluation.* New York: McGraw-Hill.

de Landsheere, V. 1977. "On Defining Educational Objectives." *Evaluation in Education: International Progress* vol. 1, no. 2.

Harrow, A. 1972. *A Taxonomy of the Psychomotor Domain.* New York: David McKay.

Henry, N. (ed.). 1946. *The Measurement of Understanding.* Yearbook of the National Society for the Study of Education. Part I. Chicago: University of Chicago Press.

Kibler, R., et al. 1977. "Behavioral Objectives." In *Curriculum Handbook: The Disciplines, Current Movements and Instructional Methodology,* edited by L. Rubin. Boston: Allyn anbd Bacon.

Krathwohl, D., et al. (eds.). 1964. *A Taxonomy of Educational Objectives: Handbook II, The Affective Domain.* New York: David McKay.

Smith, E. and Tyler, R. 1943. *Appraising and Recording Student Progress.* New York: Harper.

Struenig, E. and Guttentag, M. 1975. *Handbook of Evaluation Research,* vols. 1 and 2. Beverly Hills: Sage Publications.

Walberg, H. (ed.). 1974. *Evaluating Educational Performance.* Berkeley: McCutchan Publications, 1974.

4

RELATING EVALUATION PROCEDURES TO OBJECTIVES

The identification of general and specific objectives for courses, programs, or curricula is critical to the evaluation enterprise. Without a clear and detailed set of objectives it is impossible to ascertain whether an educational enterprise is accomplishing what it has set out to do. In the framework for evaluation presented in chapter 2, the first two classes of information require data about learner performance at the start of an educational treatment and at a later period: often the conclusion of the program. The objectives provide specifications for much of the information to be collected. Any educational enterprise seeking to bring about changes in learners is duty-bound to collect information about the extent to which such changes have occurred.

Measurement of learner performance—in relation to a set of objectives—is not limited to the measurement of factual information acquired during a period of instruction. Neither is it limited to paper-and-pencil tests or formal instruction. Evaluation is a continuous and comprehensive process, utilizing a variety of evidence-gathering procedures. It is inextricably linked to the objectives and learning experiences of an educational venture.

In the previous chapter attention was focused on the process of formulating and expressing a set of educational objectives. In this chapter attention will be paid to the problem of identifying those evaluation procedures which provide the best and most direct evidence concerning the attainment of general and specific objectives.

Relating evaluation procedures to general and specific objectives requires logical analysis and judgment. There are, however, several principles to guide such an activity. Figure 4.1 sets forth the relationship between general objectives, specific objectives, and evaluation procedures.

The important point to be made about the information presented in

FIGURE 4.1

Relationship of Evaluation Procedures to Objectives

↓General Objectives[a]
Specific Objectives[b]
↓Evaluation Procedures[c]

[a]Goals which direct educational courses, programs, and curricula.
[b]Learner behaviors accepted as evidence of the attainment of objectives.
[c]Procedures for obtaining evidence of learner behavior described in the specific objectives.
Source: Adapted from N. Gronlund. Measurement and Evaluation in Teaching, 3rd. ed. New York: Macmillan, 1976, p. 61.

Figure 4.1 is that a clear and logical relationship must be established among the three elements—general objectives, specific objectives, and evaluation procedures. The direction of the arrows shows that general objectives serve as the specifications for the development of the specific objectives; specific objectives are the determiners for the selection of evaluation procedures. This close logical relationship must be maintained if the evaluation enterprise is to have validity.

In selecting evaluation procedures, three general principles hold. First, an evaluation procedure should be appropriate; that is, the evaluation procedure chosen must produce the requisite information about learner behavior. Second, of several possibly appropriate evaluation procedures the one that is most efficient and practical should be employed. This is to insure that the evaluation enterprise is realistic and manageable. Third, wherever possible but especially with objectives that are considered to be critical, *multiple* measures be used. The purpose of this practice is to fortify the validity of evaluation results by obtaining relevant data (1) in several different ways; or (2) on several occasions. Any particular evidence-gathering procedure is bound to have its own irrelevancies: a specific format, procedures for administration, specific item content, etc. The use of more than one procedure or occasion for evidence gathering should supply a variety of information bearing on the same objective or set of objectives.

Of all three principles the one concerning appropriateness is critical. (*Appropriateness* means that the evaluation procedure requires the learner to perform the behavior specified in the objective.) If an evaluation procedure is not appropriate for a particular objective, the resulting information is irrelevant at best and misleading at worst. For example, if a specific course objective requires learners to produce a plan for testing a hypothesis in a certain subject area, then the evaluation procedure must see that students produce such a plan. Nothing less and nothing more will do. Questions asking students which of several plans would be most adequate for testing a hypothesis are invalid; the objective requires that students construct a plan, not select one from a number of alternatives. Clearly, the ability to select a plan correctly is no guarantee that the learner will be able to construct one.

It frequently happens that inappropriate evaluation procedures are selected for evidence gathering. The use of objective written tests, for example, is relied on overheavily in the evaluation of educational endeavors. Such tests include a number of item types among which are true-false and matching questions; one-or-two-word fill-in items, and multiple choice questions. Objective written tests are, generally, highly efficient in sampling learner performance on a wide range of subject matter. They can also be used to test for a variety of objectives. They become appropriate, however, when the specific objective of a course, program, or curriculum specifies that the student identify, recognize, or select a correct response. They are inappropriate whenever an objective requires that the learner recall an item of information or develop his own response. It is, clearly, the evaluator's responsibility to make sure that every evaluation procedure used is appropriate for each objective.

The principle of choosing the most *efficient* evaluation procedure is important for practical reasons: an evaluation enterprise should be as unobtrusive, practical, and economical as possible. To achieve this goal, one should use evaluation procedures that (1) are inexpensive; (2) require a minimum amount of time (from both learner and teacher) for obtaining the necessary evidence; and (3) yield the most reliable estimates of learner behavior.

To illustrate this principle, consider an objective that requires learners to identify prime numbers. There are three general ways in which learners can be tested on this objective. First, they can be given an objective written test, consisting of a list of numbers, and asked to make an *x* next to the numbers that are prime. Second, learners can be asked to list all prime numbers between two given numbers. Last, they can be questioned orally by a teacher or assistant as to which numbers in a given set are prime and which are not. All three ways of gathering the requisite learner-performance information are appropriate to the objective. Of the three, however, the objective written test is most efficient: it requires the least amount of time on the part of both learners and teacher. Administered in a matter of minutes, it can be scored quickly by the teacher, an aide, or even a machine. What's more, it can be administered to an entire class at the same time. *For this objective* an evaluator would be wise to use an objective written test.

Table 4.1 relates a variety of educational objectives to their appropriate evaluation procedures. Listed on the left side of the table are 16 different objectives. The list is not exhaustive—merely suggestive of a

TABLE 4.1

Procedures for Evaluating 16 Objectives

Objective		Evaluation Procedures									
	Objective Written Test	Objective Self-reports of Feelings	Objective Self-reports of Past Actions	Essay Written Test	Oral Questioning	Planned Observation by Checklist or Rating	Paper, Theme, or Report	Product, Scored or Rated	Performance, Observed and Rated	Incidental Observation by Teacher or Evaluator	Situational Test
1. Recalls, recognizes, identifies specific facts, concepts	X	—	—	X	X	—	—	—	—	—	—
2. Idenficies, describes, names orders	X	—	—	X	X	—	—	—	—	—	X
3. Makes set of plans, devises procedures or experiments	—	—	—	X	—	—	X	—	—	—	X
4. Communicates through writing	X	—	—	X	—	—	X	—	—	—	—
5. Communicates orally	—	—	—	—	X	X	—	—	X	X	—
6. Comprehends oral communication	X	—	—	X	X	—	—	—	—	—	—
7. Judges, compares, interprets	X	—	—	X	X	—	X	—	—	—	X
8. Carries out task or process	—	—	—	—	—	—	—	—	X	—	X

9. Produces product to meet certain criteria	—	—	—	—	—	—	—	—	X	—	—	—	—
10. Displays specified attitudes, values	X	X	—	—	—	—	—	—	—	—	—	X	—
11. Displays specified interests	X	X	—	—	—	—	—	—	—	—	—	X	—
12. Displays specified character traits (honesty, loyalty, etc.)	—	—	—	—	X	—	—	—	—	X	—	X	X
13. Displays leadership	—	—	—	—	X	—	—	—	—	X	—	X	X
14. Displays specified work habits (initiative, promptness, responsibility, etc.)	—	—	—	—	X	—	—	—	—	—	—	X	—
15. Displays social adjustments to peers, superiors, group	—	—	—	—	—	—	—	—	—	X	—	X	—
16. Displays personal adjustment (self-esteem, reactions to thwarting, handling of anxiety, etc.)	X	X	—	—	—	—	—	—	—	—	X	X	—

Source: Compiled by the author.

range of possible objectives. In all probability a given course, program, or curriculum would not include everyone of them. The lower-numbered objectives are largely cognitive, while the higher-numbered ones are principally affective. Objectives eight and nine sometimes have a substantial psychomotor component. This distinction, considered important by many educators, is not so regarded here. The view throughout this book is that educational objectives are values; *each one* is important in its own right. Whether objectives should be classified as belonging to a cognitive, affective, or psychomotor domain is relatively unimportant.

The column headings in Table 4.1 give 16 common types of evaluation procedures. The first, the objective written test, includes a variety of item-types. Typically, a learner selects a response from several choices or supplies one-or-two-word answers to specific questions. Similarly, self-reports of feelings or past actions can be obtained in multiple ways: e.g., by having learners indicate their agreement, or disagreement, with particular statements of feeling; or by having them rank statements in order of "most-to-least descriptive" of their feelings. Each general evaluation procedure thus represents a class of technique to be used in gathering certain kinds of evidence.

Evaluation procedures may be arranged in a rough order of efficiency. The first procedure, an objective written test, is the most efficient; objective self-reports of feelings and past actions are second; and so on down to situational tests which are least efficient. The checks in the boxes in the body of Table 4.1 indicate that a particular evaluation procedure is appropriate for a given objective. The chart shows that the seventh objective, which specifies that learners correctly interpret material presented to them, could be tested by an objective written test, an essay examination, oral questioning, or a situational test. All of the checked evaluation procedures would be appropriate for gathering evidence with regard to the attainment of the objective. The objective written test, however, is the most *efficient* procedure for obtaining the relevant information. Nevertheless, while an objective written test is most efficient, an essay test might in some cases be more suitable; e.g., in a situation where the persons charged with evaluation did not have the requisite expertise to develop objective items necessary for objective testing. In effect, one uses the available resources to do a job. Many people do find it easier to develop essay rather than objective-type questions to measure complex intellectual performances. Consequently, while one would consider efficiency first by choosing evaluation procedures as far to the left as possible in Table 4.1, there are sometimes very good good reasons for not doing so. The important point is to choose an *appropriate* evaluation procedure for a given objective.

As noted above, one may choose to use a less efficient procedure for highly practical reasons. One may also wish to consider, where resources permit, using more than one procedure to determine to what extent an objective has been achieved. The use of multiple measures of outcomes is generally recommended as a means of overcoming the idiosyncracies associated with a particular evaluation instrument or procedure. In the case of an objective requiring learners to identify prime numbers (discussed earlier) three different procedures could be used to determine learner proficiency. The use of multiple measures of educational outcomes is highly recommended as a means of insuring that learner performance, after a period of instruction, is due to the effects of instruction, not to irrelevancies of specific evaluation procedures. The extent to which multiple measures of learner-performance can be employed will often depend on the exigencies of local circumstances—e.g., the amount of evaluation material that can be produced, the time available for administering and scoring tests, etc. In chapter 10 ways of collecting information efficiently are described, which will enable evaluators to gather more information than they might have thought possible. In any event, local conditions will be the overriding determiners of what kind of, and how much, information can be gathered.

The evaluation procedures listed in Table 4.1 are ones generally employed to gather data about learner behavior. A brief description of each will be given—to acquaint the reader with the general characteristics and main feature of each.*

OBJECTIVE WRITTEN TEST

Objective written tests consist of a number of different item-types. The learner operates within a highly structured situation; selects his answer from a limited set of choices, supplied by the test constructor; typically responds to a large number of items and receives a score— usually right or wrong—according to a predetermined set of correct answers. The term "objective" refers to this last characteristic, namely, that competent judges can agree on the correctness of a learner's answers. Item-types used in objective tests include true/false, matching, multiple choice and, sometimes, short one-or-two-word fill-in questions. Objective written tests have been used extensively to test for possession of factual information; they can also be used to assess ability to draw inferences; make interpretations from presented material; apply principles to novel situations; make comparisons and elementary kinds of analyses. Two examples of objective test questions that go *beyond* the testing of factual information are reprinted from Comber and Keeves (1973):

---

*Detailed presentations of each procedure can be found in general textbooks on measurement (see Gronlund [1975] and Thorndike and Hagen [1977].

(Example 1)

3. Tom wanted to learn which of three types of soil—clay, sand, or loam—would be best for growing beans. He found three flowerpots, put a different type of soil in each pot, and planted the same number of beans in each, as shown in the drawing. He placed them side by side on the window sill and gave each pot the same amount of water.

Loam Clay Sand

Why was Tom's experiment NOT a good one for his purpose?

A. The plants in one pot got more sunlight than the plants in the other pots
B. The amount of soil in each pot was not the same.
C. One pot should have been placed in the dark
D. Tom should have used different amounts of water
E. The plants would get too hot on the window sill

(Example 2)

John put some seeds on moist cotton in a dish. Jane put some seeds of the same kind into a glass full of water by the side of his. After two days John's seeds sprouted but nothing seemed to happen to Jane's. Which of the following is the most probable explanation?

A. Jane's seeds had been kept dry for too long
B. Jane did not allow her seeds enough air
C. Jane did not put the glass in a warm enough place
D. Jane should have used a different kind of seed
E. Jane did not use any cotton

OBJECTIVE SELF-REPORTS OF FEELINGS

Objective self-report measures of feeling, typically, consist of several non-factual statements which the learners are asked to respond to by indicating their extent of agreement or endorsement. Some illustrative items—intended to measure learner attitudes about science—are given by Comber and Keeves (1973):

Science is steadily destroying the world.

Science helps to make the world a better place to live in.

Science is making us slaves to machines.

For each item the learner is furnished a set of response options such as "I strongly agree" "I agree," "I am uncertain," "I disagree," and "I strongly disagree," and is asked to check the one that best corresponds to his feelings. By summing the learner's responses to a number of items measuring the same characteristic, it is possible to describe an individual's affective attitude with respect to a particular area.

Three major assumptions underlie the use of objective self-report measures of feeling. They are (1) the learner is able to read and understand the statements; (2) the learner is aware of his feelings toward the characteristic being measured; and (3) the learner is willing to indicate his feelings toward the characteristic being measured.

If one or more of these assumptions is not met, using objective self-report measures of feelings would be a questionable undertaking. For example, in a science course that seeks to influence attitudes in a particular way, learners may be reluctant to express their real feelings toward science. Evaluation workers need to be sensitive about the prospects of obtaining honest information through the use of such measures. One obvious way of increasing the likelihood of obtaining honest answers is to have learners respond anonymously. Since the goal of an evaluation is to make statements about treatments rather than individual learners, it is unnecessary for individuals to be identified by name.

OBJECTIVE SELF-REPORTS OF PAST ACTIONS

These are often employed to gather supplemental information which will help interpret results of learner performance in a particular course, program, or curriculum. For example, a social studies course may seek to develop learner interest in governmental affairs. It may achieve this goal with some learners but not with others. The use of a self-report measure of learner's previous contacts and activities in governmental affairs might reveal that those who had a history of civic activities demonstrated increased interest—while those who had not, did not. The use of an objective self-report of past actions can be of considerable help in explaining why some learners change in desirable ways when others do not. It can constitute an invaluable aid for future course-planning as well.

Questionnaires are the main vehicle for gathering information about the past actions of learners. Well-constructed questionnaires can result in the collection of a considerable amount of information in a short time. One of the major problems in the use of questionnaires, however, is that they appear easy to make. Unfortunately, this is not the case. The development of good questionnaires requires considerable expertise; anyone planning to use them would be well advised, at the very least, to study carefully the principles and procedures of questionnaire development (see Kornhauser and Sheatsley 1959, Oppenheim 1966). The same assumptions that underly the development of objective self-reports of feelings apply to instruments measuring past actions. However, it is probably less likely that individuals will withhold reporting about past actions (unless they are deemed socially undesirable).

ESSAY WRITTEN TEST

An essay written test consists of a few questions. Learners are required to organize their own answers and use their own words and style of writing (usually including their own handwriting) to produce an answer with varying degrees of correctness and completeness. The essay written test is particularly useful when what is required is that learners produce their own answers rather than merely recognize a correct one. Where objectives require that students be able to describe, give examples, make comparisons, develop a unique communication, etc., the essay written test is best suited for testing such proficiencies.

While it is generally recognized that the scoring of essay written tests can create problems, it is less widely acknowledged that the development of such tests also presents considerable difficulties. One must have clearly in mind the mental processes one wants the learner to use in answering an essay question before starting to write the query. The use of novel material, or novel methods of presentation in stating an essay question, may be necessary to test proficiencies beyond mere recall of knowledge. The learner task, however, must be clearly presented and unambiguously defined. In scoring essay questions it is generally recommended that qualities on which answers are to be judged be defined in *advance* of scoring and, where multiple criteria are employed, that provision be made for a separate evaluation of each. Preparing model answers, reading all responses to one question before going on to another, and scoring questions as anonymously as possible; all are recommended practices for achieving maximum accuracy in scoring.

ORAL QUESTIONING

Oral questioning is in some ways similar to essay questioning. Learners are presented with problems which require them to organize answers and express themselves in their own words. Answers, of course, can have varying degrees of completeness and correctness; however, oral questioning permits an examiner to ask follow-up questions and elaboration on the part of respondents. As such it is a highly flexible method of assessing learner proficiency. On the negative side, it is often difficult to judge the quality of a learner's answers; unless the questioning is tape-recorded, no permanent record exists which can be studied in detail while making a thoughtful appraisal. Judging learners' responses, as they occur, places a considerable burden on an examiner. The flexibility of oral questioning also poses problems; actual questions asked of one learner can differ markedly from those asked of another, resulting in a basic noncomparability. As a method, oral questioning is comparatively inefficient; only one learner can be examined at a time.

PAPER, THEME, OR REPORT

The use of an assigned paper, theme, or report as an evaluation procedure is often undervalued. It has a number of the same features that essay written tests have. The learner organizes his own answers and expresses himself in his own style of writing. In addition, the learner ordinarily has the opportunity to review and edit his work so that the resultant product usually represents his best effort.

In many cases the learner is given some latitude in selecting the particular topic he will write on, thus introducing a certain degree of non-comparability into the situation. However, this can be remedied somewhat by specifying the limits within which choices for topics can be made, or by having an approval procedure before learners are allowed to begin to work in earnest. Another difficulty in the use of papers, themes, or reports prepared outside of a classroom setting is that it is seldom possible to know how much the product represents the learner's own efforts, and how much the efforts of others. For this reason, it is usually considered wise to supplement papers, themes, and reports with evidence gathered under supervised conditions.

PRODUCTS, SCORED OR RATED

Educational enterprises, having among their objectives the production of objects, will necessarily require product evaluations. Products that are scored or rated resemble essay questions in that the learner produces an object in his own style. The product can have varying degrees of correctness or completeness. For example, in a course in carpentry a learner may be required to build a sawhorse, according to a set of specifications. The product can then be judged on the basis of several criteria—stability, sturdiness, closeness of fit of joints, etc. Separate scores or ratings can be given for each criterion. In appraising learner products it is usually not possible to make judgments about the process used in production. In the construction of a sawhorse, for example, we cannot rate the learner's proficiency in using a T-square, saw, or hammer merely by observing the finished product; only tentative inferences can be made. These, of course, would need confirmation in another situation where process can be directly observed.

PERFORMANCES, OBSERVED AND RATED

Some objectives demand that learners carry out a particular kind of performance. Making a speech before a group, playing a musical instrument, or performing some athletic feat are examples of behaviors that can only be evaluated by direct observation and rating of the performance. In judging learner performance in this way, time and effort must be taken to closely observe the performance and—either while it is going on or immediately after its conclusion—rate it, according to previously determined criteria and standards. The usual device employed is a scale, with one or more characteristics, on which the performance is to be rated. In addition, for each characteristic there is a set of graded categories, representing different levels of quality. Observing and rating performances is often laborious and time-consuming. It also demands that the individual doing the rating is sufficiently familiar with the rating scale to use it as intended. Usually, this requires training in the use of rating scales so that various kinds of errors can be avoided. Used properly, rating scales can be important sources of information about learner behavior; in some cases, they may be the only source available.

INCIDENTAL OBSERVATION

Unlike planned observations and ratings of learner performance, incidental observation—often coupled with rating—is employed to assess typical learner behaviors. Planned observation and rating could be used, for example, to appraise learners' speaking or oral reading performances. In these cases, learners know they're "on"—i.e., called on to perform. Social skills, use of time and equipment, initiative, persistence, adaptability, and other similar behaviors are best appraised when the individual is unaware of being observed and when observation occurs over a prolonged period of time. Incidental observation by a teacher or evaluation worker, coupled with some procedure for recording such as rating scales, can yield useful information about a number of important objectives in the areas of skills, work habits, social behavior, interest, and adjustment.

The main requirement for the use of incidental observation is that the observer should be conscious of the characteristics and behaviors singled out for observation and sensitive to their occurrence. Observation normally occurs during the course of regular activities in the educational situation, placing a real demand for versatility on the part of the

TABLE 4.2

Procedures for Evaluating Objectives for High School Science Course

General and Specific Objectives	Evaluation Procedure
1. Knows common terms	
Defines common terms	Short answer essay test
Distinguishes between correct and incorrect use of terms	Objective written test
Identifies meaning of terms when used in context	Objective written test
2. Understands principles and generalizations	
Recognizes major principles and generalizations	Objective written test
States principles and generalizations in own words	Short answer essay test
Given a principle or generalization, identifies situation using it	Objective written test
Given a situation, identifies principle of generalization that applies	Objective written test
3. Applies principles to novel material	
Identifies elements in situation needed to establish problem type	Short answer essay test
Selection of abstraction (principle, method or idea) suitable to problem type	Objective written test,
Use of abstraction to solve problem	Short answer essay test
	Short answer essay test
4. Plans and carries out a study to test a hypothesis	
Develops a plan for hypothesis testing which can yield unequivocal results	Paper
Carries out study in a technically correct way	Planned and incidental observation Product (Laboratory notebook)
Prepares a report of results of the study	Paper and Product (Laboratory notebook)

Source: Adapted from N. Gronlund. *Measurement and Evaluation in Teaching,* 3rd ed. New York: Macmillan, 1976.

educational worker. If observations are to have any validity, they should be made during the normal course of educational activities when the individual being observed is least aware of being observed. Observation should also continue over some period of time, since the behavior sought after may not occur naturally in many situations. Heavy requirements are placed on observers; they must detect the behaviors considered important and keep a record of their occurrence. Incidental observation frequently requires more time and effort than usual testing procedures, and it is more subjective than one would wish. However, if the behaviors being assessed are considered educationally important, there is no alternative but to gather evidence about them, however fallible the methods employed may be.

SITUATIONAL TEST

The situational test is a mixture of a standard testing approach and a real-life situation. It is created as naturally as possible to evoke particular kinds of learner behaviors that are considered educationally important. At the simplest level, the teacher may call upon a learner to read unfamiliar material in order to note the kinds of errors made. At a more complex level, a group may be set up to discuss a particular topic, and learners are observed for the incidence of particular discussion-group behaviors such as clarification, facilitation, reaction to different points of view, etc. The difficulty in developing situational tests is making them appear spontaneous and making sure the learners are unaware that they are in an evaluation situation. This sometimes requires elaborate efforts. A situation test is useful for assessing character traits, such as honesty and loyalty, and various social skills and leadership qualities. Along with a system for recording performance data, it can be used to gather evidence about types of behavior that might otherwise go unassessed.

The special feature of the situational test is that it is intended to elicit certain kinds of learner behavior. One can wait for a learner to display these behaviors in an educational setting and not see them occur, because nothing in the situation happens to evoke them. The situational test attempts to overcome this by structuring the situation in such a way that conditions *call* for a demonstration of the required behavior. For example, if one wanted to know whether a learner knew the meaning of the word "eleemosynary," one could follow the learner around for a year and never hear him utter the word. Still, it would be unwarranted to infer that he did not know it. The occasion for its use never arose. The situational test is intended to remedy this by arranging conditions in the situation so that the only way the learner can perform successfully is by using the word "eleemosynary."

SUMMARY

The above sketches of major evaluation procedures are intended to acquaint the reader with a variety of ways of gathering information about learner behavior with regard to educational objectives. The key to relating objectives to evaluation procedures is appropriateness. An evaluation procedure should be selected on the basis of its chances of yielding the kind of evidence that will permit an evaluator to make an unequivocal statement about the extent to which a particular objective has been achieved. Table 4.2 was developed to assist in accomplishing this goal.

The tendency to equate evaluation with formal testing has been an unfortunate development. Critics of testing have charged for some time that formal testing procedures are severely limited as to kinds of educational outcomes that can be effectively measured. While there is certainly some truth in this charge, such critics go too far when they claim that *only* acquisition of information can be measured by formal paper-and-pencil testing procedures. To emphasize the variety of evaluation procedures and show how objectives can be related to them, Table 4.2 has been developed. This table presents four general objectives for a high-school chemistry course (the actual course would probably have more). Each general objective is broken down into a group of specific objectives. One, and sometimes two or three, evaluation procedures are presented for each specific objective. For each specific objective the evaluation procedures selected are those that will provide the most direct and adequate evidence of learner behavior. Such a table should be developed in connection with the planning of any evaluation enterprise.

REFERENCES

Comber, L. and Keeves, J. 1973. *Science Education in Nineteen Countries.* New York: Halstead Press (John Wiley).

Gronlund, N. 1976. *Measurement and Evaluation in Teaching,* 3rd ed. New York: Macmillan.

Kornhauser, A. and Sheatsley, P. 1959. "Questionnaire Construction and Interview Procedures." In C. Sellitz, et al., *Research Methods in Social Relations,* revised ed., edited by C. Sellitz, et al. New York: Holt, Rinehart and Winston.

Oppenheim, A. 1966. *Questionnaire Design and Attitude Measurement.* New York: Basic Books.

Thorndike, R. and Hagen, E. 1977. *Measurement and Evaluation in Psychology and Education,* 4th ed. New York: Wiley.

ADDITIONAL READINGS

Bloom, B. (ed.). 1956. *Taxonomy of Educational Objectives: Handbook I, The Cognitive Domain.* New York: Longmans Green.

Bloom, B., Hastings, T. and Madaus, G. (eds.). 1971. *Handbook of Formative and Summative Evaluation.* New York: McGraw-Hill.

Harrow, A. 1972. *A Taxonomy of the Psychomotor Domain.* New York: David McKay.

Henry, N. (ed.). 1946. *The Measurement of Understanding.* Yearbook of the National Society for the Study of Education, Part I. Chicago: University of Chicago Press.

Krathwohl, D., et al. (eds.). 1964. *A Taxonomy of Educational Objectives: Handbook II, The Affective Domain.* New York: David McKay.

Smith, E. and Tyler, R. 1943. *Appraising and Recording Student Progress.* New York: Harper.

Struenig, E. and Guttentag, M. 1975. *Handbook of Evaluation Research*, vols. 1 and 2. Beverly Hills: Sage Publications.

Walberg, H. (ed.). 1974. *Evaluating Educational Performance.* Berkeley, Cal.: McCutchan Publications.

5

GATHERING EVIDENCE
ABOUT LEARNER PERFORMANCE

The importance of information about learner performance in evaluating an educational course, program, or curriculum cannot be overestimated. Properly gathered, analyzed and interpreted, it will enable an educator to determine to what degree an educational enterprise has succeeded in doing what it set out to accomplish. What it "set out to accomplish" involves invariably changing the behavior of learners in directions considered educationally desirable: an increase in knowledge, skills, and problem-solving abilities; a change in attitudes; or other more complex performances.

In former chapters we have discussed and explained (1) the processes by which objectives were formulated and specified; and (2) how appropriate evaluation procedures are chosen for gathering evidence as to learner achievement of these objectives. In this chapter we will attempt to describe a number of the more relevant aspects of the actual process of gathering learner behavior information. (Detailed descriptions of procedures for evidence-gathering, however, will not be dealt with: they are readily available in conventional works on measurement and testing.) Of paramount importance here is the vital role it plays in the evaluation of educational courses, programs, and curricula. Evidence-gathering, it cannot be noted too often, refers not only to conventional testing: a whole range of procedures is available for the accumulation of relevant information about learner behavior relative to educational objectives.

The formulation of a set of general objectives and its elaboration in the form of specific objectives, although crucial, is only an initial step in the evaluation process. For each specific objective, one or more suitable evaluation procedures must be selected. Evaluation exercises, items, tasks, questions, observational forms, and so on are then developed to elicit relevant learner performance information. Conventional procedures for instrument development are followed, fidelity to the objectives being the overriding consideration. Occasionally, concessions have to be made for practical reasons—such as limitations on time, lack of expertise with a particular technique, or because of difficulties of application in an actual situation. For instance, a specific objective might, ideally, require the use of extensive observation of learner performance but practical considerations might lead one to settle for a self-report instrument. Of course, once one decides to use a less direct means of gathering information for a more direct one, *some* check should be made to obtain assurance that the two procedures yield essentially similar results.

The actual development of evaluation instruments is often undertaken jointly by those charged with the evaluation of educational courses, programs, and curricula and those charged with developing and conducting them. Evaluators should bring to the task a body of professional and technical expertise in the development of evaluation instruments; those who develop and conduct the programs should bring a body of substantive knowledge about the material they will teach and the nature of the learners they will serve. Their joint efforts (in some limited endeavors it might be simply two individuals) should produce a set of evaluation instruments that are relevant for the program and reasonable for learners.

Ideas for evaluation exercises can come from program, personnel, or evaluation specialists; whatever the source, they would need to be reviewed by everyone involved in evaluating. Such a review would decide whether (1) an evaluation exercise or procedure is faithful to the objective being measured and (2) suitable to the learners. These are crucial considerations. If security is a factor, evaluators and program personnel can develop prototype exercises and procedures to serve as models for development of parallel material by evaluation specialists. While less than ideal, such arrangements are sometimes necessary. It will protect the professionals most closely associated with the operation of the program by insuring that whatever beneficial program effects are found cannot be ascribed to overfamiliarity with the actual test questions, items, and exercises.

Once developed, the material should be grouped on the basis of similarity of procedure, *not* objective being measured. Thus, objective written questions would be grouped in one pile, regardless of objective being tested, essay questions in another pile, and so on. In doing this workers should make sure that the objective being tested is not lost sight of: at some later date all information items bearing on a single objective will have to be reassembled.

WHEN SHOULD EVIDENCE BE GATHERED

Information about learner performance must be obtained on at least two occasions—before instruction gets seriously underway, and after a specified period of instruction. The phrase "before instruction gets seriously underway" indicates that an estimate of learner performance *before* a treatment begins is important. Specifically, educators not only need to know that learners are not already proficient in what they are expected to achieve; they require some estimate of how unaccomplished they are. To this end measures of achievement—e.g., objective written tests, essay tests, etc.—could be administered during the first few sessions that learners are together. The administration of such measures at the beginning of a set of learning experiences is a somewhat delicate undertaking: teachers and learners will not have developed a working relationship yet, and learners presumably will be answering questions and items covering unfamiliar material. One commonly used procedure is to include in the test directions a statement acknowledging the learner's general lack of familiarity with the material, but requesting them to try to do their best. It can also be announced that information resulting will be of assistance in planning specific learning experiences for the group. Often, assurance that these test performances will not influence individual marks is given; however, this may cause individuals not to put forth their best effort in answering various questions and items. Here is a real problem, and there is no easy solution. Some assurance should be offered that performance will not influence the learners' marks. Frankly given, it may even contribute to the development of a sense of trust between teachers and learners. It should not be assigned undue prominence. Instead, educators should emphasize that information, representing the best efforts of the learners, will be of great practical importance in planning an appropriate set of learning experiences for the group.

Information relating to intellectual outcomes can be gathered during the beginning sessions of a course, program, or curriculum. For several reasons information about nonintellectual outcomes should probably not be gathered until somewhat later—perhaps three to four weeks after a program has started. First, learners may be reluctant to respond frankly to measures dealing with attitudes, feelings, and interests. Rather than run the risk of obtaining incorrect information or no information at all, it seems wise to hold off a little until some positive relationship has been established. Second, some measures—notably those dealing with social relationships—cannot be administered until a group of learners has been together for a period of time. For example, socio-metric measures cannot be administered until a group has been together long enough for social relationships to develop. If a program has objectives dealing with social aspects associated with learning, this will usually be the case.

The chief danger in delaying information-gathering about student performance is that the information, at length obtained, may have already been influenced by the program. Called "confounding," this unlooked-for influence can cause considerable confusion in the interpretation of results from evaluation studies: it should be avoided if possible; minimized, if necessary. As a rule, initial information should be gathered as early as possible. However, in regard to nonintellectual outcomes, it may be useful to delay administering some instruments for a few weeks until the learners have adjusted to the situation and feel comfortable enough to give frank answers to items of a personal nature.

How much information should be gathered about the initial performance of learners is an open question. While some would advocate as much as possible, a good case could be made for obtaining as little as possible; keeping the amount of testing time down to a minimum at the beginning of an instruction period has distinct advantages. First, the less time is taken for testing, the more time is left for learning. Second, the chief purpose of measuring learner performance at the beginning of a course, program, or curriculum is to obtain a rough estimate as to learners' proficiencies regarding program material. Third, one would expect that minimizing testing time at the beginning of a treatment period would increase the likelihood of learners making an all-out effort to answer questions and items and to respond frankly to attitudinal items and the like. That is to say, increasing the test burden is likely to *decrease* the willingness of learners to furnish useful information. In a few special cases, most initial information gathering can be dispensed with entirely: programs to train welders, electricians, joiners, computer programmers, health technicians, and the like involve such specialized knowledge and skills that it is safe to assume that entering learners have little, if any, initial proficiency. The same holds true for *beginning* courses in foreign languages or specialized math and science programs. In programs that are developmental in nature, however, learners typically enter with some previously acquired proficiencies: reading, mathematics, and a number of other school subjects are examples of programs where entering learners have already attained some proficiency. In such cases, it is important to make some assessment of initial proficiency. To sum up, assessment of the initial proficiency of learners with respect to the objectives of the course, program or curriculum is usually important. The sole exception is programs that are highly specialized in nature, where prior competence can be presumed low, if not nonexistent.

In addition to all this, information descriptive of the learners to be served must be gathered. Data on sex, socioeconomic status, or previous educational history of the learners can either be gathered directly from the learners themselves or from institutional records. Depending on the nature of the educational enterprise, additional items of information descriptive of learners should be collected. Such information serves three purposes. First, educational workers should be able to characterize their learners correctly. Interpretations of the results of evaluation studies must take into account the nature of the learners. Second, educational courses, programs, and curricula are designed to serve a particular group of learners (usually referred to as the intended, or target, population). The question is, are the intended beneficiaries of an educational venture the ones actually being served. Only by systematically gathering information about the learners themselves and comparing this with the defined target population can a determination of a match be made. From time to time it does happen that the actual learners being served by a program are not the ones for whom the program is intended. Voluntary educational programs such as "Sesame Street" and "The Electric Company" have experienced such outcomes; it can even happen in institutional settings. Thus an important feature of any evaluation study is determining whether the intended group of beneficiaries is being reached. A third reason for gathering information describing the learners being served by an educational enterprise is to detect shifts in the nature of the group over a period of time. While it is usually hoped that a program, course, or curriculum— found to be reasonably successful in one institution at one period in time—will continue to be effective with succeeding groups of learners, any rapid changes in learner populations would appear to signal a need for reexamination. Systematic collection of descriptive information about learners being served can be useful in detecting whether changes in the nature of the group occur. Appropriate modifications in the program can then be considered.

Collecting information about learners and how proficient they are relative to what is to be learned is a relatively straightforward matter compared to the gathering of subsequent information. Even the phrase "after a period of instruction" is vague, although for good reasons. *When* subsequent information is collected is largely a function of the *purposes* to be served by evaluation. If the purpose of evaluating a course, program, or curriculum is to improve it, then it will be necessary to gather information repeatedly. Each time would be deemed critical in the life of the enterprise, representing a major decision point or milestone. In a science course, for example, it might occur at the end of each major unit of work or even at a critical point within a unit—e.g., when the basic principles of a given class of phenomena have been presented and discussed, and learners are about to move into an application phase or embark on a series of laboratory experiments. The function of evaluation in such a situation is to track learners through a series of activities so as to determine group progress, identify problems in learning, and so on. As previously noted, such activity is termed "formative" evaluation and is undertaken with the explicit intent of program *improvement.* In contrast with this, collecting information at the *end* of a program is done to decide about the effectiveness of the program in terms of its objectives. Here, information is gathered as close to the end of the program as possible so that learners can be tested with regard to the attainment of all the program's objectives.

It sometimes happens that decisions regarding the future of courses, programs, and curricula cannot await the completion of a program. Budgets for most educational institutions need to be drawn up months in advance, requiring programmatic decisions well in advance of full and final information. While it is highly desirable that decisions be made on the basis of complete information, it may not always be possible. In such circumstances—even in the case of summative evaluation—it is well to gather evaluative information before the close of a program. It may be necessary to collect information halfway through a program. This is far from an ideal state of affairs; but it is sometimes unavoidable. Better something than nothing; in the words of Sir Robert Watson-Watt, the inventor of radar: "Give them the third best to go on. The best never comes, and the second best comes too late."

In summary, decisions about when evidence should be gathered is an open-ended question. The collection of information about the nature of the learners and their initial level of proficiency is a relatively clear issue. The purposes to be served by the evaluation govern the collection of subsequent information. The program developer must work these out as he goes along. All in all the purposes to be served by an evaluation study should be clarified as early as possible and a schedule for collecting information about learner performance that is consistent with these purposes should be developed. It is because there is no universal set of purposes for evaluation that the ambiguous phrase "after a period of instruction" must be retained to characterize when subsequent information about learner performance should be gathered.

HOW SHOULD EVIDENCE BE GATHERED

Some mention has already been made about the conditions under which learner-performance information should be gathered. For example, for objectives which involve evaluating the learner's typical behavior in a group setting, unobtrusive procedures—such as planned or incidental observations—should be employed; for objectives demanding the best efforts of the learner, a task must be specified, and the learner encouraged to do his best.

There are a number of other considerations in the collection of information about learner performance. Of paramount importance is time. One should always try to keep the time down to a minimum. There are a number of obvious reasons for this, the chiefest being: the less time used for evidence-gathering, the more time available for teaching and learning. In most cases, fortunately, this is not a major problem: it is simply not necessary to examine each learner with respect to each general or specific objective. One can, for example, divide a group of learners at random into four equal parts and gather $\frac{1}{4}$ of the required information from each quarter: this represents a saving in time of 75 percent—not an inconsiderable economy. Details as to how such procedures can be developed and implemented will be described in chapter 10. Clearly, it is not necessary to gather information on every learner—with regard to every objective—when evaluating an educational enterprise. These economies, beside allowing more time for teaching and learning, will intensify cooperation by reducing the testing burden for each individual learner. In many evaluation situations it will be possible to gather the bulk of the required, learner performance information in about thirty to forty minutes. Observational procedures or out-of-class learner productions would, of course, require additional time; but they would, at least, not interfere with normal teaching and learning operations.

The use of procedures that require each learner to respond to only a fraction of the total amount of evaluation material has several important consequences. One, the scope of an evaluation study need not be unduly limited because of time restrictions. In fact, it should be possible to gather full information with regard to all objectives without making excessive demands either on teachers and learners or the time allotted for instruction. Two, through judicious allocation procedures, the same set of instruments for gathering information about learner performance may be used *before* instruction gets underway and *after* a period of instruction. If the total amount of testing material has been divided at random into quarters, a learner can be asked to respond to one set of exercises before instruction began and a different set after a period of instruction. In this way, a single set of material could be used several times; at the same time no individual would be required to respond to the same material more than once. In fact, if it is decided that information about learner performance is required at *four* points during the course of an educational enterprise, then a single set of material, appropriately divided into quarters, and carefully assigned to learners, could suffice for an entire class. The saving in time, effort, and expense from not having to develop parallel sets of instruments should be obvious.

The idea of not administering the same set of questions, exercises, etc. to every learner may appear to be somewhat unusual. However, when one remembers that the purpose of evaluating an educational treatment is to say something about the worth of the treatment, and not to describe the performance of each and every learner, the procedure makes eminent sense. Just as we routinely accept the results of surveys that poll a small sample of persons, we should be prepared to accept studies in which 20 to 25 percent of the learners respond to any given item or exercise. (A more detailed discussion on procedures for allocating evaluation exercises among learners and analyzing the results will be found in chapters 10 and 11.)

ISSUES IN THE GATHERING OF INFORMATION ABOUT LEARNER PERFORMANCE

Testing each learner on only a fraction of questions, items, and exercises immediately raises the issue of non-comparability: it will not be possible to compare one learner's performance with another if they have not been tested on the same set of material. This is quite correct. However, evaluation and learner-appraisal are two distinct enterprises. The former is much broader in scope; it considers not only treatment effects on learners but matters of cost; reactions of learners, teachers, administrators, and others; and even consideration of the worth of the objectives being pursued. Learner appraisal, on the other hand, involves assessing the progress of learners in terms of a set of stated objectives, which is normally the responsibility of the teachers. (In some cases external testing and certifying by accrediting boards—as in professional schools and certain vocational programs—constitutes normal practice: this, however, is the exception, not the rule.) The appraisal function is generally best handled by those who work closely with learners and are therefore in the best position to observe and record their progress; these would obviously be the teachers. However, the evaluation enterprise is one apart; it should not be confused with the appraisal of learner performance.

If the evaluation of courses, programs, and curricula is handled separately from the appraisal function, then those charged with appraising learning performance must organize and conduct such activities themselves. Evaluation personnel may furnish teachers assistance, if requested and if time and resources permit but, in general, the latter will have to bear the major responsibility for appraising learner performances. In carrying out this responsibility, teachers should keep in mind that the gathering of learner-performance information for evaluation purposes will not contribute to the appraisal function. This is obviously true if not all learners are given the same set of questions, exercises, scales, etc. The distinction between evaluation and learner-appraisal should be clarified from the beginning; otherwise false or unrealistic expectations will develop and the professional integrity of each kind of educational worker—teacher, evaluation specialist—may be jeopardized. Systematic evaluation of educational programs by teachers does not alter the basic responsibility of teachers which is learner appraisal. In many cases, evaluation will not facilitate it, either.

Another issue of import which has been raised in connection with evaluation in recent years is the place of norm-referenced and criterion-referenced measurement of learner performance. Considerable confusion still surrounds the basic conception of what criterion-referenced measurement is. This is partly due to the novelty of criterion-referenced measurement (although it has been shown that the basic notion has existed for years) and partly to the confusion that naturally surrounds a newly presented technical concept (Airasian and Madaus 1974). The presentation of rather idiosyncratic views and interpretations of what criterion-referenced measurement is or should be has not helped the situation, either.

Criterion-referenced measurement has two major characteristics. First, the domain measured is limited to a very clear but narrowly defined topic or skill. The one hundred basic addition facts and the use of commas in series are examples of such clear and narrowly defined domains. Second, there is a predetermined standard which separates acceptable from unacceptable performance. In addition, a number of other characteristics exist which serve to distinguish criterion-referenced measurements from norm-referenced. However, these are generally either minor ones or stem from the two major characteristics noted above or involve technical issues of no concern here. By having a predetermined dividing line between acceptable and unsatisfactory performance (some writers use the terms mastery and non-mastery), it has been possible to obtain results from criterion-referenced testing, showing that all learners have achieved an acceptable level of performance on a particular topic or skill. The prospect of obtaining such results has probably been one of the major appeals of criterion-referenced measurement. Learners are not judged on the basis of how they stand in relation to the rest of the members of a group but, rather, in terms of whether they have met a predetermined level of acceptable performance. No fixed percent of a group must be consigned to a low level of performance: every learner can be a winner!

The use of criterion-referenced measurement in the evaluation of courses, programs and curricula is not especially recommended. On the contrary, evaluation studies need to determine learner performance at several levels of proficiencies rather than a single one. In evaluating a special reading instruction program for seventh graders, for example, it would be well to know how learners perform on simple material, on material of average difficulty, and on difficult material. Since performance information, gathered in connection with evaluation studies, is generally not used to appraise individual learners, there is little danger that learners will be harmed by responding to material at varying levels of difficulty and complexity. Indeed, considerable benefit may accrue from ascertaining the range of attained proficiency. The situation here is similar to a high jumping contest where the bar is set at three feet eight inches. Finding that all contestants can jump that high is far less instructive—in terms of information gained about jumping proficiency—than having contestants continue to jump at successively greater heights until they reach their maximums. It is this latter kind of information that is particularly important in evaluation studies: evaluators seek to measure actual levels of achievement, rather than some single arbitrary level.

Another problem with the use of criterion-referenced measurement in evaluation studies arises because many of the objectives of instruction do not meet the specifications of a clear and narrowly defined domain. Important educational objectives are highly complex—even specific objectives are—and require the use of several concepts, skills, and abilities. A relatively clear objective—e.g., the preparation of a report on some aspect of Greek civilization—requires the use of a broad range of competencies. In contrast, criterion-referenced measurement necessitates narrowly defined domains if the results are to be clearly interpretable. Faced with a variance between the nature of educational objectives and a method of testing, educators should put objectives first. Testing procedures must be appropriate for the objectives, not vice versa.

This does not mean that criterion-referenced measurement has no place in instruction; it doubtless does. But its place is restricted to those areas where there are clear and narrowly defined domains. Indeed, such measures seem best suited for making instructional decisions about individual learners.

A third issue in the gathering of evidence about learner performance in evaluation studies centers on the use of nonlocally produced questions, exercises, tests, scales, and so on. This would include the use of published instruments as well as standardized tests. Opinion in this area varies greatly. On the one hand, some will argue that only locally produced measures, tailored to the objectives of a particular program, can be used with confidence. The use of externally developed measures can be exceptionally unfair if they measure proficiencies not emphasized in a particular program. To judge a program on the basis of such irrelevant measures, they argue, is not only a disservice to the program but poor evaluation practice. Situations have been known where only ten to fifteen percent of the questions in a standardized test measured proficiencies relevant to course objectives. The maxim "test what you teach" is a strong one and particularly germain in evaluation.

In contrast to this position stands the view that non-locally produced measures are not only useful and desirable but essential. Several reasons have been cited for this position. First, it is unlikely that there will be enough resources available locally to produce all the instruments needed to gather information about learner performance. Judicious selection and use of nonlocally produced measures is considered not only desirable but essential. Second, it is unlikely that the objectives of a particular program are so specialized or idiosyncratic as to make nonlocally produced instruments inappropriate. Third, for a number of educationally important objectives—e.g., reading comprehension and math computation—

published standardized tests are substantively and technically better than measures locally produced. Finally it is argued that—when the goal of evaluation is to find out what changes a course, program, or curriculum produces in learners—measures should *not* be limited to the specific objectives of instruction. "An ideal evaluation," Cronbach (1963) writes, "would include measures of all the types of proficiency that might reasonably be desired in the area in question, not just the selected outcomes to which this curriculum directs substantial attention." This, of course, opens the door to any and all measures that bear relation to the program under study.

While the two positions would appear irreconcilable, the problem may be handled in a fair and evenhanded way. The selection or development of measures for gathering information about learner performance should be based on the objectives themselves. If the objectives are the governing factors whether the measures are locally developed or not is simply irrelevant. Most efficient would be to use already developed measures, including published ones if such are available, and supplement these with locally developed ones. As long as the results are analyzed and reported separately, measures not directly related to the specific objectives of the program can be used to gather information about other kinds of learner proficiency in the general area of study. In terms of the framework for evaluation presented in chapter 2, such results would more appropriately be regarded as belonging to the class of supplemental information. If the evaluation enterprise is appropriately and judiciously managed, distinctions between locally and nonlocally developed measures, and measures related to program objectives and measures not related to objectives, lose much of their importance.

A TECHNICAL NOTE

For several reasons the discussion in this chapter has avoided any detailed consideration of the issues of validity and reliability. In the first place, these subjects are dealt with at length in standard works on measurement and evaluation (Thorndike 1971; Gronlund 1977). Second, it was felt that the evidence-gathering considerations, issues, and problems discusssed in this chapter were the important ones for evaluation studies and often received inadequate treatment. Third, the issue of validity—the paramount one in testing—has been emphasized throughout. This has been done, however, in context: wherever the importance of choosing or devising measures of educational objectives which faithfully and fully reflect the intentions of the objectives has been emphasized, the notion of content validity has been central.

The issue of reliability, in contrast, has not been considered for two reasons. First, the precision with which a characteristic is measured is a secondary consideration to validity. Second, conventional notions of reliability do not apply to the evaluation of course, programs, and curricula in the same way as to the measurement of *individuals*. Reliability theory and procedures for estimating the reliability of measures developed out of a concern for the latter. When a reading test is administered to a single learner, it is important to know how accurately the learner's reading proficiency is being measured. This involves knowledge of the standard error of measurement. In evaluation studies, however, concern focuses on estimating performance for a *group* of learners—from a particular subgroup exposed to a treatment to all individuals exposed to the treatment. Thus, in evaluation studies, concern centers on the reliability of group estimates of performance.

Typically, the reliability of group performance estimates is higher than the reliability of individual estimates (Wiley and Block 1968), principally because individual differences among members of a group are treated as errors of measurement in estimating group performance, and formulas for estimating the reliability of group measures are readily available (Wiley 1970). The practical import of the heightened reliability of estimates of group performance is twofold. First, one can use instruments with reasonable confidence in evaluation studies which would be marginally acceptable, or even unacceptable, for purposes of individual measurement. Thus an attitude scale with a reliability coefficient of .60 for individual measurement can be reliably used to estimate the attitude of a class of twenty to thirty learners. By shifting the focus from individuals to groups, a greater range of measures becomes available. The second consequence of the greater reliability of group estimates is that it permits one to use subscores and even single items to characterize group performance in fairly reliable fashion. This is especially important in evaluation studies where performance information in relation to program objectives is sought. In contrast, total scores which summarize several aspects of performance may mask more than they reveal. The average score of an arithmetic test, administered to a group of learners, tells one nothing about how the learners performed with regard to particular topics. Using subscores and even single items can provide program personnel with important information about successful and unsuccessful aspects of the program, and furthermore such information *for a group* will be fairly dependable. Thus the concern for reliability of measures of learner performance is nowhere near as critical in group evaluation studies as in individual measurement.

SUMMARY

This chapter has set forth a number of important considerations in the collection of evidence about learner performance in evaluation studies. Issues regarding the nature of the evidence to be obtained, the points at which it should be gathered, and the ways in which it can be gathered, have been taken up one by one. In addition, several important theoretical, procedural, and practical considerations have been introduced and discussed. Throughout emphasis has been placed on the importance of using appropriate evaluation procedures and collecting relevant information. This is the critical point in all evaluation work. Details of instrument development were not given since they are readily available in conventional texts on testing.

REFERENCES

Airasian, P. and Madaus, G. 1972. "Criterion-referenced Testing in the Classroom." *Measurement and Education* 3. Reprinted in R. Tyler and R. Wolf (eds.) *Crucial Issues in Testing*, edited by R. Tyler and R. Wolf, pp. 73–88. 1974. Berkeley: McCutchan Publishing Corporation.

Cronbach, L.J. 1963. "Course Improvement through Evaluation." *Teachers College Record* 64: 672–683.

Gronlund, N. 1976. *Measurement and Evaluation in Teaching*, 3rd edition. New York: Macmillan.

Thorndike, R. (ed.). 1971. *Educational Measurement.* Washington: American Council on Education.

Wiley, D. 1970. "Design and Analysis of Evaluation Studies." In *The Evaluation of Instruction*, edited by M. Wittrock and D. Wiley. New York: Holt, Rinehart and Winston.

Wiley, D. and R. Bock. 1968. "Quasi-experimentation in Educational Settings." *School Review* 75: 353–366.

ADDITIONAL READINGS

Bloom, B. (ed.). 1956. *Taxonomy of Educational Objectives: Handbook I, The Cognitive Domain.* New York: Longmans Green.

Bloom, B., Hastings, T. and Madaus, G. (eds.). 1971. *Handbook of Formative and Summative Evaluation.* New York: McGraw-Hill.

Harrow, A. 1972. *A Taxonomy of the Psychomotor Domain.* New York: David McKay.

Henry, N. (ed.). 1946. *The Measurement of Understanding.* Yearbook of the

National Society for the Study of Education, Part I. Chicago: University of Chicago Press.

Krathwohl, D., et al. (eds.). 1964. *A Taxonomy of Educational Objectives: Handbook II, The Affective Domain.* New York: David McKay.

Lake, D., Miles, M. and Earle, R. (eds.). 1973. *Measuring Human Behavior.* New York: Teachers College Press.

Shaw, M. and Wright, J. 1967. *Scales for the Measurement of Attitudes.* New York: McGraw-Hill.

Smith, E. and Tyler, R. 1943. *Appraising and Recording Student Progress.* New York: Harper.

Struenig, E. and Guttentag, M. (eds.). 1975. *Handbook of Evaluation Research,* vols. I and II. Beverly Hills: Sage Publications.

Walberg, H. (ed.). 1974. *Evaluating Educational Performance.* Berkeley, Cal.: McCutchan Publications.

6

MONITORING THE IMPLEMENTATION OF THE PROGRAM

While information about the effects of courses, programs, and curricula on learners is widely accepted as an essential part of an evaluation enterprise, the collection of information about how programs are actually carried out has not received adequate attention. This is indeed unfortunate since it is critical to any systematic evaluation study. The collection, analysis, and interpretation of such information must be viewed as vital to the success of any evaluation enterprise. How many educational undertakings have been judged unsuccessful because the intended program was never really carried out can only be guessed at. In recent memory, a sizable number of ESEA programs for the disadvantaged as well as Headstart programs were considered to have failed when, on closer examination, they were found not to have been carried out at all. Whether the programs would have succeeded had they been carried out is a question for speculation only. The fact remains that in many instances they were neither adequately nor fairly tested.

Information about the way an intended course, program, or curriculum has been implemented is needed for two major reasons. First, it is vital to the interpretation of information about learner performance. If an intended learning sequence was not properly executed or in certain cases not executed at all, information about learner performance with regard to the objectives in question is open to serious misinterpretation. For example, in one school district, a fifth-grade mathematics curriculum called for teachers to teach a unit on prime numbers. An end-of-grade, locally devised mathematics test revealed that learner performance on this topic was abysmally low. This was in marked contrast to the other topics in the curriculum where learner performance was generally high. Only the most casual investigation was needed to uncover the reason for the low performance of students: the unit had not been covered in instruction.

Further inquiry showed that the teachers were not knowledgeable enough about prime numbers to feel comfortable teaching them and consequently omitted the topic from their classroom instruction. The remedy for this situation was simple. A single workshop on prime numbers was conducted for the fifth-grade teachers in the district. Not surprisingly, learner-performance on problems involving prime numbers on the end-of-grade mathematics test improved markedly the next year. The learners, in fact, performed as well on that topic as they did on the others. Clearly, it is vital to know what has gone on in the teaching-learning situation in order properly to interpret learner-performance information with regard to the objectives of instruction.

A second reason for gathering information about the way in which an educational treatment has been carried out is even more basic. Evaluation involves more than the assessment of learner performance in terms of objectives. One of the additional elements in evaluation is an examination of the relationship between objectives, learning experiences, and appraisal procedures. Judgments need to be made about the relationships among these three elements of the educational process. For instance, are the learning experiences consistent with the stated objectives? What are the relationships between the learning experiences and the evaluation procedures? Answers to these questions require information about the learning experiences themselves.

Unfortunately, this aspect is often overlooked. While many people accept the tripartite characterization of the educational process formulated by Tyler and outlined in chapter 1, a corresponding effort has not been made to gather information about the extent to which an intended program was implemented or the way in which this was done. The principal exception to this in the field of evaluation work was the book *Thirty Schools Tell Their Story*, which was part of the Eight-Year Study of the Progressive Education Study (Van Til 1943). (Ironically, this volume chronicles the fact that when the thirty schools constituting the experimental group were freed from traditional college and university entrance requirements, they did not modify their programs sufficiently to institute an innovative treatment. In light of this the failure to find any significant differences between the graduates of the experimental and control schools can hardly be viewed as surprising.)

Information about the actual set of learning experiences undergone is needed as part of the evaluation enterprise so that an analysis of the relationship between objectives, learning experiences, and appraisal procedures can be made. Discontinuities between objectives and learning experiences may easily arise. For example, in a college course in the biological sciences the *objectives* called for students to be able to write about conceptual issues in biology, to analyze problems, design experiments to test hypotheses, etc. The *learning experiences*, in contrast, consisted exclusively of lectures and set experiments in the laboratory. Failure to achieve the objectives could be traced in large measure to this basic discontinuity. Similarly, elementary school mathematics programs often espouse an intention to have students develop problem-solving abilities. In contrast, the learning experiences may contain an inordinate amount of computational work and simple drill, leaving little time to devote to solving the more complex kinds of problems stressed in the statements of objectives.

There are numerous instances of educational courses, programs, and curricula that failed to achieve all their objectives. Unfortunately, evaluation work often does little more than document such failures. Good evaluation work should not only establish the extent to which objectives have been attained; it should attempt to explain why they were attained or not. This is extremely difficult to do. Education does not have a well enough established body of theory to allow one to say unequivocally why a program succeeded or not. The evaluation specialist, with the assistance of other educational specialists in curriculum, administration, and the teaching of particular subjects, should be able to offer *some* reaons for why educational ventures turned out as they did. Such explanations may have to be strongly presumptive and based on logical analysis, as contrasted with empirical analysis. They will probably also need to be strongly qualified, regarded as suggestive rather than definitive. The important point is that some attempt in this direction should be made, if evaluation studies are to be more than a box score of the successes and failures of educational treatments.

METHODS OF GATHERING INFORMATION ABOUT THE EXECUTION OF EDUCATIONAL PROGRAMS

There are three principal ways of gathering information about how an educational treatment has been carried out. The purpose of this section is to describe each one and state how it can be used to obtain the information necessary.

The first way to obtain information on the extent of program implementation involves the use of observational procedures. Information about aspects of learner performance is not being sought; observational procedures will be focused on the learning activities and instructional materials. Ideally, a highly trained observer would be present at all times to observe and record what occurs in the learning situation: the organization and conduct of activities; the grouping of learners; the kinds of learning materials used and the ways; teacher behavior; and so on. Such information, systematically recorded, could furnish the basis for sound evaluative judgments. But, obviously, few if any programs can afford to have full time, highly trained observers present for the duration of the treatment-period. It is possible that periodic visits can be made, however. Weekly, bi-weekly, or even monthly visits can be made to programs; observation periods of from one half hour to several hours in duration are clearly within the realm of possibility. Exactly how much observational work will be undertaken would be determined to a large extent by available resources. Given a limited amount of resources, the most productive deployment would probably be to have a substantial number of periods of observations, each of limited duration, rather than a small number of observations of extended duration. If resources were available for ten hours of observation for a course lasting an academic year, it would be preferable to hold forty observations of fifteen minutes each than to have say ten one-hour observation periods spread throughout the year. Each short observation period yields fresh information: all other things being equal, the more observations the better.

Another highly practical reason for employing a large number of observation periods involves the perceptions of learners and teachers. Infrequent visits will tend to be perceived as official inspections whereas shorter, more frequent visits can be accepted and handled more casually. As long as it is made clear at the outset that the purpose of such observations is not to judge the effectiveness of the teacher but to gather information about the program and that a number of short visits are essential for this purpose, apprehensions can be minimized. Certainly assurance should be given to teachers that no information obtained from such observations will be included in a formal evaluation report, until the teachers, whose classes are observed, have had an opportunity to read and react to it.

Once a schedule for observation has been established and cooperation elicited from teachers, attention must be devoted to the form in which observational information is to be recorded. Few observers are qualified to record observational information in a discursive form. Too much occurs in any learning situation for even the most sensitive observer to capture and record everything. Accordingly, some guidance must be furnished to the observer. An observer may be presented with a brief guide or pilot, indicating in very general terms what to look for in the learning situation. In other cases, an observer may be presented with a series of general dimensions to direct the observation. These dimensions might be (1) activities engaged in by learners; (2) grouping procedures employed; (3) instructional materials used; and so on. More specific guidance may be provided: scales for rating specific aspects of the learning situation, for example, or a checklist covering a substantial number of features of the learning situation. Rating scales will be used to rate the strength or quality of particular aspects of the learning situation; checklists will be employed to determine the presence or absence of particular items.

Which features of the learning situation are attended to and which are ignored will hinge to a large extent on the nature of the objectives and the nature of the program. Consequently, specific prescriptions about what to observe cannot be given. At a minimum one needs some information about the physical setting in which the learning takes place, the kinds of activities and materials used, and how the learning situation is organized and conducted. Beyond these minima, the *specific objectives* of the program and the *learning experiences* related to their attainment would determine what is of interest and ought to be observed and recorded.

Whatever form of recording is employed, even a detailed checklist of items, it would need to be supplemented by observer comments. It is highly unlikely that any recording system could be devised so comprehensive that comments, which amplify and qualify the formal record, would not be needed. On the contrary, it is recommended that forms for recording observations provide ample room for comments. Comments should be encouraged as much as possible.

While there have been a number of attempts in recent years to develop observational instruments for classroom use and an anthology of such instruments has even been produced, it seems unlikely that any existing instrument will be entirely adequate for use in a particular evaluation enterprise (Simon and Boyer 1970). Existing instruments, however, can furnish suggestions and in some cases be adapted for use in a specific situation.

A second way of gathering information about the way in which a course, program or curriculum is being implemented is through the use of teacher reports. These might come in the form of teacher lesson plan books, supplemented by elaborating comments or log/diaries which teachers are asked to submit on a regular basis. The latter are intended to serve as records of what happened in the learning situation and to preserve teachers' comments on those events.

Using what is essentially a kind of self-report information from the teacher is not without drawbacks. As in self-report information about personal characteristics, such instruments are limited by the nature of the reporters: their ability to observe and comment objectively, and by their willingness to do so. This is not to suggest that professionals would wilfully engage in deception; rather, it might occur unconsciously. It is generally presumed that people wish to think well of themselves and what they do: this could easily influence their ability to report fully and accurately about what occurred in the learning situation. Furthermore, maintenance of a log/diary or an elaborated set of lesson plans with supplemental comments is laborious and time-consuming. It may be unreasonable to expect teachers to bear such a reportorial burden. To rely heavily on such teacher reports seems questionable. Their use should probably be quite restricted; they should never provide the sole, or even main, basis for describing what occurred in the learning situation.

The third way to gather information about the extent of implementation of educational programs is through reports by the learners themselves. These reports, usually termed participant observations, call on the group members, in this case the learners, to observe and comment on a number of aspects of the situation in which they find themselves. While the pioneer work in the methods of participant observation occurred in the field of anthropology—in the work of Margaret Mead and others—such methods have been adapted, systematized, and applied to the field of education. The work of C.R. Pace and G. Stern on the measurement of psychological characteristics of college environments (1958) was one of the first attempts to apply psychometric principles to the measurement of environments. Pace's subsequent development of the College and University Environment Scales (CUES), modified and extended this original work (1969). Recently, descriptive scales have been used in connection with the studies conducted by the International Association for the Evaluation of Educational Achievement (IEA). The scales consist of a number of short items which call upon the learner to indicate whether certain activities or events occur in their classroom. Some illustrative items, from a scale descriptive of science teaching and learning, are given by Comber and Keeves (1974):

> We use a testbook for science.
>
> Our science teacher tests us only on what is in the textbook.
>
> The main aim of our science lessons is to understand our textbooks.
>
> Our science lessons include laboratory experiments in which we all take part.
>
> We make observations and do experiments during our science classes.

The three response categories were "always or almost always," "sometimes," and "hardly ever or never." The purpose of such items is to have the learner serve as a reporter about what has occurred in the learning situation. If a number of learners respond to a set of such items and there is substantial agreement among the learners' responses in a single setting (as a rule of thumb two-thirds agreement is regarded as acceptable), then it should be possible to use such information to characterize aspects of the learning situation.

While descriptive scales are a relatively new development, they promise to furnish important information about the nature of the learning experiences of an educational course, program, or curriculum. Since this information has often been lacking or, at best, inadequately gathered, in most previous evaluation work, a clear need exists for the further development of descriptive scales. One can easily envisage the development of several dozen items that attempt to characterize important aspects of an educational program. Such items can be included in a questionnaire, to be administered to learners at periodic intervals as part of a systematic information-gathering operation. Further, to achieve economy in information gathering, a collection of such items can be randomly split into several subsets, in much the same way that a pool of items measuring learner proficiency can be. Thus, no individual learner would need to respond to more than a fraction of the descriptive items yet the resultant information could be used to characterize the learning situation.

There is an ethical question that can be raised about the use of participant-observer reports. Such reports call on learners to observe and report on their learning environments. To a large extent this entails responding to statements intended to describe instructional procedures, learning activities, use of materials, etc. It sometimes becomes difficult to separate items descriptive of such aspects of classroom life from evaluations of the teacher; thus, learners may end up serving as reporters on teacher behavior. With the growing acceptance of course evaluations in recent years, the use of participant-observer instruments may not seem objectionable. But unless it is made clear at the outset that learners will be asked to respond to descriptive items from time to time, there is a strong possibility these instruments could be viewed as an unwarranted invasion on the learning situation. To counter the possibility of such an objection, it is suggested that all items used to describe the learning situation be carefully scrutinized and any that are possibly offensive be eliminated. In addition, teachers should be informed as early as possible that learners will be asked to respond to items intended to describe the learning situation. It is the responsibility of evaluation personnel to make sure that information so obtained is used to describe the learning situation and not to judge individual teachers. Such precautions are necessary if ethical problems are to be avoided and a climate of trust, so needed for evaluation work, is to be maintained.

MULTIPLE SOURCES OF INFORMATION

The need for information about the execution of an educational treatment can not be overstressed. Not only is information needed regarding the availability of learning materials and supplies; actual amount of instruction given; and adequacy of resources in the learning situation; the faithfulness with which a designed treatment was carried out must be known. The assumption that an intended treatment was executed as planned is one of the most naive ones that can be made in education. Recent educational history is studded with examples of programs that were not carried out as intended.

Given the importance of information regarding the execution of educational treatments, as much information as possible should be obtained. Yet evaluation endeavors must generally operate with meager resources. The practicing evaluation specialist realizes that resources devoted to the collection of information concerning program execution usually means fewer resources for gathering learner-performance information. Consequently, difficult decisions have to be made regarding the amount of resources to be allocated to the gathering of each kind of information.

Rather clear costs are associated with each type of information concerned with program implementation. Observational information obviously will involve the heaviest costs. At the same time, it can be expected to yield the highest quality information. Self-report information from teachers is least costly to gather. Considerable effort, however, must be devoted to analyzing, organizing, and summarizing such information. Moreover, as noted, self-report information can be less than complete and less than accurate. Participant-observer information—in the form of descriptive items—requires some time and effort to develop but generally little time to tabulate, summarize, and interpret. Certainly, a mixture of all three kinds of data would be highly desirable in an evaluation study: each would provide a partial picture of the nature of the treatment dispensed. Collectively, they should furnish a fairly complete description of an educational treatment as implemented.

When different methods of gathering information about program execution are used, inconsistencies will occur. Two principal kinds are to be expected. The first is within a data source, the second between data sources. Differences of the first kind—e.g., different activities and procedures observed at different times—are likely to reflect genuine differences in the program from one time to another. Similarly, differences in teacher reports of activities will usually reflect actual changes in the activities of the program. On the other hand, differences between data sources at a given time will likely be indicative of errors in the measuring process. For example, when reports by an external observer show little provision for individual differences in rate of learning, while a teacher's log or diary states that provision has been made, the evaluation worker will have to seek a resolution between the conflicting accounts.

At this point, having all *three* kinds of information about program implementation should prove valuable. Usually *two* of the data sources will be in agreement, and discrepancies can be reconciled fairly easily. However, if the external observer's report—the information with the highest presumed level of validity—is out of line with the others, it may be necessary to gather additional observational information rather hurriedly. In most cases, however, the use of multiple sources of information about program implementations can be expected to *fortify* the validity of the results obtained. Discrepancies can be expected to be small and erratic in comparison to the agreement; where they do occur, they should be resolved with reasonable dispatch.

SUMMARY

This chapter has stressed the importance of gathering information concerning the implementation of courses, programs, and curricula. There may be considerable discrepancies between a designated treatment and the way it is actually carried out. Gathering information relating to program implementation is considered valuable to an evaluation enterprise as gathering information about learner behavior. Information about program implementation serves two purposes. First, such it permits an evaluator to interpret more fully learner-performance information. Second, it can be directly used in assessing the relationships among objectives, learning experiences, and appraisal procedures.

Three principal ways of gathering information about implementation were discussed: (1) observations by evaluation personnel;l (2) teacher reports in the form of plan books and, sometimes, logs and diaries; and (3) student reports on activities and features of the learning situation. Each type of data has its advantages and disadvantages. All three, when systematically gathered, analyzed, and properly interpreted, should provide sufficient information to describe adequately the execution of the treatment.

REFERENCES

Comber, L. and Keeves, J. 1973. *Science Education in Nineteen Countries.* New York: Halstead Press (John Wiley).

Pace, C.R. 1969. *College and University Environment Scales.* Princeton: Educational Testing Service.

Pace, C.R. and Stern, G. 1958. "An Apporach to the Measurement of Psychological Characteristics of College Environments." *Journal of Educational Psychology* 49: 269–277.

Simon, A. and Boyer, E. 1970. *Mirrors for Behavior: An Anthology of Classroom Instruments,* vols. 1–15. Philadelphia: Research for Better Schools.

Van Til, W. (ed.). 1943. *Thirty Schools Tell Their Story.* New York: Harper.

ADDITIONAL READINGS

Boehm, A. and Weinberg, R. 1977. *The Classroom Observer: A Guide for Developing Observation Skills.* New York: Teachers College Press.

Hall, G. and Louchs, S. 1977. "A Developmental Model for Determining Whether the Treatment is Actually Implemented." *American Educational Research Journal,* 14, no. 3: 263-276.

7

PROGRAM COSTS

The area of cost has been much neglected in educational evaluation for reasons which are not very clear. Recently, however, economists and finance specialists have turned their attention to education and educational evaluation. The field of educational evaluation should benefit considerably from this attention if current work is any guide (Haller 1974).

Reckoning educational costs is an exceedingly complex and difficult undertaking. While most tend to view cost estimation as relatively hard information, specialists in the field constantly emphasize its slippery character. Few, if any educators, for example, are prepared to say how much it costs to teach the average learner to read at a given level of proficiency. At a more detailed level, it is not possible to state what it actually costs to teach a learner multiplication of fractions. Cost information is simply not kept in a way that will permit answers to such seemingly straightforward questions. And even if it were, cost experts assert, the determination of costs would require a substantial number of difficult decisions as to what should be counted as costs, and in what way they should be counted. *When* costs are determined also makes a difference. If a local school board decided to provide dental care to its employees in the middle of a school year, the cost estimate for all instructional service would immediately change even if everything else remained constant.

WHAT IS A COST?

Traditionally, costs have played a minor part in educational evaluation. To decision makers—administrators and governing boards—evaluations that make no reference to costs are rarely of much practical value, however interesting they may be pedagogically, since educational decision makers have a fairly good idea of what they could do were money no object. Their job lies in choosing among alternatives most of which are, in their own way, good. Thus value choices are involved as well as cost considerations. However, since few if any programs can be justified at any cost, cost considerations must weigh heavily on decision making. How much weight they will carry in any situation will vary enormously. The responsibility of the evaluation specialist is to see that cost considerations are explicitly included in an evaluation.

It would be desirable if a clear definition of what a cost was, and how it could be determined, existed. Unfortunately, there is no universally accepted definition and no set of procedures to guide evaluation personnel. The standard definition of a cost is that it is a lost benefit: this definition ties costs to decisions. That is to say, deciding to do one thing implies that something else cannot be done. Under this definition a set of instructional materials has no inherent value. Rather it is the *decision*—to purchase those materials and (consequently) not buy something else—which constitutes the real cost of the purchased materials. Cost determination—under such a definition—involves identifying and comparing alternative courses of action: thus the cost of a decision is tied to the various alternatives. Since every decision involves alternatives, the value of the most highly prized alternative *not chosen* becomes the cost of a decision.

One implication of this definition is that it places costs in the future. Since a cost depends on an alternative not chosen, it cannot be determined with complete accuracy; it must be estimated. As in most estimation situations, the usual procedure is to use present expenditures as a basis for estimating costs. This generally serviceable guide for cost estimation, however, cannot be depended on without reservation. Consequently, additional guides for cost estimation, including what should and should not be reckoned as costs, are required.

The notion of a cost as an opportunity foregone is generally accepted by economists and finance experts. It is not always relevant in a particular educational setting, however. For example, a local school district can obtain money from a state department of education to run a special program for gifted learners (in fact legislation may have been passed especially for this purpose.) On the other hand, the most pressing local need may be for something else. The school superintendent, with local board approval, will prepare a request and secure the funds to run the program for gifted learners. From the point of view of the local school district the program costs nothing: it is wholly funded by the state. Of course, the program has a cost attached to it, paid here by the state. Generally, however, this does not conern the school district. The point to be noted is that it is sometimes possible to obtain government money for one purpose, but not for another. Such specially funded programs cost nothing from the standpoint of the local school district.

From the standpoint of the economist, the alternatives being considered in a cost situation may be virtually limitless. There is no end to the ways in which money can be spent: in a school situation, money can be spent to improve instruction in basic subjects; for purposes of remediation; to pay off debts on buildings; to mount new programs; improve the coaching of athletic teams; field teams in new sports; purchase muscial instruments, etc. An exhaustive examination and cost estimation of every alternative is normally beyond the resources of a single evaluation enterprise. Accordingly, cost estimation in an evaluation situation is usually limited to considering alternative ways of meeting a particular set of educational needs. For example, where deficiencies exist in the reading achievement of learners at a particular grade level, alternative ways of remedying such deficiencies will have to be identified and several contemplated for trial. Cost estimation in such a case would be restricted to specific alternatives, ignoring other possible uses of funds outside the area of reading, or the grade level in question.

HOW ARE COSTS DETERMINED?

There are several ways of measuring costs. Not all of them will involve dollars. One might merely list the resources required for a particular program. Thus, if a new reading program was being contemplated, one could develop an inventory of resources, including personnel, that would be required. Such a list would give the number of teachers with specified qualifications, the space requirements, the books and other learning materials, aides, etc. The list could go on but would essentially consist of a finite set of resources required to set the program going.

A second method of measuring costs would be to formulate and describe one or more ways of meeting the same educational need. In the example of a reading deficiency identified at a particular grade level, alternatives to the installation of a new reading program might be the employment of extra reading teachers plus special supplemental reading materials; hiring several teacher aids along with a different set of reading materials, etc. For each alternative way of meeting the same educational need, it should be possible to identify the resources involved.

Going one step further, one could try to estimate the value of each alternative way of meeting the identified need. The value of an alternative is not merely a dollar cost: each alternative would have associated with it a constellation of advantages and disadvantages. These would have to be assessed; the difference between the two would constitute the net value of an alternative. The cost of adopting the alternative with the highest net value would be, in economic terms, the value of the next highest alternative. This procedure produces a measure of a choice's opportunity costs since it provides an estimate of the program benefits foregone.

The difficulty and complexity of the above procedure, here only briefly sketched, should not be underestimated. In attempting to calculate the value of a given way of meeting an educational need, one must express each advantage and disadvantage on some common scale. For some elements of an alternative this is fairly easy to do. Teacher salaries and benefits can be reckoned fairly easily; so can the cost of materials and supplies. On the other hand, the effect on teacher morale of adapting a particular course of action, or the enhancement of a learner's self-esteem by achieving at a higher level of proficiency, cannot be estimated with the same facility. There is no educational calculus which allows one to make such determinations. While economists recommend trying to measure costs through estimation of the value of alternative ways of dealing with a particular set of educational needs, this goal is not easily reached in most educational situations. As a result, evaluation workers may be forced to limit their efforts to trying to attach a dollar value to two, or several, choices. This should be done with the realization that such a procedure does not do full justice to the situation. There can often be nondollar costs associated with a course of action. If these cannot be estimated, they should at least be acknowledged.

It is important to recognize that the estimation of costs cannot be full and complete, but it is imperative that evaluation specialists try as much as they can at least to estimate the dollar costs of educational courses, programs and curricula. Failure to do this is a serious omission of an important aspect of the evaluation enterprise.

COST PROCEDURES

While evaluation specialists will quickly realize the limitations inherent in cost estimation, the task must be undertaken, even at the risk of considerable imprecision. There are procedures to follow that should prove helpful. Unfortunately, the tendency in many costing exercises is to begin considering matters of procedural detail before the larger issues are resolved. To become embroiled in details about how to estimate overhead costs of a program *before* the decision alternatives have been formulated is extremely inadvisable; in some cases, as will be shown later, it can be a wasted effort.

The first major step in estimating costs associated with educational decisions is to establish the alternative courses of action available. The particular course, program, or curriculum under consideration is, of course, one alternative. There are, however, probably several other alternative courses of action in the situation, including doing nothing.

Identification of the realistic alternatives in a situation is not a task that an evaluation specialist can undertake singlehandedly. Usually it requires an interplay between the evaluation specialist and decision makers: some discussion will be required to identify the alternative courses of action.

It is quite possible that educational decision makers will be reluctant to consider alternative ways of meeting a particular educational need. If the decision maker has made a particularly strong commitment to trying out a certain program, even on a pilot basis, serious consideration of alternative ways of meeting the educational need may be impossible. This phenomenon has been described by Campbell (1960) who characterizes such decision makers as "trapped administrators." In contrast, experimental administrators relate a particular program to the problem being addressed and not to their beliefs. They are committed to going on to other potential solutions if the first one fails. The task for the evaluation specialist is to assist the administrator in focusing on the problem, or educational need, being addressed and to explicate the alternatives as fully and clearly as possible.

Once a set of decision alternatives has been formulated, it is then necessary to ascertain the outcomes or benefits which the administrator sees accruing from each alternative. This will normally be expressed in rather general terms. While one would like to obtain as clear and specific information as possible about the goals expected to be attained by following a particular course of action, it may not be possible to do so: the administrator may not know; often, the professional staff connected with a program is in a better position to enumerate the benefits attached to an alternative. However, by focusing an administrator's attention on the benefits associated with each alternative, the relationship between costs and benefits is more clearly seen.

The benefits that one can expect to attain by choosing an alternative are embodied in the objectives of a course, program, or curriculum. For purposes of cost estimation, the general objectives should suffice. Formulating a set of specific objectives for every decision alternative would require too much time and effort. Resources for evaluation can be used more productively elsewhere. It may even be possible to use the short expository statement that describes a program instead of a list of general objectives, but this will vary from situation to situation. The essential requirement remains: one must be able to formulate a clear, if not specific, statement of the benefits for each decision alternative. Once this is done, a list of activities needed to achieve the benefits envisaged for each decision alternative should be developed. The list will furnish a basis for further cost work.

The second step in conducting a cost estimation is developing a framework for estimating the costs associated with each alternative. It is not possible at once to estimate the *total* cost associated with a decision alternative. First, a set of cost categories should be formulated; then estimates made within each category. Finally, costs within each category are combined, and a total cost can be estimated. The system of categories used for this purpose is referred to as an *input structure*. An input structure that has particular relevance for educational enterprises uses the following categories:

1. *Time* (of teachers, extra-class professional staff, administrators, students, etc.)
2. *Space* (classrooms, offices, etc.)
3. *Equipment* (movie projectors, tape recorders, etc.)
4. *Supplies* (paper, pencils, paints, etc.)

Since education is a labor-intensive activity, the time category will usually involve the greatest costs; supplies, normally the least. It is useful to keep in mind the general magnitude of each category of costs since, for example, fairly large errors in estimation in supplies will probably have a negligible effect on the total estimated cost of a program, whereas relatively small errors of estimation in the time category can affect the total cost figure considerably.

Each of the above four categories of costs occurs over a stretch of time. From the time an educational need or problem is identified until the time an operational program is dispensed with after appropriate trial, a variety of costs can be incurred within each category. One way of breaking down this temporal dimension is in terms of the three major stages of an educational program: (1) planning and development; (2) implementation; and (3) operation. The first stage—planning and development— includes activities defining the educational need with sufficient precision, formulating the general and specific objectives and selecting or developing the learning experiences, including associated instructional materials. The second stage—implementation—involves the costs of installing the program in the educational setting for the intended beneficiaries. Here the costs of teacher workshops and other in-service activities, equipment purchases and so on, would be covered. The third stage—operation— includes those costs needed to keep the treatment going—e.g., maintenance; whatever in-service activities may be needed to keep teacher performance at a desired level of proficiency; induct new teachers into service to the program; pay salaries; and other ongoing costs.

None of the stages is discrete from the others. In fact, it is usually desirable for them to overlap. Implementation costs will undoubtedly be incurred while a program is still in the planning and development stage. Similarly, operational costs will accumulate while the program is in the state of implementation. It is not inconceivable, and it may be desirable, that costs associated with planning and development—e.g., for some revision of the program—be incurred while the program is in an operational stage. Thus, while the basic input structure for cost reckoning may look tidy on paper, the reality is apt to be far messier. But this is no cause for concern. Questions can be expected to arise as to whether a certain cost should be classified as planning and development or implementation; the important thing is to make sure it is classified at some stage or another and not omitted. Similarly, one may face problems deciding whether an item is an equipment or supply cost. Such decisions should not consume much time: simply make sure that the item is included somewhere.

An unresolved issue in cost reckoning is whether to count student time as a cost. On the one hand, educational treatments intended for learners within the period of compulsory schooling can be considered cost-free since learners are obliged to be in school for a certain number of hours each day and a certain number of days each year. If a particular program is not implemented, it is unlikely that student instruction time will decrease. In this sense student time is not a cost. On the other hand, applying the economic notion of a cost to student learning, the time spent in a particular learning situation means that the learner is not learning something else. If an extended reading program were introduced, for example, the learner would have less time to learn mathematics or science. In this sense the introduction of a new program creates a learning foregone situation and consequently involves a cost. Though it may be difficult to attach a value to student time, its cost must be recognized. As one moves from compulsory to noncompulsory schooling, the case for including learner time as a clear cost becomes stronger. Here one must consider the alternate uses of the individual's time. This is what was done in one landmark study (Schultz 1953). How one treats learner time in a particular evaluation situation will doubtless depend on a number of situation-specific factors. The purpose of raising the issue is to alert the reader. So far there is no clear solution to the problem.

The last major step in cost reckoning is to measure current costs and estimate the future costs associated with decision alternatives. The input structure discussed in the previous step should furnish the framework for organizing cost data. However, before proceeding it is necessary to make several distinctions between different kinds of costs, some of which should be excluded.

SOME TYPES OF COSTS

Basic and Additional Program Costs

If a particular program is carried on in an elementary school, cost estimates derived from the school budget will be misleadingly high because of the inclusion of a number of fixed costs. Consider, for example, a nutrition education program that takes up to 10 percent of the school day. The total annual school budget is, let us say, $750,000. If there are 500 learners in the school, the per-learner cost of education is $1500. Since ten percent of the school day is devoted to nutrition education, one might divide the per-learner cost of eduction by ten—the proportion of time devoted to nutrition education—to obtain a cost of $150 per learner. This is a rather high figure. It is worth examining what it includes.

By starting with the total annual school budget in the cost reckoning, all expenditures of school operation are included. Some of these items are payments of principal and interest costs on the building, heat, light, administration, grounds keeping expenses, as well as costs associated with instruction. The $150 figure of per learner cost of nutrition education includes a number of *basic* program costs for the school which are passed on to the program by this method of reckoning.

A different way of reckoning the cost of the program is to examine the *additional* costs associated with having the program. Additional program costs are based on the presumption that if the nutrition education program did not take up ten percent of the school day, then some other activity would. (Educators do not curtail the school day if a particular program is eliminated; they either replace it with something else or increase the time allocation for the remaining learning activities.) In reckoning additional program costs, one asks what are the *additional* costs associated with having the nutrition education program. Fixed costs such as building, heat, light, grounds keeping expenses, etc., will be excluded, since they would have to be paid no matter what was taught in the 10 percent block of time allotted to nutrition education. Furthermore, if the nutrition education program is being taught by the regular classroom teacher rather than specially hired ones, there is no additional cost for teachers' salaries. In fact, the only additional costs associated with the program may be those that involve learning materials (books, pamphlets, filmstrips, etc.). Let us say this cost averages out to $10 per learner, which is vastly different from the $150 per learner total reckoned previously.

Recurring and Nonrecurring Costs

Another distinction that should be made in cost reckoning is between recurring and nonrecurring costs. Recurring costs are those that are incurred with each administration of a program. For example, if a consumable workbook is used in the above nutrition education program, the workbook constitutes a recurring cost since each entering learner must be supplied with one. A textbook, on the other hand, is a nonrecurring cost since it can be used by successive groups of learners. To take our present example, it may be that—of the $10 per learner additional cost of the nutrition education program only two dollars (the cost of the workbook) is a recurring cost, while eight dollars (textbooks, filmstrips, etc.) is nonrecurring. Thus, the administrator responsible for the program may need to spend only two dollars per learner in the second year of the program. This is a far cry from the originally estimated basic program cost of $150 per learner.

Sunk and Incremental Costs

Sunk costs refer to expenditures made in the past and consequently are of no concern in estimating the cost of decision altenatives that lie in the future. The construction of a school building is a clear example. If the building was constructed at some prior time, it cannot be considered in estimating the cost of some decision alternative lying in the future; consequently, it should be excluded from cost reckoning. On the other hand, if a contemplated program will require alterations to the building (knocking out walls seems to be the fashion these days), this would be regarded as an *incremental* cost since it does lie in the future. It should therefore be included in cost estimation.

One complicating factor in cost estimation that arises from the above distinction is that while a particular cost may be sunk, e.g., the building, there are future consequences: there may be principal and interest payments on the building that will continue for years. There will be costs involved in heating, lighting, and maintaining the building. How are these treated? Strictly speaking, such costs are incremental ones. That is, they will occur in the future. They are considered, however, to be fixed. They will be incurred as long as some use is made of the building space. Thus, they would add a constant amount to each decision alternative. Whether one should include them or not is a somewhat open question. From the point of view of decision making, it is probably not pertinent, since one is apt to be concerned with the *differences* in cost between decision alternatives. Thus, the addition of a constant value to each alternative is not likely to influence the outcome of a decision. On the other hand, from a bookkeeping point of view, such costs are real and should be assigned on a pro rate basis to all activities carried out within the building. The important consideration in handling such fixed costs, it would seem, is to be consistent with regard to each decision alternative. Thus, if fixed costs of operating a building are assigned to a contemplated program, then they should be assigned to all other alternative uses of that space.

Hidden Costs

There are often hidden costs in the introduction of educational undertakings. For example, a reading consultant may be engaged as part of a new reading program. The salary of the reading consultant is readily identifiable and will probably be routinely included in cost estimation. Less apparent are the additional costs involved. To begin with, the consultant will probably receive a set of fringe benefits, including medical and life insurance, retirement, etc., which may add between 20 and 50 percent to the actual salary cost. In addition, accommodations will have to be found for the reading consultant. An office may be needed or even an additional classroom. Failure to consider such costs can result in seriously underestimating the cost of decision alternatives. The object should be clear: try to identify hidden costs and include them in cost estimation.

ASSEMBLING COST INFORMATION

With these distinctions in mind, one can proceed to the task of measuring and projecting costs of decision alternatives. In doing so, the evaluation specialist must be careful to be consistent in following the procedures that are adopted.

Economists generally recognize four types of costs that should be considered in trying to evaluate decision alternatives (Haller, 1974). They are (1) costs that can be measured in dollar expenditures; (2) costs that can reasonably be measured in dollar expenditures, though they are not reflected in expenditures; (3) costs that are quantifiable; and (4) costs that are not quantifiable. While economists emphasize the importance of all four types and stress the necessity of gathering information about each, this chapter will deal only with the first three kinds. There are two reasons for this. First, one of the major themes of the next chapter is nonquantifiable costs and, accordingly, is better handled there. Second, while economists quite properly stress the importance of information regarding psychic costs (and benefits), the methods and procedures for assessing them are far more developed in the field of educational and psychological measurement than in economics.

Costs that can be measured in dollar expenditures—the first type of cost—have been discussed at some length already. With the previously given caveats in mind, the estimation of such costs—within the input structure already set forth—should present no unusual problems. The important point is to make sure that all costs associated with a decision alternative are identified and included in the input structure. Errors of omission constitute the greatest danger in this area. The second type of cost—costs that can reasonably be measured in dollar expenditures— should also present no special problems. Included here would be such costs as depreciation of equipment and textbooks and estimated dollar costs of space. The third kind of cost involves time primarily—time of students and other non-salaried personnel such as volunteer aides and assistants. For example, in a learner tutorial program where older learners are used to tutor younger ones, the time of both would need to be included. Such costs cannot generally be expressed in dollars. However, they can usually be expressed in time. The extent of the time commitment required by learners and other non-salaried personnel should be estimated.* The total time commitment required on the part of learners is an important component of a program's costs.

In developing cost estimates of various decision alternatives, the evaluation specialist will quickly realize that costs in the near future will be far easier to estimate than costs in the distant future. Near future costs can be measured with reasonable accuracy. For example, the cost of a set of textbooks could be quickly obtained from a publisher's catalogue. The same is true of teachers' salaries for the coming year: there is undoubtedly a salary schedule that can be readily consulted. Costs that are further in the future will be estimated with far less precision. No one can say how much a publisher is going to raise the price of his books, nor can one predict the outcome of negotiations that will result in a new salary schedule for teachers several years hence. As the evaluation specialists attempt to estimate costs further into the future, the confidence in such estimates will decrease substantially. This, of course, poses a dilemma for the evaluation specialist who is conscientious about estimating costs. The more exhaustive he tries to be, especially with regard to time, the more imprecise his estimates will be. This raises the issue of how far into the future cost estimates should be taken. There is, of course, no definitive answer but for many educational programs, the life of a textbook, roughly three to five years, should be of sufficient duration to provide some guidance with respect to projected costs. As long as each decision alternative is estimated for the same length of time, there is little likelihood that the procedure will yield grossly erroneous results.

COMPARING COSTS

The fourth major step in the consideration of costs involves the comparison of costs of different decision alternatives. Assuming that the necessary information has been gathered, or estimated, in the previous step, there are three basic ways in which comparisons can be made.

The first way costs can be compared as in terms of the *total* costs of various decision alternatives over a specified period of time. For example,

---

*In compulsory schooling, learner time cannot be expressed in dollars and is therefore properly treated in this third type of cost. In other areas of education where learners receive stipends for participating in training programs, learner time can be expressed in dollar expenditures and would therefore be included in the first type of cost.

the cost of a particular program of health education can be estimated, year by year, in terms of dollar costs and nondollar student time. Estimates of various alternatives, including a decision not to adopt a program, can be estimated and compared with the costs of the contemplated program. Comparisons like these can be helpful, and sometimes decisive, when considering adoption of a program. If money is tight, cost considerations may have a determining influence.

If the decision alternatives being considered involve different ways of meeting the same set of educational needs, then a comparison of *average* costs is helpful. This is the second basic way in which costs can be compared. Average costs are determined by dividing the total costs of a decision alternative by the number of learner hours involved so as to obtain a cost per learner instructional hour. The numerator of the equation has been discussed previously. The denominator—number of learner hours—must be carefully reckoned. There can be a considerable difference between the number of learners who begin a program and the number who actually complete it. If dropout rates are substantial, it would seem wiser to use the number of learners completing a program in calculating average costs, since they, presumably, are the only ones who have received the program benefits. This number can then be used to establish the number of learner hours involved. For example, if 100 learners complete a program that meets for one hour a day for each of the 180 days in a school year, the number of learner hours involved is 18,000 (100×180). This would serve as the denominator of the equation to establish the average cost per learner, instructional hour.

The third basic way of comparing the cost of decision alternatives involves *marginal* costs. A marginal cost is the cost required to provide one additional unit of some benefit. In educational settings, this would involve enrolling an additional learner in a particular course, program, or curriculum. Marginal costs are useful to decision makers when expansion or contraction of a service is being contemplated. There are, however, substantial problems in estimating these costs. It may be easy to accommodate an additional learner in an existing program. The marginal costs may, in fact, be negligible—perhaps an extra book. However, if an extra 100 learners are to be served by a program, the costs involved may be substantial. New teachers will have to be hired, accommodations provided, materials obtained, etc. It would seem that only when a sizable venture is being contemplated should marginal costs be considered. For example, if it is decided to quadruple the day care facilities in a community, then the calculation of marginal costs should be undertaken. In such a situation, however, it would seem worthwhile to secure the services of a highly trained cost specialist.

For most evaluation situations, the estimation of average costs should be sufficient. Since total costs are calculated as one step in the estimation of average costs, these too can be reported. Only infrequently will it be necessary to consider estimating marginal costs.

The last step in the process of cost estimation will be considered only briefly here since it will be dealt with at length in chapter 12 and is not the exclusive concern of economics. This last step involves the cost–benefit comparisons of decision alternatives. A mere comparison of the costs of different courses of action can be justified on one of two grounds. It is either important to know what the projected cost of various decision alternatives will be—so that prohibitive alternatives can be immediately excluded—or the benefits of various decision alternatives are presumed to be equal. The first justification—elimination of utterly unrealistic alternatives—is self-evident. In fact, it may not even be necessary to carry through a cost estimation exercise to see that a particular alternative is too costly to seriously consider. Sometimes only a few minutes of systematic costing will suffice to expose the hopelessness of a course of action. (Interactive, computer-based instructional programs in public school settings are often cited as examples of a prohibitive decision alternative.) The other basis for carrying out cost comparisons without regard to benefits—when the benefits of various decision alternatives are presumed equal—is not acceptable. Evaluation studies are undertaken largely to find out what the actual benefits of a course, program, or curriculum are. Presuming that the benefits of various decision alternatives are equal is the last thing a responsible evaluation specialist or educator would want to do: it is always necessary to relate systematically costs to the benefits of various decision alternatives.

Making cost–benefit comparisons on the basis of evidence or estimates has traditionally been the province of economists. There are understandable, if unacceptable, reasons for this. Economists have developed techniques for relating costs to benefits in highly systematic ways. The arsenal of quantitative techniques is impressive and, it is hoped, they will be employed more widely in the future. The glaring deficiency of traditional cost-benefit comparisons is in the measurement and estimation of benefit. This is precisely the area where evaluation specialists and educators are strongest. Much evaluation work consists of identifying and measuring the benefits—e.g., learner achievement, attitudes, etc.—which constitute the outcomes of educational enterprises. The difficulties and complexities of such work are enormous and should never be underestimated. Doing the work, however, is the responsibility of educators and evaluation specialists. Highly trained as economists may be, they are rarely in a good position to estimate benefits.*

---

*In one cost-benefit analysis of a public health program to eradicate syphilis in the United States, the "stigma" of syphilis was estimated to be 1.3 billion dollars (Mishan 1971). This estimate is, of course, utterly arbitrary.

It is unlikely that the estimation of benefits in educational situations will be readily quantifiable, although efforts in that direction are to be encouraged and should be instructive. For the foreseeable future it is likely educational decision makers will continue to decide educational questions in a judgmental fashion. Cost–benefit comparisons will undoubtedly contribute to such decision making. It is unlikely, however, that either the cost–benefit comparisons or the decision-making process will be quantitatively tractable. Nonquantifiable costs and benefits will be involved along with value positions. Since this is an extremely complex issue and goes far beyond the scope of the estimational costs, it has been accorded a separate chapter (chapter 12).

SUMMARY

In this chapter an attempt was made to introduce the reader to some of the basic considerations involved in determing costs associated with an educational treatment. The definition of a cost is the one generally accepted by economists, namely, a benefit foregone. A number of implications stem from this definition. One is that costs occur in the future. Identifying what benefits are foregone in selecting an alternative is an important step in cost determination. Other steps involve the formulation of an input structure that consists of a set of cost categories for planning and development, implementation, and operation of a decision alternative. Such a structure should facilitate cost determination. Whether learner time is to be considered as a cost is an unresolved issue at present.

The actual determination of costs for various decision alternatives should not present any unusual problems. Nevertheless, distinctions between various *kinds* of costs were made: basic vs. additional, recurring vs. nonrecurring, and sunk vs. incremental costs. Some are, properly, included in cost determination while others are not. The important point, however, is to be consistent in estimating costs of each decision alternative.

Once these have been estimated, comparisons can be made in several ways. Of these, average cost per learner seems preferable. Obviously, very high cost decision alternatives can be quickly eliminated from further consideration. While cost comparisons can be made, comparisons in relation to attained benefits would appear to be considerably more important. This topic is treated in later chapters.

REFERENCES

Campbell, D.T. 1969. "Reforms as Experiments." *American Psychologist* 24: 409–429.

Haller, E.J. 1974. "Cost Analysis for Program Evaluation." In *Educational Evaluation: Current Applications*, edited by W.J. Popham, pp. 401–450. Berkeley, Cal.: McCutchan Publishing Corporation.

Mishan, E. 1975. *Cost-benefit Analysis.* New York: Praeger Publishers.

Schultz, T. 1953. *The Economic Value of Education.* New York: Columbia University Press.

8

GATHERING SUPPLEMENTAL INFORMATION

It should be clear by now that the evaluation of educational courses, programs and curricula involves the systematic collection of a number of kinds of information, the analysis and interpretation of that information, judgments about the worth of the enterprise, and decisions about future actions. Learner-performance information at the beginning and after some period of treatment, the extent to which the designed program has been carried out, and costs are all necessary classes of information. They are not, however, sufficient. There is one additional major class of information that needs to be considered. Since this last class covers several different kinds of information, it has been named "supplemental." This does not mean that the information is in any way less important than the previously discussed classes. It may, in fact, be decisive in judging the worth of an educational undertaking. It is only that the kinds of information to be dealt with in this chapter are somewhat diverse. They have not generally received the attention that learner-performance information in relation to objectives has been accorded.

The three categories of supplemental information to be covered in this chapter are views and opinions of individuals and groups, learner performance not covered by program objectives, and unintended effects of instruction. Each category could perhaps be legitimately treated as a separate class of information since the links between them are tenuous at best. To do so, however, would mean having seven major classes of information, an undesirable outcome since it would result in a more cumbersome framework. One of the criteria of the framework evaluation advocated in this book is that it would be succinct. In any case, as will be shown later, the weighting of various kinds of information in judging the worth of educational enterprise need not be equal. This is true both between and within classes of information. Thus the inclusion of views-opinion information as a category of supplemental information does not necessarily mean it has less inherent weight than any other class of information. Also, the existence of a class of information termed "supplemental" indicates a certain fluidity which should allow for the accommodation of new kinds of information.

VIEWS AND OPINIONS

The solicitation of the views and opinions of individuals who have had some contact with an educational venture has been undertaken occasionally in connection with evaluation efforts. The reception accorded such information has been mixed. In many cases, the views and opinions of participants, teachers, administrators, and others has been judged self-serving and not much above the level of testimonials. Undoubtedly, there is ample basis for this: Individuals with some investment in a venture are apt to want to see it judged in a favorable light. Such a disposition may or may not be consciously felt. Whatever the reason, the views and opinions of individuals associated with a program have often not been given much weight. Program personnel, on the other hand, frequently give undue prominence to such information.

The schism over how much attention should be accorded information about the views and opinions of persons associated with an educational enterprise is unfortunate. The views and opinions of various groups can be critical in the evaluation of an educational program. Consider the case of a new English program that uses writings by contemporary American authors. Some parents and community members might find a few reading selections they felt contained language so offensive that it swamped all the positive features of the program. This may seem trivial, but it is precisely the stuff out of which school controversies are often made. Similarly, an after-school art program showing somewhat meager results may not only be gratefully received by learners but enthusiastically endorsed by working mothers who no longer need to worry about what is happening to their children between close of school and the time they arrive home from work. Unless some systematic attempt is made to solicit the views and opinions of persons who have some connection with a program, valuable information may be missed, resulting in incomplete or even erroneous judgments about a program's worth.

For information about the views and opinions of persons associated with a course, program, or curriculum to be useful in an evaluation study, several conditions need to be met. First, the kind of information sought needs to be carefully specified. This includes identifying what information will be gathered and what will not. For example, in a number of attempts to solicit student evaluations of courses at the college and high-school levels, learners are occasionally asked to judge the teacher's knowledge of the subject. This question is certainly inappropriate since the learner is in no position to make such a judgment. The use of inappropriate items not only produces highly questionable data but can often cast doubt on the rest of the results obtained by the use of the instrument. It is necessary, therefore, to specify carefully what will be asked of whom.

The second step in obtaining the views and opinions of persons associated with an educational enterprise is to formulate one or more questions about each aspect of the enterprise for which information is sought. Initially, the questions can be in an open-ended form, unless they immediately lend themselves to an alternative response format. Maxims for the development of such questions exist in several places and can be readily consulted (Oppenheim 1966; Noelle-Neuman 1970). A set of questions, once developed, should be tried out informally. Ideally, the questions would be tried in an interview with a small but variable sample of individuals belonging to the groups from which information is being sought. In an informal interview situation it should be possible to obtain an indication as to whether the respondents understand the questions and can supply clear, responsive answers. Ideas for additional questions and ways to improve the initial set of questions should result from a small number of informal interviews. In conducting them, the tryout nature of questions needs to be carefully explained and a clearly stated guarantee of anonymity, especially to learners, needs to be made so that resistance to giving frank answers can be minimized. On the basis of information so obtained it should be possible to (1) revise the questions so that they yield the desired information; and (2) develop response categories for those questions for which a closed-end format is considered desirable.

While several informal interviews would be an ideal way to proceed, there may not be enough time or personnel available for even this modest undertaking. An acceptable though less desirable approach would be to administer the tryout set of items to a small group of individuals in questionnaire form, asking them not only to respond to the items but also to comment on them themselves. Again, the items should be asked in open-ended form where possible. The data yielded by the tryout should enable one to revise the questions and formulate response categories for those items for which a closed-end format is desirable. In formulating the response categories, one should be heavily guided by the responses of individuals presented with the questions in an open-ended form.

The above discussion has been procedural in nature. Specific questions one would ask of learners, teachers, administrators, parents, and others will, of course, depend on the enterprise being evaluated. Generally, however, one wants to know how the program was received. Did learners feel they benefited from the course, program, or curriculum?

What did they see as its major strengths and weaknesses? What particular activities were most beneficial? What suggestions can be offered for improvement? How helpful were the learning materials? Did the expectations and standards seem realistic and fair? Somewhat different questions would be asked of teachers. For example, how do teachers view the organization of the program? Are the objectives and learning experiences appropriate for the learners being served? How should the program be modified? What objectives should be revised or eliminated? What new objectives and learning experiences should be added? Which instructional materials worked out well; which ones didn't? Separate lists of questions can be formulated for administrators, parents, and any others connected with the program.

In obtaining the views and opinions of various groups dramatic results are not to be expected; more likely, somewhat conflicting results will be found. For example, in a study that sought reactions to a number of features of a course, it was found that one-quarter of the learners thought the textbook used was too hard, one half said it was just about right, and one quarter felt it was too easy. This is quite understandable. Unanimity is not to be expected in most matters, and evaluation is no exception. Generally, however, one tends to find a fair degree of agreement among the members of a particular group. More weight, of course, will be given to such results. If, for example, a strong majority of parents of learners felt that not enough homework was assigned, this finding would warrant close examination. On the other hand, if parents were about evenly split with regard to the amount of homework that is assigned, somewhat less weight would be given to the finding. Since one is dealing with views and opinions, the resulting data will have a validity of its own which may not fully accord with the facts of the situation. It is wise not to ignore such findings.

Just as it was possible to divide a large number of questions—measuring learner proficiency with regard to objectives—into groups, so that each learner responded to only a fraction of the total set, it is possible to divide views-and-opinions questions and items in a similar way. An evaluation worker need not feel constrained from developing a substantial number of such questions and items for use with learners if he follows this procedure. Specific details on how to do this are given in chapter 10. The solicitation of such information from teachers and administrators, however, is a different matter: ordinarily, the number of teachers and administrators involved will be quite small compared to the number of learners.

In most cases it will not even be worth the effort to develop questionnaires for teachers and administrators. Semistructured interviews should be sufficient for obtaining all the information required. These can be conducted individually in informal manner in offices, classrooms or even teachers' lounges (the latter is not a recommended site because of possible lack of privacy). In all cases it is necessary to provide guarantees of anonymity. This may not mean much if only one or two teachers are involved. In such cases it may be necessary to assure respondents they will have the opportunity to review and approve the draft of sections of any written report containing their views and opinions. Evaluation workers may be reluctant to furnish such assurances if it appears to be a constraint on their freedom to do their job as they see fit. This is not the case, however; evaluation workers are not being asked to compromise their integrity. It is the way in which information is to be handled and, more important, expressed, which is at issue. Protection must be given to those whose cooperation is being solicited. In most cases assurance of the right of review and approval will probably be sufficient to get respondents to state their views and opinions in a candid manner.

Soliciting the views and opinions of parents and other adults associated with a program can be handled in a way similar to that recommended for learners. That is, several questionnaire forms can be employed so that the burden of responding is minimized. This is especially important in obtaining the views and opinions of parents. As a rule of thumb no more than five to ten minutes of time should be requested from parents. Tryouts of questionnaires—to determine the amount of time required to answer—are vital. Also, parents should be specifically instructed *not* to give their names; thus, anonymity is assured. Finally, in the course of seeking the views and opinions of parents, one must be prepared for the fact that many parents either possess insufficient information to have formed definite—let alone strong—views and opinions about a particular program; or, even being informed, do not develop strong feelings. Accordingly, instruments designed to elicit views and opinions of parents and others not closely associated with a program must provide opportunity for individuals to indicate that they have no definite opinions or feel they possess insufficient information to judge. Introductory statements and directions for responding must clearly state that these responses are acceptable. Response categories, including "no opinion" or "don't know," should be included for every item. If a considerable number of parents accept a program or even are acquiescent, this is important to know. To be avoided is any subtle (or not so subtle) structuring of questions that tends to distort responses or force reactions. The notion that if one is not for something he has to be against it may hold for certain political situations; it is not at all pertinent to the evaluation of educational programs.

SUPPLEMENTAL LEARNINGS

The second major type of supplemental information consists of learner-performance information not explicitly called for by the objectives of the course, program, or curriculum. This reflects an unsettled issue in educational evaluation. Some writers would exclude any assessment of learner performance not directly specified in the objectives—on the ground that it is inappropriate. For example, in a program of mathematics instruction that purports to develop mathematical reasoning and problem-solving abilities of learners, is it fair to test the computational proficiency of learners in the program if this area is even specifically eschewed? On the other hand, writers like Cronbach (1963) argue that it is not only proper but necessary to inquire how well a course, program, or curriculum serves a larger national interest (as well as its own objectives). The position advocated here is that it is important to gather learner-performance information going beyond the stated objectives of a program in a comprehensive evaluation, but the analysis and interpretation of such information should be handled separately from information that bears directly on the objectives. This is the reason for including such information under the heading "supplemental."

What kind of additional learner performance information should be gathered and what should be done with it? These, of course, are the critical questions and satisfactory, if not definitive, answers must be found. The additional learner-performance information to be gathered can be based on an examination of other courses, programs, and curricula in the same area as the one under study. Inspection of guides, syllabi, textbooks, and tests should produce a considerable body of material about the outcomes being promoted by alternative enterprises. Statements by specialists in the field to which the program under study belongs may also be helpful in identifying areas of learner performance that may be examined. Even a cursory study should produce ideas about areas that might be examined. The generation of material on which to assess learner proficiency is not the problem: it is the selection of material that constitutes the challenge. On the one hand, one wishes to obtain as comprehensive a picture as possible about what learners know and can do as a result of a set of educational experiences; on the other hand, one cannot go off in every possible direction. Judgments and compromises must be made.

In deciding what to study it is considered useful to examine those aspects of learner performance that are emphasized in more than one alternative program. The purpose is simply to avoid the idiosyncratic. For example, if several alternative chemistry courses stress the importance of balancing chemical equations while the course under study does not, it would be worthwhile including questions testing this competency. Thus, one guide to deciding what to test for is frequency of occurrence of proficiencies *not* emphasized by the program under study.

Another way of deciding what kind of information to gather is to exclude from study those learnings that are too clearly based on the content or terminology of a particular alternative program. Every educational program has its own specific content and terminology. To test learners on the details of an alternative program is clearly unfair. For example, in the elementary-school social studies program "Man: A Course of Study" learners devote considerable time to studying the life cycle of the salmon and the culture of the Netsilik Eskimos. The purpose of such study is not to master the details of this content but as a means of raising a number of fundamental questions and issues about man. In this context, asking learners in another program to answer questions about the life cycle of the salmon or the Nestilik Eskimos would be highly inappropriate; such information would be too content-specific to its program. One should avoid the specific content of an alternative program as much as possible and rather focus on the processes, skills, and generalized proficiencies, emphasized by alternative programs. In some cases, this may simply involve eliminating highly specific and detailed questions from tests used in alternative programs; in others it may require modification or adaptation of questions to make them suitable for learners in the program being evaluated. Whatever course is followed, one would want to include a variety of questions dealing with a range of outcomes that are emphasized in alternative programs.

The administration of questions, items, and exercises measuring competencies not specifically emphasized in a particular program is a rather delicate undertaking. If included as part of the regular collection of learner-performance information, such supplemtntal testing material could be resented and a possible a cause of outrage on the part of learners and teachers. The material is likely to be considered highly unfair—especially if it is testing objectives not at all emphasized in instruction. Consequently, it is recommended that the additional testing material be administered separately and be preceded with special instructions, emphasizing that the questions, items, and exercises are not designed to assess the objectives of the program but, rather, some general outcomes. A frank and honest explanation of the purpose of such testing material with a request for the learners' cooperation and best effort in responding is probably the best approach to the situation. Assurance should also be given that the information supplied will in no way affect the learners' grades or other appraisal of their work.

The potential reaction against answering such supplemental questions, items, and exercises can be reduced considerably by following the same sampling procedures suggested for gathering information about learner performance in relation to the stated objectives. That is, the total collection of testing material can be randomly divided into a number of different forms, each requiring about the same amount of time to answer, and passed out at random to the learners in the program to complete. The double randomization should serve to insure that the results from each form can be used to characterize all the learners in the program. The administration of this supplemental material can immediately *follow* the collection of learner-performance information relative to the stated objectives. In this way, if the collection of the supplemental performance information meets with a strong and hostile reaction, it will have no influence on the more important part of the evaluation: the assessment of learner performance in relation to the objectives of the program.

Just as the collection of supplemental performance information must be separate from the collection of performance information in relation to the objectives, the analysis and interpretation of the resultant data must also be kept clearly separate. With this single proviso in mind, there are a number of ways of handling such supplemental information. The first step—no matter what follows—is to score the questions, items, and exercises. In addition to examining the correct answers, it may be useful to study the kinds of wrong answers learners make in order to determine if the course, program, or curriculum is systematically producing certain kinds of misinformation, i.e., incorrect ways of attacking and handling certain issues or phenomena. Generally it is undesirable to try to aggregate all of the learner-performance information into a total or overall score. Such scores usually conceal more than they reveal. If one of the goals of the evaluation is program improvement, it will be worthwhile to report results item by item, including the most popular wrong answers. In this way, program developers may get useful clues for program revision. If the purpose of the evaluation is more summative in nature, it may be worthwhile to develop scores based on clusters of items that purportedly measure the same kinds of proficiencies. There would appear to be a number of ways in which such supplemental performance information can be examined, and at least several should be tried. The object in analyzing and interpreting such information is to achieve as complete a description as possible about what learners know and can do as a result of a set of educational experiences.

The timing of the administration of such supplemental assessment material has already been mentioned: it should be in a post-testing situation; that is, after some period of instruction. Whether supplemental material should be administered before instruction begins is a different and separate issue. The answer would seem to depend on how specialized the course, program, or curriculum is. For example, in a first course in neuroanatomy in a medical school, the material may be so specialized that testing prior to instruction is a waste of time. Virtually all learners are ignorant about the subject. On the other hand, in a high school course in government and politics, learners may possess considerable prior knowledge, experience, attitudes, and dispositions. Any failure to carefully assess as much of this as possible would be a gross oversight. Thus, whether instruments to measure learner proficiencies not embodied in the objectives are used on a pretest basis will depend largely on the kind of material to be learned. One will have to rely on the judgment and experience of others when deciding whether to use instruments designed to measure proficiencies not stated in the objectives of a program.

UNINTENDED EFFECTS

A third major kind of supplemental information is the unintended effects of a course, program, or curriculum. This is unquestionably the most difficult kind of information to gather since, unlike the other kinds of information, there is no clear idea as to what one is looking for. Educational programs are usually developed with some set of intentions in mind, and evaluation consists, to a large extent, in assessing the extent to which those intentions are realized. It is becoming increasingly clear in education that the adoption of a particular course of action can result in consequences that were not intended. In chapter 2, for example, we cited the adoption of a rigorous academic high-school physics program that adversely affected learner interest in taking additional course work in physics. It is but one example out of many that could be given of educational programs that had effects other than those originally intended.

It is the responsibility of evaluation specialists to assess the unintended effects a course, program, or curriculum is having. The evaluation worker may not always succeed. Limitations of time and other resources, coupled with the difficulty and complexity of the task, may prevent the evaluation specialist from accomplishing as much as he or she would like. Nevertheless, the effort must be made if the evaluation is to be comprehensive.

The assessment of unintended effects is not merely a negative matter. That is, adverse effects of educational programs are not the sole object of the search for unintended effects. Positive outcomes are also of interest. For example, a mathematics program that eschews computational proficiency because of a concern for the development of mathematical reasoning ability and problem solving may produce learners who are actually superior in computational ability. If so, this is important to know. Similarly, a program in social studies that strives to have learners acquire a great deal of content may show that learners are also developing a considerable expertise in work study skills, report writing and the like. Again this is important to know. The aim of the assessment of unintended effects is to identify as many outcomes as possible, both positive and negative, that appear to be due to the instructional treatment being evaluated.

The assessment of unintended effects has been likened to the search for a black cat in a dark room on a moonless night. In many ways it is. One has no clear idea as to what is being sought. This means that formal information-gathering devices—tests, scales, questionnaires, etc.—have little or nothing to offer since their use depends on a rather clear notion of what one is looking for. Consequently, one must use less formal procedures for detecting unintended effects. The main ones are observation, semistructured interviews, and small and large group discussions. A considerable amount of sensitivity is required in the use of these procedures. The evaluation specialist must try to place himself in the role of an anthropologist who is trying to understand a different culture, when gathering information about unintended effects.

It is useful if the specialist spends some time observing a program in action so that he can steep himself in the culture of the classroom. This can be done in connection with the observations necessary to determine whether the intended learning experiences sre being carried out. Evaluation workers should consciously set aside a certain amount of time that will *not* be devoted to assessing whether the intended learning activities are occurring; instead, they should observe the situation to see what is happening. In carrying out such loosely structured observations, the evaluation worker's focus is not on what is happening—in terms of the program's objectives—but rather on the activities occurring, the relationships among learners, and the interactions between teacher and learners. They will try to function as an anthropological field worker would. After doing this, the evaluation worker should have several observations, and possibly some hypotheses, as to what might be happening to learners that was not intended as part of the program.

While observational procedures are employed to generate ideas about possible unintended effects, it will be necessary to study them further and to test them somewhat systematically before one can conclude, even presumptively, that a program is having a particular unintended effect. For example, in evaluating a science program that had been developed in England and was being used in a developing country, several of the consultants brought in to help install the program noted that learners seemed uninvolved with the program. This was considered puzzling since the learners were the most able ones in the country, were highly motivated to do well in school, and were in fact learning the material in the program—as judged by the results of achievement tests. The condition persisted: while the learners continued to perform well, there remained a strange kind of lethargy on the part of the learners. What is more, this phenomenon did not occur in other courses.

The consultant team was able to confirm this apparent lack of involvement on the part of the learners through their own observation, although the reasons were not at all clear. The consultants, however, were able to talk with the program's teachers and shared their observations with them. The teachers agreed about the apparent detachment but could offer no explanations: they were not even sure the detachment was due to the program or to some extraneous factor. The consultants persevered. At least the teachers confirmed what they had noted, even if they were not able to provide good reasons for it. The consultants then arranged to meet with two class groups. They told the learners what they had observed as simply as they could and invited comments. The learners agreed with the observation. Further discussion revealed, somewhat surprisingly, that the feeling of distance was greater when the learners were in a laboratory situation than in a regular class situation. (This feeling of detachment, the learners agreed, was not characteristic of their other studies.) When asked to suggest reasons for this widely held feeling, one learner volunteered that he did not become highly engaged in the study of science because, after completing the required amount of study, he doubted he would ever study the subject again. Other learners concurred.

The consultants were somewhat puzzled by the learner's reason for feeling detached and gently pressed further. Did they (the learners) see no value in studying science? If the consultants felt that the learners were like C.P. Snow's humanists caught in the two-cultures dilemma, they were to be disappointed. The learners indicated that science was vitally important to the development of their nation, and they wished they could contribute. The consultants asked them why they felt that they might not be able to. It was then that one learner expressed the idea that science was a "rich man's" study and that, since he came from a home of limited means, he could never afford to engage in the study of science as fully as the subject required.

The quickness with which the others endorsed this statement indicated to the consultants that they were on to something. They continued to gently probe the learners' feelings. The study of science, the learners felt, required considerable resources. Laboratory equipment, apparatus, and supplies cost a lot of money and, *without such resources, one could not properly study science*. The reason for this feeling, the consultants soon learned, stemmed from the fact that the science program brought from England relied heavily on the use of elaborate equipment and supplies. Unless one had special resources or were so talented that they could gain them through merit, the study of science on any serious basis was beyond the reach of the great majority of learners.

The consultants left the meeting with much to ponder. The science program clearly used elaborate apparatus, equipment and supplies. This, in fact, had been one of the attractive features of the program, and the decision to adopt it by officials in the Ministry of Education was based in some measure on furnishing learners with the opportunity to work with the best materials available. It had on the whole been a costly decision. The consequences were clearly different from what had been hoped for. Instead of luring learners deeper into the study of science, the elaborate equipment and apparatus had served to convince them that science could be learned only at great expense, which placed it beyond the reach of all but the richest or most talented. Subsequent interviews with other learners and discussions with other classes confirmed this finding.

The reason for devoting so much attention to this unintended effect of instruction is to show the procedures that were used to identify, refine, and test it. Initially, casual observation was employed to sense the unintended effect, which was itself only dimly perceived. Second, discussions with teachers served to verify the observations but the meaning of these observations—let alone their reasons—was still unclear. Third, discussions with a group of learners served to define the unintended effect. Fourth, further discussion with the learners resulted in a hypothesis linking an aspect of the program, i.e., the apparatus, equipment and materials, with the unintended effect. Last, the hypothesis was tested in two ways with new groups in both interview and discussion settings.

All the steps in the above procedure were important. What is particularly critical—in the identification of unintended effects—is the sensitivity required to be able initially to identify and define such effects. It may be that evaluation specialists, chiefly concerned with determining the extent to which stated objectives are being achieved, may not be wholly receptive to unintended effects. If this is the case, then it is the responsibility of the evaluation specialists to get others to observe and report on what they see happening. Persons knowledgeable about curriculum in general or the subject being studied and who have had considerable experience could be wisely used in this capacity. Whether they should be informed about the stated objectives so that they know what *not* to be looking for is an unresolved issue. If time and resources permitted, some observers could be informed about the objectives and others not. The results of the two groups of observers could then be compared to see if it made a difference to inform observers about the program's intentions in other than a cursory way. More important, the observation notes of these external observers should provide a fruitful list of possible unintended effects.

The identification of unintended effects is extremely delicate. It is for this reason that rather loose methods must be used. Observations of the learning situation are highly recommended as an initial step. Loosely structured interviews with teachers and learners can also be used to identify and define what appear to be unintended effects. Discussions with groups of learners and teachers can also play a part. The object of this activity is to search out what might be happening that was not part of the program's intentions. But once identified, it will be necessary to adopt more systematic procedures to establish that what was thought to be an unintended effect really was. As in most validation studies, it will be necessary to establish that the unintended effect that occurred with one group of learners occurs with another. This is essential, for it may be that a particular outcome or set of outcomes, characteristic of a certain group of learners or a single teacher, is not a progrm effect at all. This requires considerable perspicacity. If an effect arises out of the peculiarities of a single situation, it would be a grave disservice to attribute it to the program. Identifying the effect in one situation and then systematically trying to establish its existence in another is one of the best ways to avoid this jumping to conclusions.

If a program, course, or curriculum is limited to a single group of learners, there is no easy way separately to establish the existence of an unintended effect. The evaluation specialist has no option but to wait for the next group of learners in order to verify the existence of the unintended effect in question. This could easily require waiting a semester or even a year. If the effect is considered to be particularly noxious, such a delay may be unacceptable. One would wish to take corrective action before the evidence can clearly establish that the unintended effect is, in fact, due to something in the program rather than arising out of specific situational factors. Such judgments and actions typically come under the heading of formative evaluation, and they present problems. Certainly, if there is something unwholesome in an educational situation, one would want to remedy it as quickly as possible. Such actions are clearly the responsibility of teachers and administrators. The evaluation specialist, on the other hand, has a more difficult task, namely, to assess whether the effect is due to something in the program or to something in the specifics of a particular situation or—as sometimes happens—to both.

An example of both program and situational factors producing an unintended effect occurred several years ago in a reading program for retarded readers at the seventh-grade level. Extensive and careful testing had been done to establish a class group of average and above average ability learners who were more than two years below grade-level in reading achievement. While the class was known to contain some learners with histories of behavior problems, it seemed to exhibit more discipline problems than had been expected. At first it was believed that assembling a number of learners with behavior problems explained the phenomenon, but continued investigation revealed that the learners were offended by the use of certain of the reading materials which, while appropriate for their reading level, were far below their interest level. Learner comments about much of the reading material being "babyish" was the critical incident that revealed the program defect. Fortunately, it was possible to secure some high interest, low readability materials fairly quickly. Once these were introduced, discipline problems declined substantially.

The use of observations, loosely structured interviews with learners and teachers, and discussions with both are ways of detecting unintended effects of a newly instituted program. The information thus obtained can be used in a formative way to remedy obvious program defects. The evaluation specialist will want to know whether such effects are due to the program or arise from a particular group of learners and/or teachers. Hence the need for independent verification with another group. If the enterprise being evaluated is one that involves several schools or several class groups, this is not a problem. Effects can be searched for in one set of schools or class groups and checked out in another. If the program is limited to a single class group, one will have to wait until another occasion for study arises with a subsequent group. This may involve a considerable delay but cannot be avoided. The evaluation worker should delay ascribing a particular effect to a program until there has been an opportunity to verify it independently. Even if verification with a subsequent group of learners is undertaken, there will still be the possibility that the effect might be due to the teacher. While learners change from semester to semester or from year to year, the same teachers may remain in the situation. Only close study of a situation, coupled with sensitive judgment, can lead to a proper ascription of a particular unintended effect.

The procedures described above are intended to ascertain unintended effects of educational programs on a prospective basis. A retrospective approach may also be used. Teachers who receive learners into the next segment of an educational program may be informally questioned and asked to comment on the significant strengths and weaknesses among the incoming learners. The learners themselves can also be asked to offer their reflections on the program they have just come through. The resultant information may offer clues about possible unintended effects. The danger in using such retrospective accounts even as a means of generating hypotheses about unintended effects is that individuals may in retrospect see the program differently from the way it actually was. One must be prepared to accept the fact that a number of false leads might emanate from these accounts. Learners, for example, might be unduly harsh or lenient in their view of the program they have just come through. Teachers may ascribe all sorts of inadequacies to the program which are, possibly, more a reflection of the teacher's idealized expectations than a function of the program. One must, of course, be as sensitive as possible in trying to detect possible unintended effects yet alert enough to realize that not every possible criticism or plaudit is true; or, if it is, it need not be a function of the program. The need for independent checking will be even greater if the hypotheses about unintended effects originates from retrospective accounts about a program.

The dangers of using retrospective accounts to investigate hypotheses about such program effects should be clear. The advantage they offer is that hypotheses about them can be checked out almost immediately. That is, if a group of learners are questioned about a program they have just come through and the teachers who receive them supply observations and comments that lead to hypotheses about possible unintended effects, these can be checked out on the current version of the program. Since there is a fair degree of independence between the program under study and the next set of learning experiences, one can conduct such investigations with a reasonable degree of confidence. If the program being studied is a terminal one—i.e., attended by graduating seniors—then obtaining retrospective accounts becomes exceedingly difficult. First, there is no single group of teachers to query about possible unintended effects. Second, the learners who have graduated from the program may be widely dispersed. Polling them about their views and reactions to the program being evaluated is difficult to do since one would almost surely have to rely on a questionnaire. A questionnaire consisting of a list of general questions and a few extended written responses may be the best one can do in such a situation to generate hypotheses about unintended program effects.

Formal follow-up studies and longitudinal studies of learners have been advocated as one way of generating hypotheses about the effects of programs. Such studies, as research undertakings, have considerable merit, increasing knowledge about what happens to learners as they move through an educational system; as such, they are strongly recommended. How much they can contribute to the evaluation of specific courses, programs, and curricula is less clear. The number and variety of influences on learners which serve to determine an individual's status on any number of variables at a particular moment is only dimly perceived. To ascribe a particular effect to a particular program is an exceedingly difficult task, considering all the influences learners are exposed to not only in school but out. Multivariate statistical procedures have been recommended as a way of identifying and isolating the effects of various variables, but the results to date have not been encouraging enough to view such proposals with much confidence. Further, such studies require careful specification and measurement of all relevant variables. Unfortunately, the current knowledge base does not permit this, as witnessed by the fact that a number of major studies of school effects have failed to detect anything of much promise.

The search for unintended effects of educational programs is an enormously complex affair and can easily consume a major portion of the resources allotted to evaluation. This should not be permitted to happen. The main concern in evaluation is first to establish whether a program was carried out as intended and, if so, how successful it was in achieving its stated objectives. The search for unintended program effects must be considered important yet supplemental to the main mission. The solicitation of views and opinions of learners, teachers, and others associated with the program may suggest unintended effects worth further study. Likewise, the measurement of learner achievement in the subject not explicitly covered by the objectives may indicate unintended program effects in the achievement area. The accumulated information from the solicitation of views and opinions, supplemental achievement data, and the deliberate search for unintended program effects will, it is hoped, produce what is sought. There are no guarantees, however, because of the uncertain and probably elusive nature of unintended effects.

How far one should carry the search for unintended program effects is an open issue. As noted earlier, one does not wish to channel too large a proportion of the resources for evaluation into what is essentially a supplemental activity. The main requirement for the identification and assessment of such effects is the time of professional personnel. Carefully designed and elaborate instrumentation is not required and would in fact be self-defeating. How far one can afford to search for unintended effects will be largely conditioned by the available time of professional personnel for the task. They could be evaluation workers or knowledgeable consultants specially engaged for the task. If the latter are used, their main job will be to identify the possible unintended effects which can be checked out more systematically by the evaluation workers. Time and personnel available will limit the extensiveness of the search.

Even with considerable resources available to search for unintended effects, there are reasonable limits as to how far the search should be carried. It would seem unlikely that program effects which are extremely subtle and escape detection by procedures recommended in this chapter will have a strong influence on learners. A long, if sometimes undistinguished, history of research in education has failed to reveal variables with such profound influences. If the evaluation worker has made a reasonable search for such effects and failed to uncover them, the most likely explanation is that they do not exist. The somewhat dramatic side effects cited in this chapter are undoubtedly the exception rather than the rule. Hardly anyone would expect the evaluation specialist to be able to show a series of profound side effects each time a course, program, or curriculum is evaluated. All that is expected is that evaluation workers make a reasonable effort in this direction.

SUMMARY

This chapter deals with the collection of several kinds of information that are supplemental to the main activities of an evaluation study. "Supplemental," however, does not mean unimportant. In some cases the information may be of such importance as to be given an overriding weight in judging the worth of an enterprise. Three main types of supplemental information to be gathered. The first consists of the views, reactions, and opinions of learners, teachers, and others associated with a program. Ways in which such informatino can be gathered efficiently and economically were given. The second type of supplemental information discussed was learner proficiency *not* covered by the stated objectives of the program. The importance of such information (along with some caveats about it) was dealt with, and procedures for gathering it were detailed. Matters of administration and timing were also discussed. The third type of supplemental information consists of unintended effects of educational ventures. The difficulties in this area were treated at some length. The lack of a search model to guide one in this kind of information was stressed, and suggestions were made as to how the job could best be approached.

How great a role supplemental information will play in any particular evaluation study will probably be a joint function of the program studied, the learners to be served, and local circumstances. No one can speak with any assurance before the fact. Nevertheless, it would seem that any evaluation study seeking to be comprehensive cannot ignore the need to obtain the kinds of information discussed in this chapter.

REFERENCES

Cronbach, L.J. 1963. "Course Improvement through Evaluation." *Teachers College Record* 64: 672–683.

Noelle-Neuman, E. 1970. "Wanted: Rules for Wording Structured Questionnaires." *Public Opinion Quarterly* 34: 191–201.

Oppenheim, A. 1966. *Questionnaire Design and Attitude Measurement.* New York: Basic Books.

9

DESIGN AND CONDUCT OF EVALUATION STUDIES

INTRODUCTION

In this chapter an attempt will be made to integrate previously presented information about the design and conduct of evaluation studies with a formal presentation of design considerations. The purpose of the presentation is to inform the reader about a number of factors to be taken into account when planning and conducting evaluation studies. It is *not* intended as a substitute for a thorough grounding in the principles and procedures of experimental design, the discipline from which evaluation design is derived.

Evaluation design refers to the scheduling of treatments and observations in order to obtain answers to evaluation questions. Generally, these questions center around the effects that educational treatments are having on learners. How the evaluation specialist is able to arrange or, at the very least, have a hand in arranging the conditions under which treatments are scheduled and deciding how and when learners are exposed to these treatments and when observations and measurements are secured will by and large determine whether statements about the effectiveness of the treatment vis-a-vis learner behavior can be legitimately made. Failure to adhere to a carefully worked out design can easily result in a mass of information that could be useless for judging the effectiveness of a program. One of the major responsibilities of an evaluation worker is to work out (often with others) the basic plan for the conduct of an evaluation study. Sometimes the planning operation is straightforward and simple. More often, however, it is quite complex. The reason for this is that educational environments are ostensibly designed to serve the needs of learners, not evaluation workers. This is perfectly understandable. An educational institution was never intended to resemble a laboratory setting where an investigator had complete control of the situation and could assign individuals to groups, groups to treatments and treatments to schedules, all on the basis of a table of random numbers.

The absence of such control requires evaluation workers to carefully plan studies within the constraints of a particular situation so that a maximum amount of information can be obtained bearing directly on the effectiveness of a course, program, or curriculum. Balancing the two requirements—the design of studies intended to yield unequivocal results about a program's effectiveness and the constraints that exist in a particular situation—constitutes a formidable challenge to the evaluation worker. Sometimes the two requirements are virtually irreconcilable. In other cases, admittedly rare, they present no problem at all. In most instances, however, there will be some tension between the two, and the evaluation worker's task will be to find some way to resolve them. This will doubtless involve some compromise but should not result in sacrificing the aims of the study: it is one of the keenest challenges that the evaluation specialist will have to deal with. While much is made of the technical aspects of the design of studies, finding a way to resolve the tension between considerations of design and the hard realities of an operational situation often requires considerable ingenuity, if not outright creativity.

What makes for a good design? This question has been a central concern of researchers and evaluation specialists for some time. Essentially, a good design is one that allows one to clearly and unequivocally interpret the results of a study. This does not mean establishing the effectiveness of a particular educational treatment; it may as easily mean clearly establishing that a program was not effective. What is important is that the evaluation specialist be in a position to state that a program did or did not have certain effects on the learners who were exposed to it.

SOURCES OF INVALIDITY

Being in a position to say something about the effect of an educational treatment means that whatever effects are detected can be ascribed to the power of the treatment and not to something else. What might this "something else" be? D.T. Campbell and J. Stanley in a famous chapter on design for research on teaching (1963) point out two sets of factors that can jeopardize the validity of experimental studies in education. The first set deals with *internal validity* and constitutes the basic minimum without which any experiment is uninterpretable. The second deals with external validity and relates to the generalizability of results from a particular experiment to different samples, populations, settings, treatment variables, and measuring instruments. The question of *external validity* presents special problems in inductive inference and is never completely answerable. It is also of no real concern in evaluation studies where the aim of an investigation is to establish what effect a course, program or curriculum is having in a particular situation—not general. Factors relating to internal validity, however, are critical and must be dealt with. The best way of doing this is to control them through careful planning. However, in evaluation studies this is not always possible, and they may have to be handled in other, less desirable ways.

Eight major factors, singly or in combination, can jeopardize the internal validity of an evaluation study and prevent any meaningful interpretation of results. The reader will need to be familiar with each factor and consider it carefully when attempting to interpret the results of a particular study. The factors are presented below.

1. *History* refers to the influence of events that are not a part of educational treatment under study but occur at the same time. For example, an in-service workshop to improve the knowledge and proficiency of teachers of reading may be undertaken by a local school district. At the same time, some of the teachers may be enrolled in graduate programs leading to an advanced degree. As part of the program, these teachers may be taking a course in the teaching of reading. It may be possible to assess the teachers' knowledge and proficiency in the teaching of reading at the end of the workshop in a variety of ways, but one would be extremely hard pressed to determine how much of the teachers' performance is due to the in-service workshop and how much to their enrollment in the graduate course in the teaching of reading. In fact, the task is impossible. The evaluation specialist, seeking to interpret the results of any study, needs to consider alternative explanations for his results. The influence of variables *not* a part of the treatment under study is a prime candidate for an alternative explanation.

2. *Maturation* refers to normal growth processes which occur while an educational treatment is in progress and not to the influence of specific events. The growth processes can be biological, psychological, or even a combination of the two. Learners growing up in a culture are exposed to a variety of stimuli and learn considerably simply as a result of such exposures. For example, learners at the third-grade level, who have mastered some of the rudiments of reading, will undoubtedly improve in their reading ability simply as a result of being confronted with printed material in a variety of situations—road signs, magazines, newspapers, TV advertisements, etc. The problem for the evaluation specialist is to determine to what extent improvement in reading for such learners is due to the effects of instruction and to what extent it is due to growing up in a culture where one is constantly exposed to reading material.

3. *Testing* refers to the effect repeating a test has on the scores of a second testing. If one administers a test to a group of learners and then

readministers the test at a later time, the second set of scores will typically be higher. Having taken the test before can account for part of this score rise. The effect of retesting can be reduced by making sure that learners are given a different set of questions to answer the second time. However, the only way to eliminate the effect of testing would be to administer a test only once after a period of instruction. This, as has been pointed out previously, is a risky undertaking and would violate one of the major precepts of an evaluation study, namely, the collection of information prior to the initiation of instruction.

4. *Instrumentation* deals with changes that can occur as a result of changes in the calibration of a measuring instrument or changes in the observers or scorers. At the simplest level, if the scorers of, say, essay tests change from pretest to posttest, differences in grades given to learners' essays may arise out of the different standards used by the two sets of scorers. If the scorers of the pretest essays are particularly stringent in grading while the scorers of the posttests are lenient, then score differences may reflect changes in the standards of the scorers more than changes in learner performance. The same situation may hold for more objective measures of learner performance too. One may simply ask easier questions on a posttest than on a pretest. This is one reason for trying to use the same instruments from one testing to another, a task that can be readily accomplished if each learner is presented with a different sample of questions at each testing but the same total set of questions is used.

There is still a problem, however. The amount of proficiency required to go from, say, a score of six to twelve may be different from the amount required to go from twelve to eighteen. Yet scores typically are treated as if the difference between score points is uniform throughout the test. The evaluation worker will have to be particularly sensitive to the nature of the instruments employed and the units of measurement in which performance is expressed.

5. *Statistical regression* arises when one deliberately seeks to select individuals on the basis of extreme scores. Later testing invariably will show that such individuals, on average, will perform somewhat closer to the average for all learners. This phenomenon was noted by Terman in his studies of gifted children over half a century ago. Terman sought to identify a group of clearly gifted children. His major criterion for classifying them as gifted was the score obtained on the Stanford-Binet. Obviously, the higher—i.e., the more extreme—the score, the more likely the child was gifted. As part of his initial follow-up, Terman had all members of his gifted group retested and found to his surprise that the average IQ had regressed rather dramatically toward the average. Such regression is now regarded as commonplace.

More recently, educational programs have been undertaken to help disadvantaged learners. A common practice in such programs is to select individuals who score extremely *low* on some measure. On later testing, these learners invariably show a higher average level of performance. While some increment in performance may have occurred, much of the apparent improvement is simply due to statistical regression: in this case the direction is upward instead of downward, as in the case of Terman's study. In both cases the phenomenon is the same: individuals initially selected on the basis of extreme scores will, on retesting, show less extreme scores.

6. *Selection* refers to the employment of different criteria in the establishment of groups to be compared after a period of instruction. The employment of differential criteria can result in biases in the selection of learners, particularly for those in the comparison groups. For example, if selection into an experimental program was based on volunteering, then it can be expected that those learners who did not volunteer, and consequently served as a comparison group, would differ both initially and subsequently from those in the experimental program. Similarly, if teachers volunteer to teach in an experimental program, they can differ considerably from teachers who opt to continue teaching in a conventional program. In this case, the act of volunteering may indicate that the volunteer teachers are looking for new challenges and may approach the teaching function with greater zeal. If differences favoring the experimental program are found, one faces the task of trying to decide how much such results reflect the effects of the program and how much the dedication of the teachers.

7. *Mortality* refers to the differential dropout rates of learners from groups being studied. Obviously, if care has been taken to establish groups that are comparable to begin with yet one group incurs a loss of low-performing learners during the course of the program, the latter's average performance level will increase, regardless of the effectiveness of the program to which it was exposed. When schooling is no longer compulsory, the effect of learner mortality or attrition can be considerable. Even in compulsory schooling it is wise to determine how much mortality has occurred to insure that inherently unequal groups are not being compared.

8. *Interactions* of some of the previously mentioned factors can occur in certain designs involving comparisons between different groups. The joint operation of several factors can lead one to conclude erroneously that a program has been effective. For example, the first year of evaluation of "Sesame Street" used four different groups to judge the instructional effects of the program. The groups were established on the basis of the time spent in watching Sesame Street. This ranged from rarely or never watching the program to viewing it more than five times a week. Scores on the Sesame Street pretests were found to be highly related to the amount of time spent viewing the program (Ball and Bogatz 1970). That is, the

higher the initial score the more time was spent in watching the program. Scores on the posttest, and hence the gains, were in the same way highly related to the time spent viewing the program. The combination of initial status and self selection into viewing category made it impossible to assess the effectiveness of "Sesame Street" from the data. (Fortunately, the flaw was not repeated in the second-year evaluation of the program.)

The presence of the factors listed above, singly or in combination, can make it impossible to determine whether learner performance is due to the effect of an educational treatment or to something else. A major goal of the evaluation studies is to interpret results meaningfully so that a clear determination of the source of an effect can be made. Failure occurs when the evaluation worker cannot say whether a particular level of learner performance was due to the effectiveness of a program, maturation on the part of the learners involved, other experiences that the learner had, or something else.

COMPARISON AND CONTROL GROUPS

One of the dominant influences on educational evaluation has been that area of method called experimental design. The origins of that field, at least in education, can be traced to W. McCall's *How to Experiment in Education*, published in 1923. This book preceded R.A. Fisher's *Statistical Methods for Research Workers* by two years and introduced educators to a number of important concepts in experimental design, among them control groups and randomization. In many respects, subsequent work in the field has consisted of refinements and extensions of the basic ideas of McCall. Campbell and Stanley (1963, p. 171) in a now standard work fully acknowledge their debt to McCall by noting that their chapter "aspires to achieve an up-to-date representation of the interests and considerations of that book. . . ."

One of the major ideas introduced by McCall and emphasized ever since was the employment of equivalent groups in educational experiments. Equivalent groups were to be established by chance—i.e., learners were to be assigned to instructional groups on a random basis. Such assignment, McCall stated and subsequent writers have echoed, would insure the establishment of comparable groups. In an educational experiment, comparable groups are established by random assignment and a random procedure is used to determine which group will receive the experimental treatment and which the alternate treatment. In the vocabulary of experimental design, the group receiving the alternate treatment would be called the control group. This designation is based partly on its receipt of the alternative treatment but—equally important—partly on the way in which it was established. Only the use of randomization procedures in the assignment of learners to groups permits one legitimately to apply the term "control" to the group receiving the alternative treatment.

There have been experiments in education in which control groups have been employed. The number of such studies is small, however, in relation to the studies using groups not established on the basis of the application of the principles of randomization. Such nonrandomly established groups are termed comparison, or contrast, groups. Ideally, comparative studies in education should employ control groups. In many cases, however, this is neither feasible nor possible. The obstacles to the use of randomization can be formidable, and heroic efforts are required to establish comparable groups on a random basis. The reasons for the objections to randomization in educational studies are generally well known. Resistance, on the part of parents, teachers, and other school officials, is deep-seated and widespread. Often there is a genuine concern for the welfare of the individual learner. School policies with regard to grouping often specify that instructional groups are to be established on the basis of ability, previous achievement, and a host of other criteria. Considerable time and effort is expended in setting up groups that are anything but random, and professionals in the schools see this as being one of their important responsibilities. None of this is intended as criticism of teachers and administrators. They are clearly trying to fulfill what they feel is an important professional function. It does, however, make it extremely difficult to establish comparable groups for purposes of evaluating the effects of different educational treatments.

The evaluation worker typically faces a dilemma. On the one hand, the use of control groups offers the best prospect for obtaining meaningful answers to evaluation questions, but the realities of educational institutions often prevents this. How the evaluation worker resolves this dilemma is critical to the success of his efforts. Accordingly, the issue needs to be discussed at some length.

There are occasions when it is possible to employ strict randomization in connection with the establishment of equivalent groups for evaluation studies. Such occasions are rare. Usually, they involve the dispensation of a treatment that does not require disruption of existing schedules, groupings and other arrangements. A notable example is Page's study of teachers' comments on students' papers (1958). In this study Page was able to have students assigned, at random, to one of three treatment groups within each of 74 classrooms. The study was even conducted without the students' knowledge that they were in a particular treatment group; nor were the students aware that a study was being conducted. Admittedly, the Page study is an example of educational research and not educational evaluation. In evaluation, the educational treatment being dispensed is, and should be, clearly known. It will typically be a course, program, or an entire curriculum. In contrast, the variables examined in a research study can be subtle and rather unobtrusive—such as the comments bestowed on student papers or other similar variables.

In some situations, the evaluation worker may have no power to influence the establishment of class groups, but he may be able to decide which groups receive which treatment. One such study involved the use of a synthetic alphabet in the teaching of beginning reading. First-grade teachers from 12 elementary schools in a midwestern city were invited to participate in a study, but no details were given. Two teachers in each school were selected from among those who volunteered. Class groups in all schools were set up according to the regular procedures followed in the school. Once established, however, it was possible, through a flip of a coin, to decide which group and teacher would receive the new reading program and which would get the regular program. The study had a number of other interesting features, some of which will be dealt with later. For now, the important point is that while there was no random assignment of learners to groups, it was possible to randomly assign the groups to treatments. Thus, it was possible to preserve the integrity of the notion of a control group.

In the above example, the class group served as the basic unit of assignment. Already established class groups were assigned, on a random basis, to one treatment or another. This is not only acceptable but often highly desirable (Poyner 1974). The study as carried out ranged over 12 schools with each classroom contributing one item of information—the class average—to the data collection for each variable studied.

There are a number of special features about this design that employed the class group as the basic unit of assignment and, consequently, the unit of analysis. Some of these features will be discussed in chapter 11 in connection with data analysis. The point is that, unlike conventional experiments in which *individuals* are randomly assigned to treatment groups, here it is possible and sometimes desirable to randomly assign *class groups* to treatments. In terms of principles of experimental design, it makes no difference whatever whether individuals or class groups serve as the basic experimental unit. It may even be desirable to use the group as the basic unit if the treatment that is dispensed is uniform for the group.

In the above example, randomization was employed as the means for assigning units (groups or individuals) to treatments. There is much to be said for randomization. It is the only way that one can insure the establishment of equivalent groups. Such equivalency is critical if one is seeking to compare groups with respect to performance after a period of instruction. Any other way of establishing equivalent groups is inferior and carries no assurance that groups can be considered equal before instruction commences.

While randomization is a sine qua non for conducting experimental studies, it is often the case that it cannot be used in evaluation studies. The obstacles in a particular setting may prohibit randomization. This can occur in a number of ways. There may be only a single treatment being studied, and all eligible learners are automatically assigned to it. For example, a local school may set up a special program to provide additional instruction for all learners found to be especially weak in reading. Withholding the program from some eligible learners may be considered administratively and politically impossible as well as educationally undesirable. Too, it may be that the total number of learners involved at any level is so small that even the use of randomization procedures is not sufficient to guarantee equivalency of groups.* Another obstacle to randomization may occur if some measure of choice is permitted to learners or, in some cases, to their parents in deciding which program the learner should enroll in. One can assume with some confidence that groups will not be equivalent if a free, or even restricted, choice is given. There are also situations arising with teachers that can undermine an experimental study. Teachers may be unwilling to participate in a study for a variety of reasons. In such situations, forced participation, even where possible, is likely to produce worthless, or at best questionable, results—if those who are responsible for giving instruction are reluctant recruits.

It may be that, in the majority of instances in evaluation studies, it is not possible to arrange and conduct a true experiment. Faced with such a prospect, what is the evaluation worker to do? Assuming that the evaluation worker will not abandon the enterprise because of an inability to conduct a true experiment, quasi-experimental procedures must be used. Quasi-experimental studies not only sound less desirable than true experimental studies; they actually are. However, while quasi-experimental studies are fairly hazardous, they are not necessarily doomed to fail.

The chief difference between true experiments and quasi-experiments is that the former, properly designed and executed, contain all the necessary safeguards with regard to those factors influencing the internal validity of the results; while the latter do not. Thus, in carrying out

---

*This would appear to contradict earlier statements about randomization providing assurance that groups are equivalent at the beginning of instruction. There is no essential conflict between the statements when one realizes that for randomization to be effective, there must be a sufficient number of units to be randomly assigned. For example, if there are only four learners who are eligible for a program, randomization will probably not result in the establishment of two equivalent groups of two learners each. A pool of only four learners to be assigned to two groups is just too few for randomization to offer assurance of equivalency. Normally, one would hope to have an initial pool of at least 30. This point will be discussed in some detail in chapter 10.

comparative studies using quasi-experimental procedures, the evaluation worker must be extremely careful to evaluate the likelihood of each possible source of bias. This requires a considerable amount of perspicacity on the part of the evaluation specialist as well as the assistance of others knowledgeable about the program under study. Nonetheless, the conclusions one draws from such studies, although often presumptive, are generally superior to no conclusions at all. Thus, the evaluation worker is urged to undertake comparative studies using quasi-experimental designs when the conduct of true experiments is not possible.

In a true experimental study, two or more groups are studied. The group receiving the major treatment under investigation is referred to as the *experimental group*, while the group, or groups, not receiving that treatment, or treatments, is referred to as the *control group*. The term "control group" can cover either an untreated group or a group receiving an alternate treatment. In pharmaceutical studies, for example, a control group will receive no medication at all, an alternate medication, or more likely a placebo. In educational studies, the usual practice is to have a control group receive a conventional or traditional program, while the experimental group receives some innovative one. Withholding any treatment from the control group—equivalent to discontinuing schooling—is not a realistic, or in most cases even a legal, alternative. Thus, in a typical true experiment, the experimental group receives some innovative treatment; the control group receives a conventional one. "Control group" is also used to denote a group that has been established on the basis of randomization. Comparative studies that are true experiments always use control groups. Groups receiving alternative treatments in quasi-experimental studies are called "comparison" or "contrast" groups. This shift in terminology is sometimes ignored in the literature but will be strictly followed here so that the reader will be constantly aware of whether the particular design being considered is an experimental or quasi-experimental one.

One of the major obstacles that an evaluation specialist faces in designing a comparative study is to locate suitable comparison groups. If, as often happens, a program is instituted in a particular setting and administered to all eligible learners, there is no readily available comparison group. The options available to the evaluation specialist in such a situation are limited and not particularly appealing. However, since the concern here is with doing the best job possible under the circumstances rather than the best possible job, the courses of action that are available shall be considered. The first possibility is to use a previously enrolled group in the same institution as a comparison group. If an innovative program is to be installed in the fifth grade of a school, let us say in 1978–79, and this is known far enough in advance, it should be possible to use learners enrolled in the school in 1977–78 as the contrast group—so long as there is no fundamental change in the nature of the school population from one year to the next. In most cases, dramatic shifts in the nature of the population of an institution do not occur from year to year. The major requirements for using a previous cohort of learners as comparison group are (1) sufficient information about learner performance can be obtained, either through direct evidence-gathering efforts or through resurrection of information from files; and (2) the learner population is reasonably stable from year to year.

A second source of groups that might be used for contrast purposes may exist in neighboring institutions. This is a rather risky venture and should be undertaken only if other attempts are not successful. The advantages of using a group in a neighboring institution for comparison purposes are (1) the group is not apt to be exposed to any of the variables that make up the main treatment being studied, and (2) evidence gathering activities can proceed concurrently for all groups being studied. The latter advantage has considerable appeal since the various measures to be used in the data collection may not be completed until the experimental program is about to be initiated. There are a number of disadvantages in using groups in neighboring institutions for comparison purposes; they would need to be carefully considered before deciding to use such groups. Unquestionably, the greatest disadvantage in using groups from neighboring institutions (either within the same school district or outside) is that they will not be comparable. If the school undertaking an innovative program is located in a middle class neighborhood and an available contrast group is located in a school drawing learners from a lower class neighborhood, the two groups are fundamentally incomparable. No amount of statistical manipulation and adjustment can be done to compensate for the fact that the groups come from inherently different populations. A sizable social class difference is fairly obvious and easily detected.

There are other ways in which groups from different institutions can differ, many of them subtle. One school may have a more transient group of learners than another. Teachers in one school may exercise fairly tight control in their dealings with learners while the teachers in another may lay a greater emphasis on independent activity on the part of the learners. All of these often subtle differences may make it difficult, if not impossible, to obtain meaningful comparisons between groups with regard to program effects. The evaluation worker will have to work hard to get reasonable assurance that groups in different institutions are basically comparable before instruction commences. Another major disadvantage in using groups from neighboring institutions in comparative studies is that the evaluation worker is in a poor position to exercise control over the groups receiving the alternative treatment. Usually, the evaluation worker is selected to serve a particular institution. The control he can exercise over groups located in neighboring institutions is quite limited.

At best, he will be able to observe groups receiving the alternative treatment and offer suggestions with regard to maintaining a certain operational program. At worst, he may be barred from entering the institution except to deliver and collect testing material. This would indeed be an unfortunate state of affairs. If the evaluation worker is not in a position to describe the nature of the alternative treatment being dispensed, he will be severely encumbered when it comes to interpreting the results of the evaluation study. If the prospect for cooperation is low, the evaluation worker should seriously consider not using groups from such institutions.

A corollary of the above disadvantage of lack of control is that the neighboring institution may decide to withdraw from the project at any time but particularly at the most critical point—when information needs to be gathered. It has not infrequently happened that a school, hard pressed by various demands, decides to drop an end-of-year testing. The plight of the evaluation worker in such a situation is obvious and painful. Although evidence-gathering requirements can often be reduced to a bare minimum by judicious sampling procedures, this may still be too much of a burden for a participating institution. It would be desirable to extract a commitment, in writing, from the institutions furnishing comparison groups, guaranteeing their participation in the study for a definite period of time. Such a written commitment would probably not be enforcable, but it might serve as an ethical reminder.

When trying to secure the cooperation of neighboring institutions participating in evaluation studies, the evaluation worker is normally restricted to the use of persusasion. While appeals to professionalism and stressing the importance of conducting evaluation studies in education may help secure participation, the prospect of more tangible benefits is likely to have a greater effect. Normally, each participating institution should be promised a full set of results and the oportunity to review and discuss them. The framework for evaluation advocated in this book, and the wide array of information to be gathered, should insure that institutions furnishing comparison groups will receive useful information about the functioning of their programs. Of course, the confidentiality of all information gathered must be assured. This means that no individual learner or teacher can be identified by name and, if requested, names of cooperating institutions must not be revealed. Such guarantees, once given, must be honored. The use of groups from neighboring institutions for comparison purposes in evaluation studies is a risky venture. It also entails considerable time and effort. It is not a first choice but it should at least be considered if there are no better alternatives.

The third source for contrast groups is riskier than the second and even more restricted in application. The use of standardized tests in educational settings carries with it an implied contrast group, namely, the norm group on which the test was standardized. Thus, if a program seeks to improve the reading proficiency of a group of learners, administration of a standardized test at the beginning of the program and again after a period of instruction allows the possibility of making judgments about program effectiveness on the basis of changes in test scores. The risks in using the norm group for a standardized test for comparison purposes are sizable. First there is the matter of finding a standardized test that is relevant to the objectives of the program being evaluated. This is not particularly difficult in reading and mathematics, but it can be impossible in other areas. If so, this approach would have to be abandoned. Second, the group receiving the course, program, or curriculum under study must be similar to the one on which the test is normed. If it is not, the use of a norm group for comparison purposes is inappropriate. For example, a reading improvement program may be initiated for disadvantaged learners, yet every eligible standardized test of reading is based on samples of *all* learners at a particular grade level throughout the country. Unless there are special norms for disadvantaged groups, the use of the norm group for the test (for contrast purposes) would not be correct. There are several reasons for this—not the least of which might be the phenomenon of regression towards the mean discussed earlier. The test, of course, could be used in connection with the evaluation of the program, but the interpretation of results—in terms of published norms—would present special problems.

The use of the norm group for a standardized test for contrast purposes is a somewhat unappetizing compromise which should probably be made only as a last resort. In a hierarchy of ways of securing a comparison group in an evaluation study it clearly ranks near the bottom. The best solution from a design point of view is to use control groups in connection with true experiments. The second-best is to use a contrast group from the same institution but from a difference year. A somewhat less desirable procedure is to use an existing group in the same institution at the same time. The use of a group from a neighboring institution is an even less desirable practice because of possible incomparability and lack of control. Using norm groups from standardized tests is an even less desirable approach but may be applicable in certain limited situations. Another alternative is to employ no comparison groups whatsoever. In the remainder of this chapter—where particular designs are considered— the question of which approach should be followed in the selection of groups for purposes of comparison will be specifically addressed.

EVALUATION DESIGNS

In this section a number of designs that can be employed in comparative studies of educational treatments will be covered. Each has certain features that warrant its use under certain conditions. In choosing a particular design, the evaluation worker will need to consider not only its special features but also the conditions under which it will be used. Frequently, this will mean that a design that is theoretically less than desirable will be employed because local conditions prevent a more desirable one from being used. The important thing for the evaluation worker to bear in mind is that each design has certain strengths and weaknesses. Knowledge of them is important, and adequate provision for dealing with the weakness inherent in a particular design is critical to the success of an evaluation study.

The designs to be presented have been drawn from Campbell and Stanley's well-known chapter (1963) and from an extension of that work by Campbell (Campbell and Stanley, 1963; Campbell 1969). Though the designs were developed primarily for research studies on teaching, their use in evaluation studies, with some modification, is clearly warranted. The reader should be familiar with the original Campbell and Stanley chapter, especially the tables listing the sources of invalidity of various designs. The symbolism employed in the presentations of various designs for evaluation studies departs slightly from that used by Campbell and Stanley. The symbols that will be used here are:

R = Random assignment of units (individuals or class groups) to treatment groups.

T_1 = Treatment (a course, program, curriculum, organizational pattern, etc.). The subscript will denote a particular treatment. For most studies, at least two alternative treatments are studied, i.e., T_1 and T_2. However, in some studies there may be only a single treatment under consideration.

P = Performance measure. This refers to some measure of learner performance. It includes measures related to specific program objectives as well as supplemental performance measures. By rights, there should be a subscript after the symbol, e.g., P_i, $i - 1$, k, denoting that there are a number of performance measures (in this case k of them). However, for the sake of brevity, the nonsubscripted P will be used. This implies that analyses will be carried out on *all* performance measures.

Pretest-Posttest Control Group Design

The classic true experimental design is the pretest–posttest control group design. It can be symbolized as follows:

$$\text{Group 1} \quad R \quad P \quad T_1 \quad P$$

Group 2 R P T$_2$ P

The design is interpreted in the following way, reading from left to right. Random assignment is used to assign units to groups and groups to treatments. (In the above schema, only two treatments are being compared. However, the design could easily be extended to additional treatments by adding more lines, one for T$_3$, T$_4$, etc. Each additional line would also contain R, P, and P.) The first P denotes that pretesting occurs before the treatment while the second one denotes testing after a period of instruction. Usually, such posttesting occurs at the conclusion of the treatment period, but this may not always be the case. When the posttesting occurs will depend largely on the purposes of the evaluation, but may be influenced by other factors. For example, while one may wish to conduct posttesting at the conclusion of the treatment period, the need to decide about future action may require that testing be done sometime earlier. This is less than wholly satisfactory but, if the results of the evaluation study are to be used in planning future action, incomplete information may be far better than no information at all.

The pretest–posttest control groups design is generally considered to be a highly acceptable design for evaluation studies. The chief reason is that it provides the basic comparability required to meaningfully interpret results. The use of randomization, provided that there are enough units, serves as an assurance that the groups receiving the different treatments are equal to begin with. The collection of pretest data serves two purposes. First, it provides information about the initial status of the groups before treatment commences, thus furnish one of the major classes of information required in evaluation studies. Second, the pretest information can be used in the analysis of the data to increase precision. This point will be discussed in some detail in chapter 11. The equal distances between the letters in the same lines denote that the treatment period is the same for all groups. In analyzing the data from the above study, the essential comparisons involve the posttest performance between the two groups after adjusting for whatever pretest performances exist, after random assignment was carried out.

Interpretation of results produced by the pretest–posttest control group design is straightforward. The use of randomization serves to eliminate history, instrumentation, statistical regression, selection, mortality, and interactions of various variables as possible explanations for whatever results are obtained; at the same time, using two or more groups eliminates maturation as a possible cause of the results. On the face of it, the design would appear to be admirably suited for determining the comparative effectiveness of alternative treatments, and the most part it is. There are, however, two qualifications. First, if the study consists of two class groups and their teachers, it is possible that any differential effectiveness might be due to the teachers instead of the treatment—materials, learning experiences, etc. The employment of randomization to establish equivalent groups of learners has nothing to do with the teachers. Even if two volunteer teachers are used, with the flip of an honest coin deciding which teacher is assigned to each treatment, one can not be sure that any differential performance between groups might not be due to the teachers involved. An investigation of the teachers themselves would have to be made to eliminate differential teacher effectiveness as the source of differential learner proficiency. Such a study would involve examination of the teachers' background, training, experience, and observed classroom performance. If one can satisfy oneself that the teachers do not differ appreciably then one can eliminate the teachers themselves as the sole source of differences between groups.

The second qualification centers on the treatments being compared. If one treatment is an innovative program involving new materials and equipment while the other is a conventional one involving used textbooks, run-of-the-mill materials and the like, it is possible that learners in the first program might outperform learners in the second because they feel they are a part of something "special." Improved performance due to a feeling of being specially chosen is referred to as the Hawthorne effect (after the now famous experiments conducted at that site for the Western Electric Company). The possibility of a Hawthorne effect in evaluation studies is very real, especially when an innovative treatment is being compared with a conventional one. There is no easy way to dispose of it: if a program is truly innovative and requires new materials, learning experiences, and the like, then these need to be present. Of course, one can wait several years until the novelty of the innovative program wears off and it comes to be viewed simply as an alternative program. However, a few administrators can be expected to wait that long. Usually administrators want to know about a program's effectiveness four months ago, not four years hence. A rather different approach is to attempt to equalize all treatments under study with respect to a possible Hawthorne effect. For example, in the previously mentioned study on the teaching of beginning reading using a synthetic alphabet, it was clear from the outset that the innovative program required new books, special in-service training for the teachers using the synthetic alphabet, and a variety of collateral materials. The novelty of the approach simply could not be avoided. To counter this, it was decided to provide teachers using the conventional approach—basal reader and associated workbooks—with additional materials, and an equal amount of in-service training, so as to make maximally effective use of the regular materials. Through an arrangement with the publisher of the basal reading series it was possible to secure the services of the publisher's consultants and a vareity of supplemental material. By the time the study began, both groups of teachers had

had equal amounts of in-service training and had their classrooms bedecked with fresh and bright new materials. In contrast, other teachers in the school who were following the conventional program had to get along with the same old materials and no special help or extra in-service training.

In retrospect, it would have been desirable to include the balance of the teachers as a second comparison group. A comparison between the synthetic alphabet classes and the conventional classes, in which the teachers received supplemental materials and additional training, afforded an estimate of the differential effectiveness of the treatments. A comparison between the specially treated conventional classes and the untreated conventional classes, on the other hand, could have provided some estimate of the extent of a Hawthorne effect. Unfortunately, the investigators did not have the foresight to build this into their study. They did, however, anticipate the possible influence of a Hawthorne effect and took active steps to control it by equalizing innovative and conventional classes with respect to it.

The above qualifications to the pretest–posttest control group design are technical ones. They can be dealt with in a number of ways, some of which have been described above. From the standpoint of the evaluation worker who must organize and conduct the study in a particular situation, there are apt to be practical obstacles to a pretest–posttest control group design. It may not be possible to assign units randomly to groups and groups to treatments, although every attempt should be made. It is also possible that there may not be a treatment alternative available for a comparative study. In such cases, the evaluation worker will need to consider another design.

Posttest Only Control Group Design

The posttest only control group design is also a true experiement and is symbolized:

$$\text{Group 1} \quad \text{R} \quad \text{T}_1 \quad \text{P}$$
$$\text{Group 2} \quad \text{R} \quad \text{T}_2 \quad \text{P}$$

The difference between this design and the previous one is the absence of the pretest measure. This design is considered acceptable from the point of view of specialists in experimental design since it controls for all major sources of invalidity. It is not, however, acceptable from the standpoint of educational evaluation advanced in this book. This is due to the absence of the pretest, considered crucial to a comprehensive evaluation study. It is quite possible, for example, that learners in both treatment groups had already learned what they were supposed to or were well on their way to doing so with instruction commenced. The posttest only control group design does not permit one to determine this. Without such information, the evaluation worker is in no position to distinguish between what learners have acquired, as a result of exposure to the treatment under study, and what they knew and could do before instruction began. Thus, while the above design would satisfy specialists in experimental design, it should be avoided by evaluation specialists, unless one is prepared to assume that learners before treatment began knew virtually nothing about what they were supposed to learn.

This is a reasonable assumption in certain situations. When the course, program, or curriculum being evaluated involves highly specialized knowledge or competencies that are quite novel, there is little to be gained by using pretests. For example, in a *first* course in a foreign language, it seems highly unlikely that entering learners possess much, if any, proficiency. The same may hold true in a first course in algebra, biology, chemistry, or physics. On the other hand, courses in reading, English, general mathematics, social studies, and even general science are more developmental in nature and an assumption of low-to-nonexistent initial proficiency is highly questionable.

Popham (1975, p. 211) has introduced a modification of the posttest only control group design that is intended to overcome the hazard of not pretesting learners. This modification assumes that the treatment to be dispensed is of relatively short duration—e.g., a unit of instruction—and that while all learners are to receive it, there is no requirement that they all receive it simultaneously. Random assignment is used to establish equivalent groups, and the flip of a coin can decide the order of presentation. The design is symbolized as follows:

$$\text{Group 1} \quad R \quad T_1 \quad P_1 \quad P_2 \quad T_2$$
$$\text{Group 2} \quad R \quad T_2 \quad P_2 \quad P_1 \quad T_1$$

Treatments 1 and 2 refer to different units of instruction while P_1 and P_2 refer to measures of learners' proficiency associated with each unit. Random assignment and scheduling of treatments serve to establish the basic equivalency of the groups. Note also that all learners receive both treatments. The comparisons that Popham recommends are as indicated:

$$\text{Group 1} \quad R \quad T_1 \quad \textcircled{P_1}\,\textcircled{P_2} \quad T_2$$
$$\text{Group 2} \quad R \quad T_2 \quad \textcircled{P_2}\,\textcircled{P_1} \quad T_1$$

Insofar as the first treatment (T_1) is concerned, the estimate of its effectiveness comes from comparing Group 1's posttest performance with Group 2's pretest performance. For the second treatment (T_2), the situation is reversed. It would appear that the basic comparability for a clear and meaningful interpretation of results exists; unfortunately, this is not necessarily so. There would appear to be three possible sources of invalidity in this design. The first would be contamination arising from the close proximity of the two groups. If random assignment has been employed, it is more than likely that the two groups are in reasonably close proximity to one another: usually in the same school, if not the same classroom. Normal contact among members of the two groups could easily result, for example, with members of Group 2 acquiring some information about T_1 from members of Group 1. Thus, when the members of Group 2 are administered the performance measures for the first treatment (T_1), they are not in the naive state that Group 1 members were—prior to exposure to treatment (T_1). The comparison between the P_1 measures for the two groups is apt to produce questionable results since the P_1 measures for Group 2 could be misleadingly high. Whatever effect the first treatment (T_1) has will consequently be underestimated. The same will be true for the second treatment (T_2).

Another factor that is likely to introduce invalidity into the results is maturation. If the treatments are of any appreciable length—a month or more might make a change—then Group 2's performance on P_1 might also underestimate learner performance prior to treatment, adding to possible underestimation of a treatment effect. The third possible source of invalidity could arise from an interaction between the previously discussed sources of invalidity. Technically, the first source of invalidity discussed, contamination, would be termed history; the second, maturation. The joint effect of these two sources can only be guessed at. Further work would be needed to estimate its effects. Until such time as the problems surrounding this staggered design can be clarified and resolved, it is recommended that the design be avoided.

Nonequivalent Contrast Group Design

The nonequivalent contrast group design is identical to the pretest-posttest control group design in all respects except for the absence of random assignment of units to groups. It is symbolized as follows:

Group 1   P T_1 P

Group 2   P T_2 P

The absence of randomization immediately raises questions about the equivalence of the groups receiving the different treatments. From the point of view of design specialists, this design is scientifically unacceptable and does not constitute a true experiment: it is a quasi-experiment. While true experiments are certainly preferable to quasi-experiments, an evaluation worker may have no alternative but to use a quasi-experimental design. The nonequivalent contrast group design may be serviceable. In order to use the design, however, the evaluaton worker will have to conduct a number of subsidiary investigations to establish the comparability of the two groups. This is usually accomplished in two ways. First, analyses of the pretest performance measures is carried out. The goal of the analysis is to determine that there are no appreciable performance differences between the two groups. Second, other descriptive information about the two groups is gathered and analyzed—with the same goal in mind. Typical variables examined are age, sex, socioeconomic status, previous school performance, and scholastic ability. If the evaluation worker can, using the results of the two kinds of analyses, provide a fairly convincing case that the two groups are quite similar at the outset, then he will be in a reasonably good position to draw presumptive conclusions about treatment effects on the basis of the information gathered after a period of instruction.

There are two important features to note about the nonequivalent contrast group design. First, its use is dependent on establishing that groups are comparable. In a true experiment, randomization is a sufficient basis for establishing comparability. In this design, additional investigatory work is needed to establish that comparability. In some cases, it may be impossible to do so. For example, if a group of poor readers is singled out for treatment, there may be no remaining poor readers to constitute a comparison group. The use of a group of average readers would not satisfy the requirements for an equivalent group; these learners would simply not be comparable. Either another, more suitable comparison group is identified or the design will have to be abandoned. The second feature to note about the nonequivalent contrast control group design is that any conclusions drawn from the results are necessarily presumptive. One cannot attribute causality to the treatment, with the same degree of confidence, as one can in a true experiment. The point of view advocated here, however, is that presumptive conclusions, while inferior to the strong conclusions to be drawn from true experiments, are clearly better than no conclusions at all. Furthermore, presumptive conclusions can be useful in assessing the worth of an educational enterprise and planning future action. One must be extremely careful, of course, that the conclusions, albeit presumptive, are warranted. This involves necessarily considerable checking to insure the comparability of the group under study.

The Single Group Pretest–Posttest Design

This design differs from the others that have been considered in that only a single group is involved. It is characterized as follows:

Group 1   P   T   P

Essentially, the design involves identifying a group, pretesting its members, exposing them to a period of treatment, and testing them again. The difference between the pretest and the posttest measures is intended to estimate the magnitude of the effect of the treatment. However, there are a number of alternate explanations for whatever difference might be found. It may be due simply to maturation. History, instrumentation, statistical regression, selection, mortality, and interactions can also produce the obtained results. Faced with such a variety of competing explanations, specialists in research design generally dismiss the single group pretest-posttest design as useless. The evaluation worker may not be able to, because the alternative—no study at all—is unacceptable.

There is little doubt that this design presents formidable problems. If used—no matter how reluctantly—the only course open to the evaluation worker is to systematically eliminate each competing alternative explanation so that the presumptive conclusion of a treatment effect is tenable. The way in which competing explanations are eliminated depends on logic and judgment rather than on manipulations of data. In some cases the possibility of doing so is real and definite; in others not. Consider for example, a first course in chemistry at the high-school level. It may be possible to establish that entering learners showed a low initial level of proficiency but a high level at the conclusion of the course. Further, it might be possible to demonstrate that there is little chance for learners to acquire competence in chemistry elsewhere; it is simply inaccessible. It may also be possible to show that there is little learner mortality, that the learners who complete the course are the ones who entered at the beginning. The point here is that the evaluation worker must separately consider each alternative explanation for the obtained results and confirm or confute the explanatory power of each. If the explanatory power of each source of invalidity can be confuted, the evaluation worker can presumptively conclude that the obtained results were due to the effect of the treatment.

This judgmental and logical approach to dealing with the possible sources of invalidity presumes that the evaluation worker possesses considerable knowledge about the details of a particular situation. This is quite correct. The evaluation worker must spend a considerable amount of time in the situation, or have access to those who do, in order to acquire the necessary knowledge to deal with each competing explanation.

In the above example, a first course in high-school chemistry was used. This course lends itself to dealing with competing explanations rather well because of the specialized and novel subject-matter. In contrast, reading comprehension at the elementary-school level presents special problems since the subject-matter is neither specialized nor novel and is easily accessible from a variety of sources. The likelihood of eliminating competing explanations is considerably reduced if not all but eliminated. An evaluation worker would be in an exceedingly difficult position if he tried to conclude that the increase in reading performance from, say, the beginning to the end of the school year was due solely, or even in large measure, to the nature of the reading program.

The One-Shot Case Study

One of the most castigated designs is the one-shot case study. It is frequently presented first in any discussion of study designs and soundly criticized as being scientifically worthless. It is symbolized as follows:

$$T_1 \quad P$$

That is, a group, usually not drawn at random from some larger population, is exposed to a treatment, and measures of learner performance are secured. From a scientific viewpoint, it is impossible to conclude that the level of learner performance is due to the effect of the treatment. History, maturation, selection, and mortality could singly, or in combination, serve to explain the obtained results. After a fairly brief discussion, most specialists dismiss this design as being so fraught with problems as to have no value at all. While not challenging this conclusion from the standpoint of experimental design, it does seem that there are occasions when the design can be serviceable in evaluation studies. However, the conditions under which it should be used are quite limited, and the interpretations that can be made of the results are restricted.

The one-shot case study design can be employed in two ways. First, the design can be used in connection with small-scale tryouts of segments of programs to obtain a crude idea of how particular learning experiences or materials are working. The one-shot case study should be able to provide useful information about how segments of a larger program are functioning, especially in the early stages of development. While no one would wish to draw firm conclusions about a program's effectiveness from such small-scale studies, their use in formative evaluation could be exceedingly helpful, especially to program developers. In fact, a very strong argument could be made for *increased* use of one-shot case studies during the early stages of the development of courses, program, and curricula.

The second use of the one-shot case study design involves the evaluation of highly specialized programs where (1) it can be strongly presumed that entering learners are virtually ignorant about what is to be learned; and (2) it is not possible to have a comparison group. A program to train people in welding would be one place where a one-shot case study, while not ideal, could be serviceable. Entering learners could safely be presumed to lack proficiency in the area. Because of the nature of the program, pretesting would probably not only be a waste of time but potentially dangerous. The program could be initiated as soon as the learners are assembled and testing carried out after a period of time. (In the case of welding, the conventional procedure is to test learners after they have been instructed and have practiced each type of weld. Of course, a single postinstructional test, covering a variety of welds, can also be used.) The likelihood that history and maturation could adequately explain resultant learner proficiency is extremely low and could probably be rejected on logical grounds. Learner mortality, however, can easily be checked and, if low, can also be rejected. An examination of the selection procedures can provide one with information about the type of learners the results might apply to while replication can fortify the validity of the results. In short, what is typically rejected as an unacceptable *research* design can be a quite serviceable design in an evaluation study.

To be sure, the particular program selected to illustrate the use of the one-shot case study—a training program for welders—is admirably suited to this design. The example is not so far-fetched, however. Beginning courses in specialized subjects such as algebra, foreign languages, laboratory sciences and special skill courses such as pottery, silk screen printing, automotive repair, and sailing—all could make use of the design. The chief requirements for use of this design are novel and specialized subject-matter and learners without proficiency in the subject. While one would wish to see stronger design employed, it may be reasonable to use a one-shot case study; local circumstances in fact may prevent any other design from being used. It is not a design to be rejected without consideration simply because of its disrepute among specialists in research design.

The Interrupted Time-Series Design

The interrupted time-series design is especially useful when a particular treatment is introduced on an across-the-board basis. It is represented as follows:

$$P \quad P \quad P \quad P \quad T \quad P \quad P \quad P \quad P$$

Measures are obtained on a regular basis, before the introduction of a treatment and afterwards. Archival data in the form of standardized test results, average daily attendance rates, learner referrals for various purposes and, in the case of morale studies, teacher turnover statistics are examples of information that are gathered on a regular and routine basis, and can be used to obtain an estimate of the effect of the introduction of a particular treatment. While the procedures for analyzing the data from interrupted time-series studies are rather complex, a graphical representation often provides a reasonable basis for judging the efficacy of the treatment. Consider the examples in Figure 9.1.

FIGURE 9.1

Possible Outcomes in an Interrupted Time-Series Design

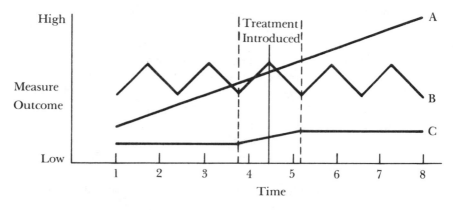

Source: Adapted from D.T. Campbell and J. Stanley. "Experimental and Quasi-experimental Designs for Research on Teaching." In *Handbook of Research on Teaching*, edited by N.L. Gage, pp. 171–246. Chicago: Rand McNally.

In the case of line A, note that there is an increase from time 4 to time 5. This coincides with the introduction of the treatment. However, as can readily be seen, the measure was increasing steadily from time 1 to time 4 and also after time 5. In fact, the various points show a clear upward trend throughout. The introduction of the treatment apparently had no effect on this trend. If inspection of the measure at only times 4 and 5 had been made, one would have been tempted to conclude that the treatment had made an effect insofar as the measure would indicate. However, the longer view—times 1 through 8—refutes this.

Line B also shows an increase on the measure that coincides with the introduction of the treatment. However, when all the measures are considered, it appears that the increase is part of a general bumping along in the level of the measure over time rather than the result of the treatment. In line C, however, there is a clear treatment effect. The level of the measure after the introduction of the treatment is considerably higher than before. In this example there is no overlap in the average level of performance before the treatment is introduced and afterwards. It would be reasonable to consider the possibility that the treatment did, in fact, result in a higher average level on the measure. This does not, however, mean that the treatment was responsible for the effect. There are at least two other possibilities to consider: namely, history and instrumentation.

It is possible that another event occurred at the same time that the treatment was introduced and was responsible for the increased level on the measure. This, of course, is history, the influence of an extraneous variable. An evaluation specialist would need to carefully check on the likelihood of such an event.

The second alternative explanation, instrumentation, exposes a fundamental flaw in the interrupted time-series design. Educational institutions routinely collect and store all kinds of information. However, there is no guarantee that the procedures used and the information gathered will remain uniform over time: the chances are they will not. Learner attendance data, for example, has been used from time to time as an indirect indicator of a program effect. Changes in state laws with regard to the gathering and reporting of such information do occur, often as a result of political factors. Such changes can result in an apparent treatment effect when, in fact, there was only a change in the way records were kept. A change in data-gathering procedures can also affect the assessment of a treatment results: the re-norming of an existing test, or the introduction of a new edition of a test, can do it. For example, educational institutions are expected to use tests with up-to-date norms (and usually do). The introduction of a renormed test or a new edition of a test can produce an apparent treatment effect or mask a real one, depending on the relationship between and new and old norms. To illustrate, the 1972 renormed Stanford-Binet has a higher set of norms for individuals up to age six and above 13 than the previous edition; That is, it now takes a higher level of performance to attain an IQ of (say) 100 than it did previously at these age levels. In a different direction, the norms for the 1973 edition of the Stanford Achievement Test (Stanford Research Report 5, 1973) are lower than the norms for the 1964 edition of the same battery. A school which routinely installed the 1973 edition as part of its testing program would show a dramatic jump in average performance among its learners, and this higher performance level would continue even if learner performance itself had remained stable. This spurious effect arises solely out of the introduction of the new edition of the test. If a new curriculum were instituted at the same time as the changeover in test editions, results would be identical to those shown in line C in Figure 9.1: this would occur even if the new curriculum had no effect whatsoever on learner performance. The lesson is plain: any shift in the instrumentation employed in an interrupted time-series design can affect the results one obtains. It will either be to mask a real treatment effect or produce a spurious one, depending on the nature of the shift. The evaluation worker clearly needs to consider carefully the nature of the instrumentation and the uniformity of procedures employed in gathering data about possible treatment effects.

There are two other issues surrounding the interrupted time-series design that can strongly influence its possible adoption. First, the design assumes that a treatment is instituted at a particular time. In Figure 9.1, this is indicated by the verticle line designating "Treatment Introduced." If this condition is met, the design can be considered for use. If the innovation is introduced over a period of time in phases, then the design is inappropriate, since it will not be possible to separate a treatment effect from whatever secular trends there are in the data. A second major issue that must be dealt with—when considering an interrupted time-series design—involves the relevance of the measures to be used. While educational institutions routinely collect and store all kinds of information the relevance of such information to a particular course, program, curriculum, organizational pattern and the like can vary enormously. In some cases, archival data may bear directly on the planned innovation; in other cases they may not. If the information has no relevance to the treatment, the design simply has no attraction. The evaluation worker will need to carefully study existing data sources; the nature of the treatment to be introduced; the scheduled introduction of the treatment; and the relationship between the treatment and the data sources—before deciding to employ an interrupted time-series design.

Regression Discontinuity Design

The regression discontinuity design most closely resembles the nonequivalent contrast group design with one major exception: in the latter, the two groups are comparable, while in the former they are not. The regression discontinuity design was developed for use in situations where a treatment is intended for all eligible learners. The treatment could range from a program of remedial instruction to an enrichment curriculum. In using a regression discontinuity design, a strict and orderly procedure for assigning all eliglble learners to a treatment is employed. For example, all learners at a given grade with test scores below a certain point are assigned to a remedial program. In another situation, all learners above a certain cutting score are given an enrichment program. The ineligible learners constitute a contrast group. Unlike the nonequivalent contrast group design, however, the ineligible learners are not presumed to be directly comparable to those in the treated group. One of the chief differences between the nonequivalent contrast group design and the regression discontinuity design lies in the way in which the resulting data are analyzed. In the nonequivalent contrast group design, some procedure for comparing the average level of performance between the treatment groups is used. This may involve one of a number of techniques, including the analysis of covariance.* In the

---

*Statistical procedures are discussed in chapter 11.

regression discontinuity design, however, the techniques of regression analysis are used. This is illustrated in Figure 9.2.

FIGURE 9.2

Regression Discontinuity Design: Genuine Effect

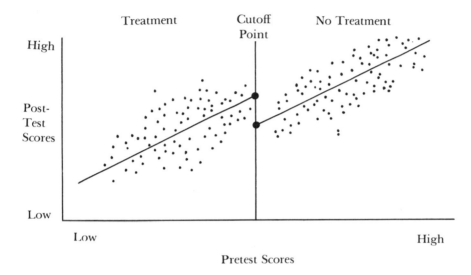

Source: Adapted from D.T. Campbell. "Reforms as Experiments." *American Psychologist* 24: 409-29, 1969.

All learners were administered a pretest. The resulting scores were strictly used to decide which learners received the treatment and which did not. (In the example illustrated in Figure 9.2, the treatment might be a remedial program in reading.) After a period of instruction, a posttest was administered to all learners. The regression of posttest scores on pretest scores was calculated for each group separately and the regression lines plotted. The distance between the points where the two regression lines intersect the vertical cutoff point line provides an estimate of the treatment effect.*

---

*The determination of the statistical significance of the distance between the points remains a problem. While no definite procedure has been established, Campbell (1969) cites a suggestion by Abelson that seems a reasonable one. This involves fitting a regression line for a body of data extending above and below the cutting point in equal amounts. Column means are then expressed as deviations from the single regression line. A t test is used to statistically evaluate the columns just above and below the cutting point. Just as the design is properly labeled quasi-experimental, the analysis can perhaps best be characterized as quasi-statistical!

Obviously, proper execution of a regression discontinuity design requires strict adherence to the use of a cutoff point for selection into treatment. Any fuzziness in the selection procedure will cloud the results. There is also at issue the relationship between the posttest measure and the pretest measure. It is not obligatory that the pretest and posttest measures be identical, only that they are related. If the relationship between them is high, the regression discontinuity design will be a reasonably strong one. If it is low, the design more closely resembles the nonequivalent contrast group design. If the relationship is zero, the design resembles the pretest–posttest control group design. It is only a resemblance, however.

The regression discontinuity design is a relative newcomer in the field of evaluation. Its origins can be traced to the work of Thistlewaite and Campbell (1960) in attempting to assess the effects of receiving a fellowship. While originally envisaged as a way of estimating a treatment effect through the use of tie-breaking procedures, it has now developed as a general approach for the estimation of effects when a scarce boon must be distributed to the most needy or the most meritorious or when all eligible members of a group are to be given a treatment. Quantification of need or merit makes the regression discontinuity design an excellent candidate for evaluation studies. There are, however, a number of outstanding problems with regard to the analysis and interpretation of results. Considerable progress in resolving them can be expected in the near future.

REPLICATION

The designs presented above should furnish the evaluation worker with a sufficient array of procedures to effectively study most educational treatments. As noted, each design has its own strenghs and weaknesses. Some of these are theoretical, some methodological, and some practical. The evaluation worker will need to consider the nature of the course, program, or curriculum to be evaluated, and the existing conditions in a particular setting, before choosing a particular design. Even after a design has been selected, some modifications may be necessary in order to use it in a specific situation. If modifications are introduced, this may result in increasing the possible invalidity of results.

One way of improving the validity of evaluation studies is through replication. In evaluation studies, replication can occur in three ways. The most familiar is when a number of learners are exposed to each treatment under study. The presentation of each design routinely referred to *groups* receiving one or another treatment. Little was made of the fact that each group is composed of a number of individuals and that the purpose of studying a number of individuals is to obtain more precise estimates of treatment effects. Thus, the study of a number of individuals receiving a certain treatment is considered a replication.

There are two other ways in which replication can occur. An evaluation study may be carried out with successive cohorts of learners. A program may be initiated one year and evaluated and a second trial and evaluation carried out the next year with a new group. The results of the two separate evaluation studies can be compared and judgments and decisions then made. Those responsible for deciding what course of action should be followed are apt to feel more comfortable basing their decisions on the results of at least two separate evaluation studies rather than a single one. Of course, problems can arise. The results of the two studies may be inconsistent, the program may have been modified from one year to the next, etc. However, there problems can be handled within the context of the framework for evaluation emphasized throughout this book. The framework explicitly includes provision for monitoring the treatment being dispensed, the learners being served, the objectives being pursued, etc. It would seem clear that the advantages of having two separate evaluation studies as a basis for making judgments and deciding on future action is much superior to having the results of a single study only. What is required, however, is that those responsible for deciding on future action willingly postpone such decisions until the needed information is in hand. Decision makers willing and able to postpone such decisions have been termed "experimental administrators" by Campbell (1969). Such administrators have effected a posture in which they advocate the seriousness of a particular need and persistence of effort in seeking ways to meet it. "Trapped administrators," according to Campbell (p. 409) fall into the snare of advocating a specific reform ". . . as though they were certain to be successful." According to Campbell (p. 410), the experimental administrator says in effect: "This is a serious problem. We propose to initiate Policy A on an experimental basis. If after . . . two . . . years there has been no significant improvement, we will shift to Policy B." Not only will such a posture permit honest evaluation of the outcomes of a treatment—Campbell's main point—but it should buy time for the kind of sequential replication advocated here.*

The last way in which replication can occur is when a treatment is simultaneously introduced into a number of units in an institution and separate evaluations are carried out in each unit. A particular innovation may be introduced into a number of elementary schools in a single district, for example, and separate studies can be conducted in each

---

*A notable example of the use of successive replication can be found in the evaluation studies of Sesame Street. See S. Ball and G. Bogatz, *The First Year of Sesame Street: An Evaluation* (Princeton, N.J.: Educational Testing Service, 1970); and G. Bogatz and S. Ball, *The Second Year of Sesame Street: A Continuing Evaluation*, 2 vols. (Princeton, N.J.: Educational Testing Service, 1971).

school. Simultaneous evaluation of a treatment in each of its implementations should produce a series of replications which fortify the validity of results. Furthermore, replication over units should produce a considerable time saving which may be critical if the need for action is acute. Whether an evaluation worker adopts a procedure of replication over time—successive replication—or replication over units—simultaneous replication—will undoubtedly depend on conditions in the local situation. Either procedure is clearly better than a single trial, no matter how elegant the design.

SUMMARY

In this chapter a body of information has been presented regarding the design and conduct of evaluation studies. While the main source of knowledge about this topic is that branch of applied statistics called experimental design, some revision has been made to render it suitable for educational evaluation. Accordingly, the treatment here differs somewhat from some of the standard works on the topic.

While differing in a number of details, the general principles of experimental design hold for evaluation studies. The threats to the validity of results in both experimental and evaluation studies are the same: history, maturation, instrumentation, statistical regression, selection, subject mortality and selection–maturation interaction. These factors were first described and then presented and discussed in relation to each design.

The importance of equivalent groups for the purpose of comparison was examined at length. Ideally, procedures of random assignment are employed to establish equivalent comparison groups. In evaluation studies, such procedures are often not feasible, and the problem of locating groups that could be considered equivalent was discussed. Considerable attention was given to the identification of comparison or contrast groups for use in evaluation studies.

Specific designs for evaluation studies were considered in detail: strengths and weaknesses of each design were noted. Emphasis was placed on the logic of each design rather than formal details. Throughout the discussion practical considerations concerning the use of each design in an educational setting were taken up. Finally, the value of replication in evaluation, as a way of fortifying the validity of results, was shown.

REFERENCES

Ball, S. and G.A. Bogatz. 1970. *The First Year of Sesame Street: An Evaluation.* Princeton: Educational Testing Service.

Campbell, D.T. 1969. "Reforms as Experiments." *American Psychologist* 24: Designs for Research on Teaching." In *Handbook of Research on Teaching*, edited by N.L. Gage, pp. 171–246. Chicago: Rand McNally.

Fisher, R.A. 1925. *Statistical Methods for Research Workers.* London: Oliver and Boyd.

McCall, W. *How to Experiment in Education.* 1923. New York: Macmillan.

Page, E. 1958. "Teacher Comments and Student Performance: A Seventy-four Classroom Experiment in School Motivation." *Journal of Educational Psychology* 49: 173–181.

Popham, W.J. 1975. *Educational Evaluation.* Englewood Cliffs: Prentice-Hall.

Poyner, H. 1974. "Selecting Units of Analysis." In *Evaluating Educational Programs and Products,* edited by G. Borick. Englewood Cliffs: Educational Technology Publications.

Thistlethwaite, D.L. and Campbell, D.T. 1960. "Regression–Discontinuity Analysis: An Alternative to the Ex Post Facto Experiment." *Journal of Educational Psychology* 51, 309–17.

10

SAMPLING CONSIDERATIONS

In his primer on sampling (1960), M. Slonim points out that anyone who has poured a highball into a potted plant after taking one sip has had an experience in sampling. We are bombarded almost daily with the results of polls which make routine use of sampling procedures. The goal of all sampling is to make accurate and meaningful statements about some group on the basis of a study of a subset of the group. The group may be a collection of individuals (as in a Gallup or Harris poll) or it may be a collection of objects as in, e.g., an industrial process such as the manufacture of lightbulbs. Whether the group consists of individuals or objects is of no consequence; the principles and procedures of sampling remain the same. The object is to select a subset or sample of a group in such a way that it will be representative of the whole.

Sampling can be undertaken for several reasons. First, it is usually more economical to study a subset of a group than a total group. Second, it is generally more efficient to examine a sample than a larger group. Third, it is often impractical to study an entire group, especially if it is widely dispersed.

The two key terms in sampling are population and sample. A population, previously referred to as the total group, is defined as a collection of elements (people or objects) having one or more characteristics in common. Typically, a population is defined by specifying those common characteristics. Thus, one can define a population as broadly as "all students, age 13.0 to 14.0, enrolled in full-time schooling in the United States," or as narrowly as "all boys enrolled in the fifth grade in the Watson Elementary School." Both are acceptable definitions of populations. Each defines a population by specifying the characteristics that the members of the population have in common. A sample is a part of the population. In selecting a sample we usually wish to select that part of the population which is representative of the total population. How this is done best to insure representativeness—at the lowest cost—is the business of sampling.

There are three general types of samples. The first is often referred to as a chunk sample. It involves selection of some fraction of the population for closer study, often on the basis of availability, or economy. Chunk samples are considered to be scientifically worthless, since there is no assurance that the sample is at all representative of the population and usually there is no way to find out. When an investigator chooses to study a group of children because of accessibility and tries to draw conclusions from his findings about children in general, he is on dangerous ground. The sampling procedure is open to serious criticism: there is nothing about it worth recommending except its convenience. It will sometimes suffice for pilot studies, when one is interested in testing out instruments and data collection procedures, but it should not be used as the basis for drawing substantive conclusions about a population.

A second type is the judgment sample. Here, members of the population are selected for inclusion in the sample on the basis of the judgment of the investigator. The aim of a judgment sample is to select a subset of the population that will be representative of the total population. A judgment sample may or may not be representative. Unfortunately, there is no way of knowing this: it is the chief weakness of judgment samples. One must depend solely on the judgment of the person who has selected the sample. In certain instances, judgment sampling may be the best available way of obtaining a represenative sample. For example, if resources are extremely limited, forcing the selection of a very small sample, it may be better to use a judgment sample than some other procedure such as random selection. The sample size may not afford enough of an opportunity for a randomization principle to operate. Usually, however, judgment samples should be avoided, since there is no way of gauging their accuracy.

The third type is a probability sample. A probability sample is one in which every member of the population has a known and nonzero chance of being included in the sample. There are two general kinds: simple and complex. The best known type of simple probability sampling is a simple random sample. Here, each member of the population has an equal chance of being selected for the sample. *Simple* random samples are selected in one of two equivalent ways. Each member of the population is assigned a unique identification number, and enough members to constitute a sample are selected through a lottery procedure or—more likely—a table of random numbers. Detailed procedures for selecting a simple random sample can be found in the references at the end of this chapter. The most well known form of sampling, it is routinely taught in introductory statistics courses and usually is easily understood. How widely simple random sampling is actually used is another matter. In large-scale studies of educational effects—such as Sesame Street or Harvard Project Physics—simple random sampling could not be used: there did not exist a single list of all the individuals in the population, and constructing one would have been an extraordinarily difficult task. Furthermore, even did such a list exist, it would be highly impractical to use in selecting a sample. Random selection from such a master list might result in having to test one student in, say, Grand Marais, Minn., another in Odessa, Tex., another in South Pasadena, Calif., etc. Resources for evaluation would not likely be available to support such a scheme. Accordingly, a variety of *complex* sampling procedures have been developed. Despite their complexity, they are highly practical to apply. Among complex sampling procedures there are multistage sampling, either random or with probability proportional to size; stratified sampling; cluster sampling; and sequential. Also, various combinations of complex procedures can be used. Detailed discussions of each procedure can be found in the Kish text (1966) cited at the end of this chapter.

In selecting a sample, there are two major concerns. First, the sample should be representative of the population. If any part of the population has a very low or zero chance of being selected for inclusion in the sample, the sample is likely to be biased. Considerable effort often has to be made to insure that every segment of the population has a known and non-zero chance of being included in the sample. Sometimes, special provisions are made to insure that groups that make up a very small fraction of the population are included in the sample. Usually this is accomplished through stratification. The second concern in sampling is precision; that is, estimates of characteristics of the population based on sample results should have as small a margin of error as possible: furthermore, these estimates of error should be known. The two major reasons for using some form of probability sampling are that (1) it offers the best guarantee of obtaining representative samples, and (2) it is possible to obtain estimates of the precision of a sample's statistics. We know, for example, that in well-conducted polls by the Gallup or Harris organizations, voter preferences in the sample are likely to be within 2 percent of the population values. In studies of educational effects, it is similarly possible to obtain estimates of the precision of sample statistics.

The precision with which characteristics of a population can be estimated from sample data depends largely on the size of the sample. The larger the sample, the more precise the estimates of population characteristics. (The limiting case occurs when the sample is 100% of the population. Sample statistics in that case have zero error, being population values.) The important point to note is that of the three major types of samples—chunk, judgment, and probability—only probability sampling offers a way to determine the precision of statistics based on information obtained from a sample. Probability sampling, correctly done, also furnishes the best assurance that the sample selected for study will be representative of the population, i.e., free from bias.

Sampling is widely used in research. Often it is necessary to obtain information about some large population when exhaustive testing of each and every member of the population would be prohibitive. In evaluation studies, the situation is often quite different. A course, program, or curriculum has been developed for a particular group in a certain institutional setting. A new social studies program, for example, may be introduced at the sixth grade in a school district. Selecting a sample for study would be a questionable undertaking for several reasons. First, all the learners in the program are likely to be available, so sampling is unnecessary. Second, sampling would create administrative problems. E.g., if a sample were selected, what would the remaining learners do while data were being gathered? Furthermore, how would the learners feel about selective testing? Administratively, it is easier to treat all learners uniformly. Thus, sampling, in the traditional sense, is not only often unnecessary but is likely to be a source of problems for the institution.

If sampling in evaluation studies is not used in the traditional way, how is it used? There are two answers. First, a group of learners currently enrolled in an educational program in a particular setting may be regarded as a sample from the population of all learners, current and future, who are to undergo a program. Thus, the present group is used to help make decisions about the program for future cohorts. Sampling *per se* is not carried out; the current group of learners is taken to be representative of the population of all learners to be served and, consequently, is used as a basis for inference. This is reasonable as long as there is no substantial change in learners from year to year.

The second way in which sampling is used in evaluation studies has been suggested previously. Now is the time to discuss it in detail. The collection of all information required in an evaluation study could place enormous burdens on learners, teachers, and administrators. It is not unusual to develop a series of data-gathering instruments and procedures which, if fully answered by every learner, would require five to ten hours of response time. Since time is a commodity usually in short supply, expectations of 100% response to every question, item, task, or problem are unrealistic. Accordingly, some sampling scheme must be undertaken. The term for the scheme that is increasingly used is *multiple matrix sampling.** While originally formulated as an efficient way of developing norms for tests, its use in evaluation studies was recognized early, and

---

*Various terms have been used to describe this development—e.g., item sampling, item-examinee sampling, and matrix sampling. Since the only test in the area uses the term *multiple matrix sampling* (Shoemaker 1973), and since it seems to be most apt, this term will be used.

considerable developmental work and research have been directed towards its use in evaluation studies. The case for the use of multiple matrix sampling in evaluation studies has been well stated by K. Sirotnik (1974):

> ... If an evaluator wants to examine the effects of an instructional program, there is no reason why every student in the program must answer every item related to the outcomes of the program. In fact, obtaining data from every examinee on every item is often a waste. To make decisions about programs one needs data on the programs. If a population of examinees is exposed to an instructional program and a population of items is developed to assess the effects of that program, then the evaluator needs to know how well the population of examinees does on the population of items. The individual student is important to himself, to his teacher, to his parents and even to the evaluator, but he is not, in this case, the object of the evaluation—the program is.

There are several important notions embodied in Sirotnik's statement. First, it is not only unnecessary but unwise to have every learner answer every item. Second, in evaluation work, the program is the object of attention. Third, two kinds of sampling can occur in a data-gathering enterprise: sampling of items and sampling of learners. This dual sampling can be represented as shown in Figure 10.1.

Box A in Figure 10.1 represents an item-learner population. If every learner in the population answered every item in the population of items, the cells of the matrix would be filled with the responses. For example, if the item population consisted of questions that were scored as correct (1) and incorrect (0), the matrix would be filled with 1s and 0s. Inspection of the matrix would allow one to determine quickly how every learner performed on every item. As noted earlier, such a scheme is highly impractical. In evaluation studies, the situation presented in matrix C is the more likely case. Here, all learners are administered a sample of items to answer. The size of the item sample is usually developed on the basis of the time alloted for testing. That is, the time available for testing is determined first and enough testing material to fill that time block is generated. Unfortunately, the item sample so developed is often a chunk sample. Whether the item sample is representative of the population of items which could be developed to cover the domain represented by the objectives is, alas, not usually considered.

The situation represented in Box B is a theoretical one. A sample of examinees is administered a population of items. This rarely occurs because (1) few investigators have ever developed a population of items and (2) it is typically not possible to administer a population of items to even a single examinee. The reason for this is that a population of items would, by definition, be composed of all possible items measuring an educational outcome. Except for a few extremely limited outcomes—the

FIGURE 10.1

Sampling Schemes for Items and Examinees

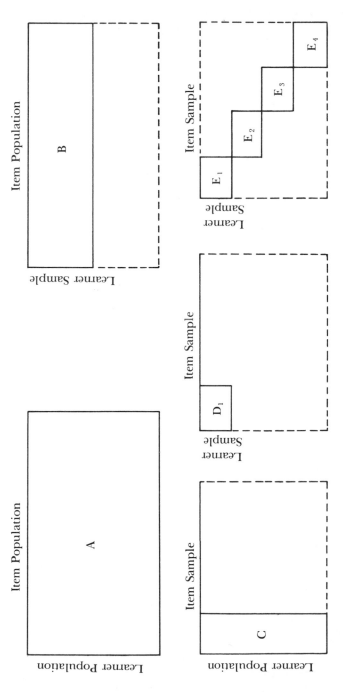

Note: (A = matrix population, B = examinee sample, C = item sample, D = matrix sample, E = multiple matrix sample).
Source: Adapted from K. Sirotnik and R.J. Wellington, "Scrambling Content in Achievement Testing: An Application of Multiple Matrix Sampling in Experimental Design," *Journal of Educational Measurement,* II, no. 3, pp. 179–88.

100 basic addition facts would be an example—one usually does not develop a population of items. The notion of a population of test items for even narrowly defined educational goals is almost always a theoretical idea; it is rarely a practicable alternative.

The sampling notions represented in the D and E boxes are especially important for educational evaluation studies. Box E is one example of a multiple matrix sampling scheme. A matrix sample is a representation of the responses of a group of learners to a set of items. In the example given (Figure 10.2), seven items were administered to ten students and responses were scored as right (1) or wrong (0). The matrix thus contains a total of seventy responses. The procedure is not dependent on item type. One could use essay questions—graded on a continuous scale ranging from 0, say, to 100—as well as attitudinal items in which learners indicate their degree of endorsement of statements—from "strongly agree" to "strongly disagree." The use of items scored right or wrong is only a simple example of a matrix sample.

FIGURE 10.2

Example of a Matrix Sample

Learner Sample

		1	2	3	4	5	6	7
	1	1	1	1	0	1	1	0
	2	1	1	0	1	1	1	1
	3	1	1	1	1	0	0	0
	4	0	1	0	0	1	0	1
Item Sample	5	0	0	1	1	1	1	1
	6	0	1	1	0	1	0	1
	7	1	1	1	1	0	1	0
	8	0	0	0	1	0	1	0
	9	1	0	0	0	0	0	1
	10	0	0	0	1	1	0	1

Source: Adapted from K. Sirotnik, "Matrix Sampling for the Practicioner." In *Evaluation in Education: Current Applications,* edited by W.J. Popham. Berkeley: McCutchan Publishing, 1974.

In matrix sampling procedure, a sample from a pool of items is administered to a subset of learners. While it would be possible to obtain a score for each examinee, this is rarely done, the reason being that the sample of items answered is usually too small to yield a reliable score for an individual. Also, the sample of items taken by a learner is an inadequate sample of the total pool of items and, further, it is of no special interest for evaluation purposes to know how each learner responds. The program is the object of concern.

The notion of matrix sampling has been considerably extended in the E Boxes. In this case, a pool of items has been divided into four sets and each set is administered to a different sample of examinees. One obvious advantage of this scheme is that no learner responds to more than 25 percent of the items for the total pool. This represents a considerable savings in testing time, an often critical consideration. A somewhat less obvious feature of the multiple matrix sampling scheme is that it is a rather straightforward matter to estimate the performance for the total group on the basis of the matrix samples.* That is, the information that would be obtained by the testing scheme represented in Box A can be closely approximated by the sampling scheme set forth in Box E. What is less apparent is that estimates of a population (Box A) based on multiple matrix sampling (Box E) will be more precise (less variable) than those based on learner sampling (Box B). Yet that is the case: the standard errors obtained with multiple matrix sampling will be less than those obtained with learner sampling.

While the representation of multiple matrix sampling set forth in Figure 10.1 may look complicated, the procedures involved in carrying out such a scheme are straightforward and easily executed. Consider a simple example. An evaluation worker wishes to obtain information on 100 test questions, dealing with mathematical problem-solving and proficiency, from 400 learners enrolled in an innovative fifth-grade mathematics program. Time does not permit each learner to respond to 100 items. Accordingly, the evaluation worker randomly divides them into five piles of 20 each. Each pile is organized into a test booklet and assigned a letter A through E. Eighty copies of each booklet are reproduced. An equal number of booklets of each form are given to each classroom teacher who shuffles them and passes them out at random for learners to answer.

The double randomization—random assignment of items to booklets, and random assignment of booklets to learners—serves to insure that the results are unbiased. Each learner answers one-fifth of the total pool of items—an 80 percent saving in testing time. The resulting information can be easily assembled in the form represented in Box E in Figure 10.1, the chief difference being that there will be five matrix samples instead of four. Furthermore, if both initial and final levels of proficiency are to be

---

*Detailed procedures, including formulae and computer programs, for estimation of characteristics for the total group are supplied by Shoemaker (1973).

assessed, it is a simple matter to see that the particular form a learner receives at the end of the program is *different* from the one he is given at the beginning. Thus, the likelihood of specific reactive effects of instruments is minimized, if not eliminated.

There are a number of technical considerations in developing a set of procedures for multiple matrix sampling in a specific situation. These are discussed in considerable detail by D. Shoemaker (1973) and Sirotnik (1974). Two important questions that need to be dealt with are (1) how many subtests should be assembled from a total pool of items, and (2) how should items be allocated to subtests. In the example given above, random assignment of items to booklets was used, but stratified random assignment could also be used. Stratification can be done in several ways. The difficulty of the items, the objectives being tested, or a combination of the two can be used to stratify. In deciding how many subtests to use, some of the considerations will be: (1) the size of the total pool of items; (2) the amount of time for testing; (3) the size of the learner group to be tested; (4) the expected distribution of scores; and (5) the judged importance of certain items. In the case of the last variable, it may be that certain items in the pool are judged so important that it is decided that the performance of *all* learners, and not just a sample, be obtained. In that case, the critical items would appear in all test booklets; thus, it will be necessary to cut down on the number of remaining items to be used if testing time is to remain constant. Given an item pool of a fixed size and a limited amount of time for testing, the only way this can be done is to increase the number of subtests or booklets. Technically, this procedure, referred to as sampling with replacement, introduces some complications into the multiple matrix sampling procedure which would need to be considered. It is mentioned to let the reader know that, while multiple matrix sampling is a highly efficient way of gathering information, it is not without problems. Nonetheless, it is a highly useful development and well worth considering in evaluation studies because of the economies it offers.

In addition to these benefits, there are other features to multiple matrix sampling which make it especially attractive for use in evaluation. First, research to date on multiple matrix sampling suggests that scrambling of cognitive test items in a multiple matrix sampling scheme has minimal or no effect on average learner test performance or on any of the statistical estimates obtained from analysis (Sirotnik and Wellington 1974). The implications of this finding are extremely important for evaluation work. Typically, a program, course, or curriculum will consist of a number of objectives, some rather diverse. While multiple matrix sampling was originally developed with a view for use with tests that were homogeneous with respect to what was being tested and the way in which it was tested, the findings of Sirotnik and Wellington and others suggest that the scheme is more robust and can be used with different content, item types, and other context factors. Thus, the evaluation specialist need not be excessively concerned that the test forms or booklets, administered to learners, may be highly varied with regard to what is being tested and the item types employed.

Another benefit of multiple matrix sampling that is not readily apparent is that it can be combined with traditional learner-appraisal procedures so that the twin goals of appraisal and evaluation can be served through the administration of a single instrument. In the International Educational Achievement Association's study of science achievement in 19 countries, for example, every high school senior tested received one of six booklets. The first 25 test questions were the same in all booklets and were used to obtain a score for each learner. The last five questions, which differed over the six test forms, were used to obtain an estimate of school performance on a number of additional science achievement objectives. Assignment of test forms was carried out at random within each classroom. Since twenty-five items were common to all forms, the random distribution had no effect whatsoever on the measurement of individual learners.

Another benefit of multiple matrix sampling has already been hinted at: it allows for the collection of a maximum amount of information in a minimum amount of testing time. In addition to this obvious economy, multiple matrix sampling makes it possible to gather information with respect to *every* objective being pursued by a course, program, or curriculum. It was noted earlier that obtaining learner performance information about every objective is important if major judgments and decisions are to be made. Multiple matrix sampling enables this important goal to be realized.

A last benefit is highly practical but not immediately obvious. One of the difficulties in conducting comparative studies in education is obtaining the cooperation of contrast groups. Time demands are made on the contrast groups, and there is no obvious benefit for cooperation. Administrative edicts may produce contrast groups when required, but securing cooperation does not follow. The use of multiple matrix sampling with contrast groups may not generate enthusiasm, but it can minimize the intrusiveness of the data-gathering effort by reducing the time demand to a level deemed tolerable by the members of the comparison group, notably the teachers. While "hit and run" data collection procedures are not generally recommended in any kind of educational study, consideration should be shown to the groups that are used for purposes of comparison. One way of doing so is by keeping the time demands of data-gathering down to the lowest possible level. Multiple matrix sampling meets this requirement admirably.

LIMITATIONS OF MULTIPLE MATRIX SAMPLING

While the benefits of multiple matrix sampling far outweigh its limitations, they do exist and should be noted. The most serious has already been mentioned in passing: multiple matrix sampling does not produce scores for individual learners; only estimates for groups are obtained. Individual learner appraisal must either be undertaken separately or (as described earlier) in *connection with* a multiple matrix sampling scheme. A second limitation is that there are no theoretical guidelines for determining the most efficient multiple matrix sampling design for a particular situation. There is, however, a growing body of evidence, based on empirical studies and simulation work, being used to establish working guidelines for an evaluation worker to follow (Sirotnik 1974). Nevertheless, the lack of a set of *theoretical* guides at the present time is regrettable.

Three other limitations are more specific in nature. First, multiple matrix sampling does not seem to be appropriate for speeded tests. A learner's responses are not independent of the context of the set of items he is answering, and estimates of group performance will not be valid when tests are speeded up. Second, multiple matrix sampling cannot be used with orally administered tests, unless learners are segregated by test forms. To do this would at minimum require that learners be randomly assigned to test form, segregated into different rooms, and an administrator would be needed in each room to carry out the testing procedure. Such an arrangement can pose serious logistical problems. (On the other hand, if the different forms consisted of written tests, there would be little problem in giving general directions to a class of learners and setting them to work, even though different learners answered different questions.) Finally, the testing of reading comprehension poses some interesting problems in multiple matrix sampling. Typically, a reading comprehension test is composed of a number of passages, each followed by questions. Random assignment of questions to test forms would be highly inefficient: it would probably result in one, or at most, two items, based on a particular passage, being included in the same test form. The learner would have to read an entire passage to answer one or two questions, a rather inefficient use of learner time. It can be overcome by using the passage and associated questions as the unit to be assigned to a form. Whether this produces a particular context effect, undermining the estimation procedures of multiple matrix sampling, is not known at present. The issue requires further study.

SPECIAL SAMPLING CONSIDERATIONS FOR EVALUATION STUDIES

The preceding presentation has tried to indicate how sampling activities in evaluation studies typically differ—often markedly—from sampling procedures used in conventional research studies. Since evaluation studies are normally undertaken to assess the worth of a particular program in a certain setting, the production of generalizable knowledge is often of no concern. Furthermore, since the group of learners enrolled in a program, course, or curriculum are generally available to participate in data-gathering activities, there is no reason not to include all of them. Certainly, it is better to have information about all members of a group than a part, no matter how carefully selected. There are also good practical reasons for testing every learner enrolled in a program. If some selection process is used, those chosen for testing may wonder why they have been chosen; those who haven't may wonder too. A uniform treatment is likely to arouse the least amount of questioning or resistance. Selective questioning could lead those chosen to put forth less than their best efforts. Also, selecting some learners for testing (rather than others) would require segregating them for the testing period: the administrative and logistical arrangements involved might be considerable. Consequently, it is better, for theoretical, methodological, and practical reasons, to test all learners enrolled in a program rather than draw a sample.

The testing of all learners currently enrolled in a course, program, or curriculum is highly desirable for evaluation purposes. The group, however, is not a population. It is a sample of all learners who *have* or *will be* exposed to the program. Thus, the testing of a cohort of learners one academic year is used as the basis for estimating the present effects of a program so that judgments and decisions with regard to the future operation of the program can be made. Any subdivision of the cohort enrolled in a single year is made to improve the efficiency of the data-gathering operation. Random distribution of testing forms to learners (as in the case of multiple matrix sampling) is not a sampling exercise but an assignment one. The clear intention is to test all available learners at any point in time.

If the sampling of learners is not a major consideration in evaluation studies, what is the major sampling consideration? The answer, usually only dimly realized, is the domain of learning outcomes. Virtually every data-gathering enterprise involves sampling. A ninth grade mathematics program, for example, may include among its objectives the ability to solve two simultaneous equations, involving two unknowns. Teachers or evaluation workers may construct a series of problems testing learner ability to solve for the two unknowns. A set of such problems would constitute an extremely small sample of all problems that could be formulated to test this proficiency. It should be clear that it is not possible to ask a learner every question that could be generated for even a single objective. The sole exception would be in connection with an extremely narrow and limited objective—such as the 100 basic addition factors or the names of the 50 state capitals. For most objectives, however, only a limited sample of items can be asked.

Yet the conception of a population of items or questions, testing a single objective or domain, exists: it is in fact one of the basic tenets of testing theory. Testing practice, however, does not generally follow testing theory. That is, we do not usually define a domain with clarity and precision, generate an exhaustive list of problems, tasks, or questions, testing competency in that domain, and then select a sample of these to administer to our learners. There are good practical reasons for not doing so. It would be a waste of time and effort to produce a wealth of testing material and use only a tiny fraction in an actual testing situation. Even in multiple matrix sampling, which allows for a broader sampling of each objective, the number of items that can be administered for each objective is extremely small compared with the number of items that can be produced.

It is in this respect that the notion of sampling must be carefully examined. The set of items administered to a learner in a testing situation is considered to be a sample from the population of items that could be asked. It is also considered to be a representative sample. Yet how is this sample of items determined? The answer is clear: it is a judgment sample. Test developers, working from a set of specifications, produce test items that—in their judgment or the judgment of specialists in the subject— measure the outcomes stated in a given objective or set of objectives. Sometimes a comparison of test items and test specifications is made to assess the content validity of the test material, sometimes not. Even when a systematic comparison is carried out, it is usually confined to determining whether the test items fall within the domain specified by the objectives and test specifications. Usually, little attention is devoted to the issue of the representativeness of the items.

The evaluation worker must be particularly sensitive about the relationship between items, questions, tasks, and problems used to obtain information regarding the attainment of educational objectives; and the objectives themselves. In earlier chapters, attention was given to the need for careful specification of objectives and to the importance of selecting appropriate evidence-gathering procedures. Here, the importance of sampling, or more accurately, the generation of testing exercises likely to produce a representative measure of learner performance in the domain specified by an objective, is stressed. Unfortunately, there is no well developed set of procedures to follow that will assure representativeness. Unlike the sampling of individuals from a population, the sampling, or production, of items from a domain remains largely a judgmental matter and open to considerable subjectivity. Cronbach (1971) has recently addressed a number of these issues and has proposed procedures for test validation which could lead to a number of improvements in test development. While many of Cronbach's proposals are rather technical and will involve extensive and intensive investigations, there is a heightened recognition of the importance of judgment in the process of test development. It will involve an explication of the types of judgments to be made at each step in the process; identification of the information needed to form such judgments; and the setting forth of principles for the making of such judgments.

Much work, of course, remains to be done. The evaluation worker may feel uncomfortable with the knowledge that the sampling or generation of items for assessing the attainment of objectives is a somewhat haphazard and unscientific affair and is likely to remain so for some time to come. Such discomfort will be a good thing if it results in greater attention paid to the development of test items and exercises for evaluation studies and to the development and application of procedures that will yield the best judgment of representativeness. Judgment sampling, as noted previously, may be very good or very bad. Steps to insure that it is good must be carefully and deliberately taken. This means that the production of item pools for objectives must be carried out with extreme care and constant checking must be the order of the day. Once a pool of items is developed for an objective, however, the same procedures used for random assignment of learners to forms can be used to assign items to forms in a multiple matrix sampling scheme.

Multiple matrix sampling was originally developed as an efficient way of norming tests of ability and achievement. Its obvious attractiveness in evaluation work was recognized fairly early, and a great deal of important work has already been done to establish its utility. While the notable accomplishments to date have been in the area of achievement testing, there are no conceptual reasons why the procedure cannot be extended to the assessment of affective outcomes of educational endeavors and the collection of background information. Attitude scales, opinion polling, and questionnaires of one form or another can be accommodated within the framework of multiple matrix sampling. In addition to the obvious economies and efficiencies, there may be sound theoretical and methodological reasons for doing so. For example, in the testing of affective outcomes, various biases are known to influence responses. By exposing individuals to only a fraction of the items normally responded to, and mixing them up with items measuring other outcomes, it may be possible to reduce considerably certain kinds of response bias frequently encountered in assessing affective states. Obviously, more research and development work needs to be done with multiple matrix sampling. Fortunately, interest in this relatively new development is running high, and the prospects for the needed work getting done appear good. In the meantime, multiple matrix sampling can be used in most cognitive areas where speed is not a major consideration. Of course, when individual appraisals are needed for grading, certification, and licensure, conventional testing procedures must be employed.

SUMMARY

This chapter introduces the reader to a number of concepts associated with sampling and relates them to evaluation work. The traditional notion of sampling, for the purpose of estimating population parameters, does not generally hold in evaluation work in the same way it does in research studies because of the extremely limited generalizability associated with evaluation studies. In addition, the limited scope of such studies often makes sampling of individuals not only unnecessary but, for practical reasons, undesirable.

The dimension of sampling that often does not receive adequate attention in educational studies deals with the sampling of items from domains of interest. (In educational studies these domains of interest are the objectives of the program, course, or curriculum under study.) The large role played in this area by judgment was stressed in this chapter.

Multiple matrix sampling is presented as an efficient, economic, and practical way of gathering learner response information in evaluation studies. Its advantages are stressed; its limitations noted. While originally developed as a means of developing test norms, multiple matrix sampling serves as a highly useful assignment vehicle for gathering a broad range of information in a minimum amount of time. Formulas for estimating program effects are readily available in standard works on the subject.

REFERENCES

Cronback, L. J. 1971. "Test Validation." In *Educational Measurement*, edited by R.L. Thorndike. Washington, D.C.: American Council on Education.

Kish, L. *Survey Sampling.* 1966. New York: Halstead Press (John Wiley).

Shoemaker, D. 1973. *Principles and Procedures of Multiple Matrix Sampling.* Cambridge, Mass.: Ballingor.

Sirotnik, K. 1974. "Matrix Sampling for the Practitioner." In *Evaluation in Education: Current Applications*, ed. by W. J. Popham. Berkeley: McCutchan Publishing.

Sirotnik, K. and Wellington, R. J. 1974. "Scrambling Content in Achievement Testing: An Application of Multiple Matrix Sampling in Experimental Design." *Journal of Educational Measurement.* Vol. 11, No. 3, pp. 179–88.

Slonim, M. 1966. *Sampling.* New York: Simon and Schuster.

11

ANALYZING AND INTERPRETING EVALUATIONAL INFORMATION

An evaluation study will involve the collection of a sizable body of information. The emphasis thus far in this book has been on the classes of information needed for a comprehensive evaluation of educational courses, programs, and curricula. Considerable attention was also given to the procedures for gathering such information. In this chapter, attention will be paid to the organization, summarization, analysis and interpretation of this information. While a number of excursions into statistical issues will be made, the central objective of data analysis must not get lost, namely, to obtain answers about questions of educational worth.

The material in this chapter focuses on the analysis and interpretation of information gathered in evaluation studies. A strong emphasis will be placed on the logic of analyzing and interpreting such information, relatively little attention will be given to statistics *per se*. There are so many textual treatments of statistical procedures available that it would be not only wasteful to repeat standard presentations but also a little distracting. (The reader who does require knowledge about standard statistical methods can find them in the references listed at the end of the chapter.)

The first step in the analysis and interpretation of evaluation information is the organization and summarization of data. In the conduct of a study, information about a large number of variables was gathered in each of five major classes. These will need to be organized and summarized, one variable at a time. Many of the variables are quantitative, or readily quantifiable. For example, age and sex of learners, scores on various tests and scales, cost information, ratings, opinions and reactions, and attitudinal responses can be readily classified into categories, organized into frequency distributions and, in some cases, averages and measures of variability can be computed. The nature of the scale of measurement underlying each variable will dictate the statistical operations to be used. For nominal scale variables, a count of the number of individuals in various categories can be sufficient; percentages in each category can then be easily determined. E.g., if learners have been categorized in terms of the type of study they are pursuing (academic, vocational, or general), simple counts and percentages in each category can readily be made.

Data on ordinal scale variables such as socioeconomic status can be organized in the same way. In addition, the median of such an ordered distribution can be computed along with the interquartile or semi-interquartile range as a measure of dispersion. For variable measured on an interval scale, the mean and standard deviation can be computed. It is generally wise, however, to obtain a frequency distribution for *every* quantitative variable included in an evaluation study as well as for every variable that can be quantified without undue difficulty. For example, learners may be judged according to whether they meet the highest, second, third, or lowest level of proficiency of some desired educational outcome. The number of learners in each category can readily be determined.

It is expected that all variables in the first two major classes of information—initial and later status of learners—can be quantified without undue difficulty. It may not be easy to quantify variables in these two categories, especially when the variables of interest are highly qualitative in nature; but research, experience, and a vast history of previous practice indicates that it can generally be done. Ratings of the quality of learner products such as essays, term projects, and oral presentations can be and are made routinely. Similarly, the quality of a process can be observed and rated.

The summarization of information about the way in which a course, program, or curriculum has been carried out will undoubtedly have to be handled differently from the summarization of learner-performance information. Much of the information about the execution of the program will probably come from observation and will be in the form of written descriptions. This will need to be summarized into short essays about the main features of the treatment as executed. Statements about the organization, relative frequency of various instructional procedures and the quality of execution of each, the kinds of learner assignments, rapport between teacher and learners, and other salient aspects of the learning experience will need to be covered. Since much information will be based on observational information that cannot be easily quantified, verbal summaries and analyses will need to be made. If descriptive scales have been employed, however, it is possible to summarize the information from them quantitatively. The summarization of such information is handled differently from the way in which learner-performance information is treated. In the latter case, the mean or median serves as a best summary of learner performance and the standard deviation or semi-interquartile range, as a description of learner variability. In the case of items from descriptive scales, the standard deviation or interquartile range provides important information bearing on the quality of the information obtained. If a high degree of agreement obtains among learners about the presence or absence of particular features about the program, e.g., the use of multiple texts vs. a single text, then one can have much more confidence in the obtained results than if there were not this agreement. On dichotomously scored items, for example, Pace has recommended two-thirds agreement as a rule of thumb for evaluating learner responses (1969). That is, unless two-thirds of the learners enrolled in a particular institution, curriculum, program, or course agree about the presence or absence of a particular feature, one would not report the result in the same way that other results are reported. If more than two-thirds agreement is found, then the modal response would be reported. Even if descriptive scales of the kind developed by Pace, Stern, and the International Educational Achievement Project are used, it is expected that observational information about the execution of the program will also be obtained. Both qualitative and quantitative information would need to be aggregated into a written summarization about program execution.

The presentation of cost information can also be treated discursively, although considerable financial information would necessarily be included. Tables, setting forth expenses by category, can be produced, and estimates of costs associated with alternative means of meeting a program's needs can be included. As noted earlier, estimates of basic and additional program costs, fixed and variable costs, as well as other kinds, can be presented. The goal, as in all presentations of information, is to provide as full a picture as possible about the treatment.

The presentation of data from the class of supplemental information can be handled rather straightforwardly. Information or opinions, views, reactions, and attitudes towards the program by various groups can be summarized and presented either in terms of measures of central tendency and variability or in percentage form, expressing the extent of endorsement or rejection. Obviously, the form of presentation will hinge to a large extent on the manner in which the data were gathered. If particular scales were used, then summary statistics would be appropriate; if single items about particular features of the program were asked, then percentage responses could be used, and results reported in the same way that opinion-poll results are presented in newspapers and magazines.

Information about learner performance, not covered in the stated objectives of the program, can be summarized and presented in several ways. The choice of procedure will depend largely on how questions and items were framed and asked. If items can be grouped into clusters that define a particular proficiency, then reporting them in this way would be suitable. Thus, if a mathematics program aspiring to develop learners' concepts and problem-solving abilities paid little attention to computational abilities and supplemental learner proficiency data were gathered in this area, it would be quite natural to report performance on each of the four major computational processes—for whole numbers, fractions, and decimals—if these were frequently taught in *other* programs at the same grade level.

Besides reporting information by item clusters, it may even be worthwhile reporting results for individual items. Some specialists, notably Cronbach, recommend doing so. The reason for presenting results for individual items is that it provides the reader with a fairly clear picture of how well learners are succeeding at various tasks. On the negative side, it is often hard to digest the mass of information generated by presentation of individual item results. There is no easy way to resolve the issue. Item results may furnish clues as to what proficiencies are being developed in an educational venture, but wholesale reporting of such results may be unproductive. They should be obtained and studied; reporting, however, should probably be selective. The chief beneficiaries of such information may be program personnel who may find it instructive for purposes of program improvement.

Information bearing on unintended program effects is apt to be the most limited section of any evaluation report. Reasons for this have been discussed earlier. Paramount are lack of any clear idea of what to look for; limited resources to spend on searching; and the fact that such effects may not become apparent until some later time. Few evaluation enterprises can afford to wait around to detect such effects. Thus, any section on side effects of educational programs is apt to be extremely restricted. Whatever can be done, nevertheless, should be.

PRESENTATION OF DESCRIPTIVE INFORMATION

The presentation of information about an educational program, course, or curriculum is a rather knotty problem. The aim is to give a reader not only the main results of an evaluation study but the full range of findings. A full disclosure policy is important for two reasons. First, if various consumers of evaluation reports disagree with the conclusions and judgments of the evaluation specialist, they should have available an information base which would permit them to draw a different set of conclusions. Second, a policy of full disclosure will minimize the likelihood of a loss of credibility in the work of the evaluation specialist. Educational evaluation is a field of specialization that is struggling to establish itself. Every evaluation worker should contribute to the establishment of the field by seeing to it that work is reported as fully and accurately as possible. Anything less is apt to raise doubts in the minds of other educators and the public.

While full and accurate reporting is critical in evaluation studies, complete reporting is not without its problems. The chief is to avoid burying the reader in a mass of results. Unfortunately, there is no easy solution to this problem. Judicious organization and presentation of results can help considerably, however. For example, while questions, items, and exercises may be administered in a haphazard fashion to learners, it makes good sense to report learner-performance information by *objective*. Further, information on a number of specific objectives coming under a general objective should be grouped and presented together. Such organization can greatly assist the reader in digesting a large body of results. In addition, if information bearing on initial and later performance of learners are combined and presented together, it will provide the reader with a more comprehensible picture of learner progress.

The manner of presentation of results is critical. Generally, graphical presentations are preferable over tabular. They are easily understood by those who constitute the audience for evaluation reports. Tabular presentations more properly belong in technical appendixes where the quantitatively minded reader can seek them out. Two major types of graphical presentations which can convey considerable information are bar graphs and line graphs. Examples of each (for the same set of results) are presented in Figure 11.1 and 11.2. The results were taken from a numbers test administered to learners, before and after a year of viewing Sesame Street (Bogatz and Ball 1971). The various subtests (eight) asked different kinds of questions. To present the results in a meaningful and comparable way, group means were transformed into percentage-correct scores. For each subtest, average initial and final performance levels are given.

In Figure 11.1, the clear section of each bar represents initial performance; the shaded portion, the increment from initial to end-of-year performance. The height of each bar represents the final level of achievement on each topic. In Figure 11.2 the same information is presented in a slightly different manner. Here, the solid line describes average beginning-of-year performance on each topic, while the broken line describes average end-of-year performance. The distance between the lines for each topic measures the gain. In both presentations, a single graph describes initial and final learner-performance for all specific objectives (as well as the general objective) for a major outcome of Sesame Street. Even a relatively unsophisticated reader would encounter little difficulty in reading and digesting the results in Figures 11.1 and 11.2.

The graphical presentations of these figures can be easily expanded to

FIGURE 11.1

Pretest and Gains on Number Subtests and Number Total Test for Sesame Street

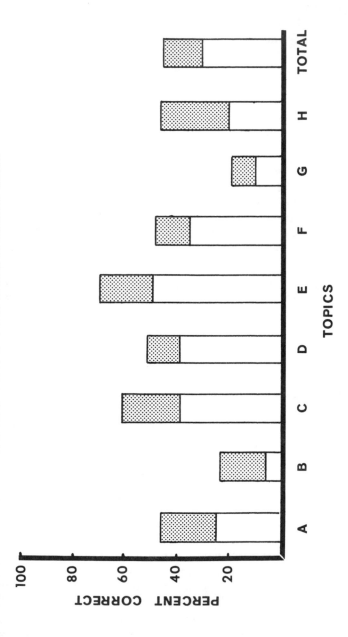

Source: Adapted from G. Bogatz and S. Ball. *The Second Year of Sesame Street: A Continuing Look,* vol. 2. Princeton: Educational Testing Service, 1971.

FIGURE 11.2

Pretest and Posttest Performance on Number Subtests and Number Total Test for Sesame Street

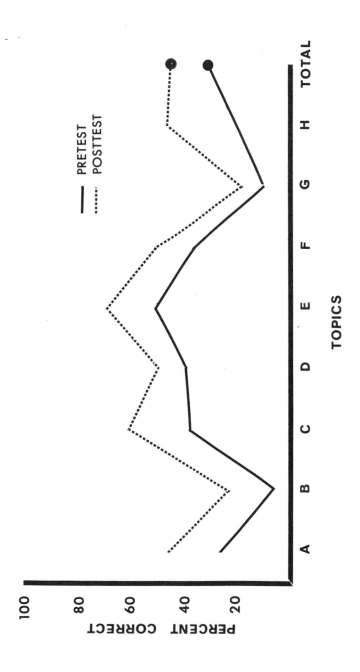

Source: Adapted from G. Bogatz and S. Ball. *The Second Year of Sesame Street: A Continuing Look*, vol. 2. Princeton: Educational Testing Service, 1971.

accommodate results for both a treated group and a comparison group. In the Sesame Street study, for example, there was a group that was encouraged to watch Sesame Street and a group that was not. The later served as a comparison group. Figures 11.1 and 11.2 presented results for the treated group only. Figure 11.3 presents results for both.

This graph is instructive for several reasons. First, the general closeness of the two groups, with regard to initial performance, on most objectives furnishes some assurance that the groups could be considered comparable at the outset. Second, the greater increment in performance for the encouraged group is suggestive of the effectiveness of Sesame Street in teaching number concepts (the actual evaluation of differences between groups will be treated later). Third, the failure of the encouraged group's performance to shoot up to near 100% after viewing the program is tempered somewhat by viewing the increment in the contrast group. In summary, the graphical presentation of results in the form shown in Figure 11.3 can serve to present a considerable amount of information. In this figure alone, initial performance, gain and final performance, for both an experimental and control group, on eight specific objectives and a general objective are displayed. Most readers would have little difficulty understanding such presentations.

A series of line graphs (see Figure 11.2) can communicate considerable amount of information in a fairly small amount of space. One procedure, used with considerable effectiveness, is to construct one graph for each objective. Each graph presents results for a general objective and all associated specific objectives. A summary graph is then developed which contains the results for the various general objectives of the program. It would represent the most compact summarization of learner-performance with regard to the attainment of the objectives of the program, course, or curriculum.

While graphs of the sort described above provide a wealth of information about what happened to learners in an educational treatment, they will need to be supplemented by other kinds of information. Similar kinds of graphs can and should be developed to summarize the views, reactions, and opinions of learners and others. Information about other kinds of learning, not specified in the objectives, may also be summarized in rather similar ways. Observational information about program execution, supplemented by summarizing expository statements, will also be needed—if correct interpretations of results are to be made. Finally, cost information will have to be reported, usually in tabular or expository form. There are two goals for all such reporting activities. The first is to describe what was found: such descriptions should be as clear and as cogent as possible. The second goal is to make the presentation of information as comprehensive as possible.

FIGURE 11.3

Pretest and Gains on Number Subtests and Number Total Test for Encourage and Not-encouraged Viewing Groups: Sesame Street

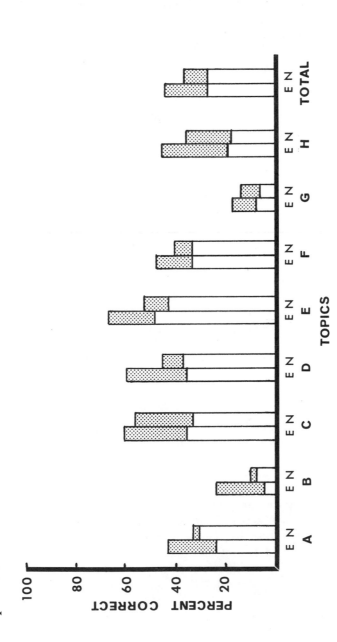

Source: Adapted from G. Bogatz and S. Ball. *The Second Year of Sesame Street: A Continuing Look,* vol. 2. Princeton: Educational Testing Service, 1971.

ANALYSIS AND INTERPRETATION

The focus in the previous section was on description. In this section, attention will be given to the analysis and interpretation of information produced in evaluation studies. This involves both statistical and judgmental considerations. To illustrate something of what is involved, the results for the total score on the Numbers Test in the study of encouraged versus not-encouraged children viewing Sesame Street will be analyzed and interpreted. Inspection of Figure 11.3 shows that the initial and final performance levels for the encouraged group were 27 and 42 percent, for the non-encouraged group, 27 and 35 percent. Since the initial performance levels were identical for both, no further attention need be given to the matter of whether the groups were equal to begin with.*

The first question to answer is whether the difference in final performance for the two groups could have occurred by chance or not. This question is answered by using a *statistical* procedure to test for the significance of the difference between the final performance levels for the two groups. Since the evaluation report provides (1) the mean performance for each group, (2) the number of individuals in the two groups (130 in the encouraged, 153 in the not-encouraged), and (3) enough information to estimate the standard deviation for each group, it is possible to test the significance of the difference between means for the two groups. The statistical procedure for doing this is the t test. Formulas for the t test are available in many statistical texts. In the present case, the use of the t test produced a t value of 4.35. Reference to a table of percentiles of the t distribution in a standard statistical textbook will quickly show that the chances of obtaining a t value of 4.35 purely by chance—with 283 participants—is less than one in 1,000. This is usually expressed by the representation $p < .001$, or by the statement in the text that the difference between the means is significant beyond the .001 level. Whatever the manner of expression, the meaning is the same: the difference between the means is too great to be attributed to chance alone at the chosen level of significance.

In comparative studies, it is important to know whether the performance differences between one group receiving a certain treatment and another receiving an alternate one can be ascribed to chance or not. This is not sufficient, however. It is necessary to go further and determine whether an obtained difference, once its statistical significance has been established, has practical educational importance. This is largely a

---

*Other information from the study provides convincing evidence that the groups were, in fact, comparable. Some of that evidence is based on background information about the individuals in the groups but, more important, is how children were assigned to a particular treatment.

judgmental matter, although statistical procedures can be used to assist one in reaching a judgment. In the present example, it is possible to estimate the strength of association between being in a particular group (encouraged or not-encouraged) and achieving a certain level of performance on the test. The statistical procedure for such an estimation is ω^2 (omega squared).* The computed value of ω^2 ranges from 0 to 1 and is interpreted as the proportion of variation in the performance scores that can be accounted for by group membership. For the above Sesame Street results, the appropriate formula for ω^2 is:

$$\omega^2 = \frac{t^2 - 1}{t^2 + N_1 + N_2 - 1}$$

> where: t^2 = the square of the computed t value (4.35 in the Sesame Street results)
>
> N_1 and N_2 = the size of the two groups involved 130 and 153 in the present case)

Substituting the values for t, N_1, and N_2 in the above formula yields a value of 0.06 for ω^2. This can be interpreted as meaning that 6 percent of the variation in the test scores can be attributed to the treatment effect, the remaining 93 percent to individual differences among learners. Thus, while there is a statistically significant difference between groups, the *strength* of the treatment effect is small.

As W. Hays notes (1963, pp. 328-29):

"... Statistical significance is not the only, or even the best evidence for a strong statistical association. A significant result implies that it is safe to say some association exists but the estimate of ω^2 tells how strong that association appears to be. It seems far more reasonable to decide to follow up a finding that is *both* significant *and* indicates a strong degree of association than to tie this course of action to significance level alone. ... In most experimental problems we want to find and refine relationships that 'pay off,' that actually increase our ability to predict behavior. When the results of an experiment suggest that the strength of an association is low, then perhaps the experimenter should ask himself whether this matter is worth pursuing after all, regardless of the statistical significance he may obtain by increased sample size or other refinements of the experiment.

The use of a measure of strength of association can help the evaluation worker judge the efficacy of treatment effects. There are,

---

*For extended discussions of strength of association measures, see W.L. Hays, *Statistics for Psychologists*, 2nd (New York: Holt, Rinehart and Winston, 1973) and E.A. Haggard, *Intraclass Correlation and the Analysis of Variance* (New York: Dryden Press, 1958).

however, two additional data analytic considerations in evaluation studies: one conceptual and the other statistical. The conceptual issue is well illustrated in the Sesame Street Numbers Test results. While the encouraged group outperformed the not-encouraged, neither group's performance is particularly noteworthy. Considering that the test questions were specially designed to measure the instructional effects of Sesame Street, the average performance level of the encouraged group is, at best, unimpressive. Presumably, the developers of the Numbers Tests had large expectations about learner performance when they developed their tests. The failure to achieve a high level of performance in the experimental group, no matter how much it exceeds the performance of a comparison group, is significant.

In evaluation studies one is particularly concerned about whether a treatment succeeds in achieving its objectives. If it fails to do so, the fact that it outperforms some alternative may not be important. While comparisons between one program and another may be useful, one must also attend to the level of performance achieved by learners exposed to a program being evaluated.* While there may not be a clearly defined level of performance to be achieved, it should be possible to make some kind of judgment about whether a program is succeeding in what it set out to accomplish. Such judgment is critical, and the evaluation worker, using what assistance he can get, will need to render such judgment. If previously set levels of performance have been specified, the task will be considerably easier. In most instances, however, this will not be the case. The necessity for making a judgment, nevertheless, remains. While comparisons with alternatives and measures of strength of association can be determined, there are only means to an end: the end is a judgment about the effectiveness of a program, course, or curriculum. Statistical analyses can and should inform one's judgment; they cannot replace it. In arriving at such a judgment, the level of achieved performance will be a crucial consideration. In the case of the Sesame Street results described above, the generally low level of achievement, relating to numbers, is certainly of greater importance than the performance differential between the experimental and comparison groups.

A second issue frequently faced in evaluation studies involves the number of comparisons to be made. Throughout this book, stress has been placed on gathering evidence about a large number of outcomes.

---

*One may also wish to extend one's analyses by examining the performance of various sub-groups of learners. For example, how does the program succeed with the most and least able learners; do learners of one sex respond differently to the program than members of the opposite sex? Such analyses are examples of attempts to examine trait-treatment interactions and may provide fruitful leads about how a program is working (D. Berliner and L. Cohen 1973; Cronbach and Snow 1977).

General and specific objectives; attitudes, views and reactions of learners, teachers, administrators and others associated with educational programs; all have been emphasized. Each element can involve a number of comparisons, especially if one follows Cronbach's recommendation and uses clusters of items and single items, as well as total scores, in analyses of evaluation data. One hazard in making a large number of comparisons is that some may turn out to be statistically significant simply through chance. For example, if one hundred comparisons are made between an innovative and a conventional program, some of the differences can achieve statistical significance through chance factors only. This hazard can be avoided by employing multivariate statistical procedures, which allow for a large number of comparisons but contain appropriate safeguards against false significance. In the Sesame Street evaluation study, the investigators employed multivariate analysis of variance and covariance to test their hypotheses of program effectiveness. These were appropriate procedures since dozens of comparisons were involved. It may be necessary to seek statistical counsel in analyzing data from evaluation studies, and it is almost certain that computers will need to be used, if multivariate procedures are employed, because of the complex calculations. a relatively modest investment in such services is strongly advised, and the earlier one can plan for such assistance the better. Ideally, plans for data analysis should precede data collection. If this admonition is followed, many problems associated with data analysis can be avoided.

Some comments about the interpretation of results of data analysis have already been made. Statistical significance, by itself, is not a major consideration. A measure of strength of association between treatment and performance is likely to be useful in judging the importance of results. Judgment, however, is necessary. Such judgment will involve a comparison between an achieved level of performance and an expectation of performance. Obviously, the clearer one's expectation is about how learners should be performing after a period of instruction, the easier it will be to adequacy of performance. There are, however, a few simple procedures that should facilitate the judgmental process. First, all evidence bearing on a single general objective should be brought together. A single table should generally be sufficient to accommodate means, standard deviations, number of items and/or percentage correct of all items, as well as t or F ratios and a measure of strength of association, for each specific objective for a single general objective. It is also useful to leave some room for comments. Table 11.1 contains an example of such a summarization for the Sesame Street Numbers Test results.

The table indicates that significant gains were made by the encouraged group in six of the eight subtests as well as on the Number Test total score. The ω^2 values are generally unimpressive, only two exceeding 0.05. Further, inspection of Figure 11.3 reveals that the encouraged group exceeded a 60 percent mastery level on only one subtest: counting strategies. The Number Test total score for the encouraged group represented a percentage mastery of only 42 percent; while significantly higher than that achieved by the not-encouraged group, it is hardly striking. One would reluctantly conclude that, despite statistically significant results, the program did not produce notable final levels of performance on the kinds of numerical proficiencies stressed in the program.*

This conclusion, while informed by the results of the analyses, is not a statistical statement but a judgmental one. Statistical analyses and interpretations can carry one only so far. Judgment must enter the scene at some point. In the above example, the critical judgments were based on gains in performance, final level of performance, F ratios, and the value of ω^2. Taken together, the relatively unimpressive final levels of achievement, the moderate gains, and the generally low strength of relationship between treatment and performance were the determiners of the judgment of an absence of strong program effects.

In the Sesame Street Numbers Test there was a total score which could be used to help make a judgment about the attainment of the general objective of number proficiency. This is not always the case. If evidence from several sources is obtained bearing on a general objective. it may not be possible to combine them into a total score. In that event, it will be necessary to proceed through the specific objectives and then arrive at an overall judgment about the extent to which the general objective has been attained. Such a judgment is made more difficult because of the increased inferential demands.

Judgments about the attainment of objectives are facilitated when a comparison group is available. As noted earlier in chapter 9, comparison groups are not always necessary. The absence of a comparison group does present some difficulties which, however, are not insurmountable. The bases for judgment would be limited to the increment in performance and the final level of performance that was achieved. To get some idea as to how this might be attained, the reader is referred to Table 11.1. Inspection of the pretest and gain results for the encouraged groups does provide information to serve as the basis for a judgment about the relatively low level of success in attaining the objectives relating to numerical proficiencies.

If a program, course, or curriculum has been initiated with a single group of learners, and neither a comparison group nor information about the initial status of learners are available, judgments about the attainment

---

*This conclusion may seem somewhat harsh, since the groups that were studied included three-, four- and five-year-olds. Inspection of results for each age group, however, indicates that none of the groups of encouraged learners achieved fifty percent on the Numbers Total.

of objectives are exceedingly difficult to make. Many researchers with an experimental orientation would argue that no valid conclusions can be drawn. In some cases this may be so. If, however, the treatment to be evaluated is so novel that the initial status of learners—and the likelihood that external events will influence learner performance—can virtually be ignored, then presumptive conclusions can be drawn on the basis of learner performance after a period of instruction. In such cases, judgments about the attainment of program objectives will contain a high degree of presumption. However, the alternative in the situation—no judgment at all—may not be acceptable if a decision must be made. Highly presumptive conclusions and judgments will be quite tentative and highly qualified, it may be that the best use for them is for formative evaluation. (Major decisions about continuation or abolition of a program should probably be postponed until more and/or better information is obtained.) Nevertheless, the need for some sort of judgment about how well a program is succeeding is necessary; if the evaluation worker fails to make it, chances are that someone else less informed will do so. In such situations Watson-Watt's adivce is still pertinent: "Give them the third best to go on. The best never comes and the second best comes too late."

TREATMENT OF OTHER INFORMATION

The preceding section, devoted to the analysis and interpretation of learner-performance information in terms of course, program, or curriculum objectives, covers the first two classes of information needed in the framework for evaluation recommended in this book. It is now necessary to describe procedures for the treatment of information in the remaining three classes: namely, execution of the program, costs, and supplemental information.

Information about the execution of a program will usually take one of three forms. The first is narrative material, collected on the basis of periodic visits to the program. The second ratings, is provided by external observers, usually members of an evaluation team. The third takes the form of program descriptions furnished by the learners. This is often obtained through the use of descriptive scales. Whatever form the information may take (one hopes that at least two will be gathered), the evaluation worker must (1) determine what actually occurred in the execution of the program, and (2) compare this with statements of intentions about what was supposed to happen during the course of the program. These are paramount tasks.

The procedures for determining what actually occurred will depend largely on the form of the information. For narrative material, it will be necessary to compare the reports of each visit and summarize this

TABLE 11.1

Evaluation of Sesame Street Numbers Test Results

Variables	Max. Poss. Score	Chance Score	Experimental Encouraged Group (N = 153)					
			Pretest			Gain		
			Mean	%	S.D.	Mean	%	S.D.
A. Recognizing Numbers	4	1.0	0.9	23	1.0	0.8	20	1.4
B. Naming Numbers	6	—	0.3	5	0.9	1.0	17	1.7
C. Enumeration	7	0.5	2.5	36	2.0	1.7	24	2.0
D. Conservation	7	2.3	2.5	36	1.5	0.9	13	2.0
E. Counting Strategies	8	—	3.8	48	2.5	1.4	18	2.8
F. Number/ Numerical Agreement	3	0.8	1.0	33	1.0	0.4	14	1.2
G. Addition & Subtraction	13	—	1.1	8	1.8	1.2	9	2.0
H. Counting	30	—	5.5	18	6.9	7.7	26	7.4
Numbers Total	54	5.4	14.6	27	8.3	8.0	15	8.7

information as succinctly as possible. Consistencies and inconsistencies in the execution of the program also will need to be noted. Obviously, such comparisons and summarization will be qualitative in nature. For information in the form of ratings, summarizations of each feature will need to be made. Averages will be useful in describing the general level of operation of the program, but standard deviations will be equally important; since they will allow one to determine how "on target" instruction was. The greater the standard deviation for a particular feature of a program over observations, the greater the variability in the execution of the program. If descriptive scales have been completed by the learners themselves, it will be necessary to obtain the extent of agreement among learners as well as the estimates of what actually occurred. Procedures for estimating the concurrence among learners have been proposed by Pace (1969). Once it has been established that the learners

Comparison Not Encouraged (N = 130)								
Pretest			Gain					
Mean	%	S.D.	Mean	%	S.D.	F†	ω²	Comment
1.2	30	1.1	0.1	3	1.3	11.5*	0.036	Significant but not important
0.5	8	1.3	0.2	73	1.3	18.6*	0.058	Significant but not important
2.3	33	2.0	1.5	21	2.3	3.3	0.009	Non-significant
2.6	37	1.5	0.5	7	2.0	2.4	0.004	Non-significant
3.4	43	2.4	0.8	10	2.9	12.9*	0.041	Significant but not important
1.0	33	0.9	0.2	7	1.2	4.8*	0.013	Significant but not important
0.9	7	1.5	0.9	7	2.0	4.4*	0.012	Significant but not important
5.2	17	7.0	5.7	19	7.7	6.8*	0.020	Significant but not important
14.5	27	7.6	4.4	8	7.6	18.9*	0.060	Significant but not impressive

†These are univariate F ratios for analysis of covariance, using pretest scores on Sesame Street tests, Peabody Picture Vocabulary test, and socioeconomic status as covariates.

*Probability: $p < .05$.

Source: Adapted from G. Bogatz and S. Ball, *The Second Year of Sesame Street: A Continuing Evaluation*, Vol. 2. Princeton, N.J.: Educational Testing Service, 1971, Tables 16 and 27.

essentially agree about what occurred, one can compute avaerages or proportions describing features of the program as executed.

Whatever the form or treatment, the outcome is a characterization of the program in operation. This then will need to be compared to statements about what was supposed to occur. This, again, is largely a judgmental matter and will probably require some assistance from those in daily contact with the program. For example, if a science program calls for considerable laboratory experience and the available evidence indicates that little was provided, it would be important to check out this result with the teachers and find out, if possible, why it did not occur. The object of this is to be able to characterize what actually happened, compare it with what was expected to occur and—should discrepancies be found—determine reasons why the program was not executed as intended. In carrying out this phase of the work, the evaluation worker will find himself functioning more like a private detective than a laboratory scientist, with even the most rigorously gathered quantitative data serving as little more than clues.

The treatment of information relating to program costs, dealt with at length in chapter 7, need not be repeated here. Some summarization of costs will undoubtedly be needed. One would hope that a one or two tables would be sufficient to present this information, along with a few pages of narrative material, describing and interpreting results.

The analysis and interpretation of supplemental information will also depend largely on the form of the data. Information in the form of responses to interview questions, testimonials, and reports of discussions will have to be dealt with qualitatively and summarized in narrative form. In contrast, information gathered from attitude and opinion measures can be analyzed and interpreted in much the same way as learner-performance information. Similarly, information about supplemental learnings—i.e., competencies not included in a program's stated objectives but considered enough a part of the program domain as to be worthy of inquiry—can be treated like other learner-performance information, even to the point of using the same form of graphic presentation illustrated in Figure 11.1. One must, however, take care to report the results of such analyses in separate graphs, separate, that is, from those based on learner-performance in terms of the stated objectives. Combining these data—of at this stage of the evaluation—is clearly a disservice to the program and will likely be perceived as unfair by program personnel. In all other respects, the treatment of supplemental information can parallel the treatment of other kinds of information.

It is difficult to specify or even suggest how to treat information, bearing on the side effects of programs. The reason for this is that is is not possible to anticipate the kind of information about side effects that will be obtained. Likely, much of the information about side effects will come in the way of comments, observations, or casual reports. If that is the case, then the most one can do—after some attempt to verify this information has been made—is to prepare a written summary. If, *quantitative* data are available, conventional statistical procedures can be used.

SUMMARY

Evaluation studies produce a wealth of information. This chapter has suggested strategies for the analysis and interpretation of such information. Stress was placed on the treatment of data in terms of five major classes of information in the framework for evaluation used throughout this book. For ease and meaningfulness of analysis, however, the first two classes of information—initial and later performance of learners in terms of a program's objectives—have been combined. The use of statistical procedures was discussed. Distinctions between statistical significance and educational importance were made, and the importance of having results meet both criteria has been emphasized. Finally, the crucial role of judgment in interpreting results in evaluation studies was stressed.

The analysis and interpretation of qualitative information was examined and the need to verify results by checking with program personnel noted. Whether information bears on the execution of the program or on supplemental information—such as opinions and reactions of persons associated with the program—the procedures to be used, it was noted, were similar: narrative summarizations need to be prepared, then compared to program intentions, and judgments made about the adequacy of various aspects of the program.

REFERENCES

Berliner, D. and Cahen, L. 1973. "Trait-treatment Interaction and Learning." *Review of Research in Education*, vol. 1, edited by F. Kerlinger. Itascoe, Ill.: Peacock.

Bogatz, G. and Ball, S. 1971. *The Second Year of Sesame Street: A Continuing Look*, vol. 2. Princeton: Educational Testing Service.

Cronbach, L. and Snow, R. 1977. *Aptitudes and Instructional Methods*. New York: Irvington Publishers.

Haggard, E. 1958. *Intraclass Correlation and the Analysis of Variance*. New York: Dryden Press.

Pace, C.R. 1969. *College and University Environment Scales*. Princeton: Educational Testing Service.

ADDITIONAL READINGS

Glass, G. and Stanley, J. 1970. *Statistical Methods in Education and Psychology*. Englewood Cliffs, N.J.: Prentice-Hall.

Guilford, J. and Fruchter, B. 1973. *Fundamental Statistics in Psychology and Education*. 5th ed. New York: McGraw-Hill.

Hays, W. 1973. *Statistics for Psychologists*. 2nd ed. New York: Holt, Rinehart and Winston.

Tatsuoka, M. and Tiedeman, D. 1963. "Statistics as an Aspect of Scientific Method." In *Handbook of Research on Teaching*, edited by N. Gage. Chicago: Rand McNally.

Walker, D. 1976. *The IEA Six Subject Survey: An Empirical Study of Education in Twenty-One Countries*. New York: Halstead Press (John Wiley).

Walker, H. and Lev, J. 1953. *Statistical Inference*. New York: Holt and Co.

Wolf, R. 1974. "Data Analysis and Reporting Considerations in Evaluation." *Educational Evaluation: Current Applications*, edited by W.J. Popham. Berkeley: McCutchan.

12

EVALUATION AND DECISION MAKING

INTRODUCTION

In the early part of this book a distinction was drawn between judgments about the worth of an educational course, program, or curriculum and judgments about future action. In this chapter both kinds of judgments will be treated. Specific questions to be addressed include: How does one make judgments about the overall worth of an educational treatment? What are the specific considerations that enter into making such judgments? How does one weight different kinds of information in making judgments of worth? What is the evaluation worker's responsibility with regards to judgments about future action? These and other related questions take the evaluation workers into areas in which they may not feel comfortable, especially if their training and background has been in more technical areas such as measurement or statistics. Having come so far in the evaluation process, however, it is necessary to take these last steps and formulate the required judgments. Otherwise, the time and effort expended in the design and conduct of an evaluation study will have been largely wasted.

The evaluation worker may be somewhat reluctant to make the kinds of judgments described above. There are two reasons for this. First, the kinds of judgments to be made will normally go somewhat beyond the evidence that has been gathered. Evaluation workers reared in a methodologically rigorous training environment may view the issuance of the judgments of the worth of educational programs as a violation of the norms of their essentially conservative training. Having been taught not to go beyond the data, they are now being encouraged to do so. While research training is often valuable for evaluation work, the rather different nature of educational evaluation requires that judgments be made. If the evaluation worker won't make them, then someone else will. It is necessary that the evaluation worker contribute judgments lest they be lost.

A second reason for reluctance to make judgments about the worth of educational programs is that others may reject them. This is a real possibility. While evaluation workers will typically feel comfortable in defending a finding that one group statistically outperformed another on a particular measure, the defense of a judgment about the overall worth of a program is much more difficult. This is because there is no agreed upon way at arriving at such judgments. Different individuals, examining the same body of evidence, can come to somewhat different conclusions. Rather than risk rejection of one's judgments, the evaluation worker may avoid making them. Again, the possible educational loss of not making such judgments would seem to be far greater than the risk that a particular set of judgments may be challenged.

It is interesting to note that evaluation workers whose background and training have been in curriculum and administration do not suffer from the same reluctance to make educational judgments. On the contrary, there is often a rush to judgment on the part of such workers. Such judgments are often made in spite of the evidence that has been gathered. What seems to happen in such cases is that evaluation workers often hold such strong views about what an educational enterprise should be like and how it should function that these override the evidence. This is indeed lamentable. Conclusions and judgments should not be contradicted by one's evidence.

The task for the evaluation worker is to draw conclusions and judgments about the worth of educational undertakings as carefully and as reasonably as possible. A major basis for doing this should be the kinds of evidence that have been systematically gathered and analyzed. This is not sufficient, however. The larger educational and social goals to be served by particular programs will also need to be considered. A specific course, program, or even curriculum will have been initiated to meet some perceived educational or social need. It will be necessary to determine how well the enterprise meets the need. Determining attainment of program objectives is important as part of this process, but a judgment of the importance of the objectives, in terms of a larger set of purposes, is needed for a comprehensive evaluation.

Since the evaluation worker will be going beyond the bounds of the kinds of conclusions that are drawn in conventional research studies, it is important that the judgments be clearly separated from the rest of the material in an evaluation report. There are two reasons for this. First, it is important to label the judgments being made in order to distinguish them from the more objective evidence. Second, if readers choose to reject such judgments, this can be done without jeopardizing the body of evidence on which they have been based. A delightful example of how this can be done is furnished by Beeby in his classic evaluation of junior high schools in New Zealand (1938, pp. 204-5). The following note appears in Beeby's book just before his recommendations.

It has become the practice for certain writers of detective fiction to interpose, just before the denouement, a page such as this, on which they state, "The reader now has all the facts necessary for the solution of the mystery, which he can, if he wishes, work out for himself. But, if for any reason he does not desire to do this, he can read on." Whilst harboring no illusions that the resemblance between this report and a "thriller" extends beyond the complexity of the plot and the multiplicity of the clues, I wish to adopt the same procedure.

At the risk of repeating what was said in the Introduction I must draw a sharp distinction between what has preceded and what is to follow. Up to this point I have confined myself as far as possible to objective facts. Admittedly, these facts are not objective in quite the sense that the detective novelist's heavy blunt instrument is objective. They are selected facts. Worse still, they are interspersed with my own personal judgments. Such judgments were necessary, sometimes because the facts themselves would have been meaningless to the reader without analysis, and sometimes because the complete segregation of fact and opinion would have meant an unjustifiable waste of time and space. If complete objectivity is denied to the facts, at least it will not be denied that up to now no constructive solution has been offered of the problems raised. Such judgments as have been made have not reflected any preconceived philosophy of intermediate education, but have been the naive reactions of an enquiring mind to the facts as they arose.

The reader now has almost all the facts that I have, the facts contained in Parts One to Four and in the Appendices. I have, perhaps, the advantage of having absorbed during three months in the schools a myriad to tabulate. Part Five contains my own solution, product of the objective facts and my philosophy of education. The reader may follow me if he wishes, or may construct a solution for himself from the same facts and his own philosophy. The main conclusions of Parts One to Four would, I believe, have been arrived at by almost any unbiased investigator, and have a value and an authority of their own that mere clash of opinions cannot affect. Every conclusion in Part Five is preceded by an implicit "I think that. . ."

Unfortunately, few evaluation workers possess Beeby's gift of language. Nevertheless, some statement that one is about to leave the relatively safe area of findings for the rather dangerous waters of judgments, conclusions, and recommendations is needed to alert the reader.

PROCEDURES IN JUDGING THE WORTH OF EDUCATIONAL PROGRAMS

Performance in Terms of Objectives

How does one go about making the critical judgments about the worth of an educational enterprise? The question appears simple yet it is extraordinarily complex. In fact, there are no clear or definitive answers. One begins with the findings and low-level judgments in each of the five major classes of information emphasized throughout this book and discussed in some detail in the preceding chapter. This serves as the raw material from which comprehensive evaluative judgments will be fashioned. The initial questions to be addressed involve the extent to which the program succeeded in attaining its stated objectives. This involves a review of the judgments about the general objectives of the program, as well as a synthesis of these judgments into an overall statement of attainment of objectives. Such a synthesis can be achieved in several ways. There is a sizable literature on the weighting of part scores (performance on objectives, in the case of evaluation studies) to obtain composite scores. Unfortunately, this literature is of little help, since most of the empirical procedures involve the use of an external criterion or, if judgmental procedures are used, every individual has been administered a full battery of instruments. Neither condition is likely to be met in an evaluation study. Thus, the evaluation worker is forced to rely on judgmental procedures.

At the simplest level, one can employ equal weights to the percentage success for each general objective, if such information is available, to compute a grand average. More than likely, however, the judgments with regard to the general objectives will not be in numerical form the Numbers Test total score in the Sesame Street study is an exception). The evaluation worker will thus be forced to employ a judgmental procedure. Discussion with program personnel throughout the study should furnish some indication of the relative weights being accorded various program objectives. Such information will be useful in deciding how much weight to accord each objective. While numerical weights would be highly desirable for aggregating information, they are not likely to exist. Also, attempts to obtain them from program personnel are likely to meet with resistance. Such resistance is due to the fact that program personnel are probably not clear as to what the weights should be. The inclusion of a particular statement in a list of objectives signifies that it has a non-zero weight. Program personnel are usually in no position to say more than that.

Program Execution

Once an overall judgment about the effectiveness of a course, program, or curriculum in attaining its stated objectives has been made, it needs to be interpreted. If an enterprise has not succeeded in achieving its objectives, the question which must be immediately raised is whether the intended enterprise was, in fact, carried out. This will involve an examination of the information about program execution. Obviously, if the program was not carried out as intended, or did not actually get underway until close to the time when later status measures were given, one cannot make any judgment about the efficacy of the treatment. It remains, at best, an untested commodity. If the program had been carried out reasonably faithfully, then the failure to achieve the objectives is a matter of considerable concern. In most instances, however, things will not be so clear cut. On an overall basis, few programs will either be a howling success or an outright failure. Moderate degrees of success or failure are more likely. Some objectives will be carried out rather well, others will be achieved with modest success, while still others are apt to show somewhat disappointing results.

While an overall judgment might indicate that the program was only moderately successful in reaching its goals, an analysis by general objectives may reveal that there is a relationship between program execution and learner performance. That is, learner performance is higher on those aspects of a program which were carried out as intended and lower on those which were not. Such direct relationships, if found, would go a long way toward accounting for learner-performance results. In some cases things may work out this way. In other cases they may not. For example, instruction may not have been carried out as intended, but learner performance may be high because so much instructional time was devoted to achieving particular objectives. This is sometimes the case in mathematics education where educationally questionable procedures may be used to get learners to master the multiplication tables—but enormous amounts of time are devoted to the task. In other cases, instruction may have been carried out as intended but learner-performance is low, because of the difficulty and/or complexity of the objectives. This frequently occurs in areas where the objectives stress higher mental processes or other complex performances (Bloom and Rakow 1969).

The kinds of patterns described above are not exhaustive. Rather, they illustrate only a very few of the possible patterns which could be found in a single course, program, or curriculum. The evaluation worker will have to examine the information resulting from his own study, develop hypotheses as to why things are as they are, and attempt to check them out (this activity will necessarily be somewhat informal so it seems best not to dignify it by labeling it as hypothesis-testing). The major classes of information which will enter into such analysis are initial and later performance of learners in terms of the objectives and execution of the treatment. The goal of this phase of the evaluation is to account for why the program did or did not succeed as a whole or in part.

Supplemental Information

Once this phase has been completed, the evaluation worker will need to proceed to consideration of the supplemental information. The first type of information within this class that should be considered is the supplemental learning information. It should be considered somewhat in conjunction with learner-performance information in terms of the stated objectives. The evaluation worker should try to determine if some kinds of supplemental learnings have been achieved to a fairly high degree of proficiency and others have not. This will then have to be related to the stated objectives, as well as to the program as executed and explanations sought. Certainly, it is noteworthy if a program that does not set out to accomplish certain objectives succeeds in doing so. Also, if a program eschews certain traditional objectives—say computational proficiency in an elementary-school mathematics program—and it is found that students are not equipped to compute, this too should be noted. Comparative information on the performance of learners undergoing *different* treatments would be highly useful in making judgments about program effectiveness in a larger educational context, one going beyond the formal program objectives. Such judgments will be part of the comprehensive evaluation of the course, program, or curriculum under study.

After an examination of the supplemental learning information, consideration should be given to affective outcomes. Opinions, views, and reactions of learners, teachers, administrators and others associated with the program, need to be considered. In viewing such information, major attention should be given to extreme results. That is, strong views or reactions, in favor or against the program, should be noted particularly. For example, if parents agree and feel strongly that a particular course is harmful, this is important to note, whatever effects it may be having on learner performance. Similarly, if teachers harbor hostile feelings toward a particular curriculum, this too is significant. (The converse is also true: considerable enthusiasm may exist for a program whose effects may be rather weak.)

In many cases there are no strong reactions for or against a particular program. This, in fact, may be the typical finding of an examination of affective outcomes. While some critics of education have reported a sense of joylessness in American education, the absence of strong positive affect should not be taken as necessarily indicating a deficiency in a course, program, or curriculum. If the enterprise is characterized by hard work on the part of both learners and teachers, it would seem unreasonable to expect participants to go around chortling about it. As long as they are not gnashing their teeth in fury, one can be reasonably satisfied. A lack of enthusiasm may not be laudatory; it need not be damning. If reactions are extreme, however, they may be of considerable import.

The last kind of information within this class to review will involve unintended effects. Here, the evaluation worker may have little to go on. Information in this area is hard to obtain, since no one has a clear idea of what to look for. One hopes that observations of the program in action; conversations with persons associated with the program; or, even better, follow-up information may furnish clues about unintended effects a course, program, or curriculum may be having. Such effects may be beneficial or harmful. While one would hope to detect them early, it is possible that they will not begin to emerge until the program is well underway. An inability to detect such effects in a program just launched need not be considered a deficiency of evaluation. What is important is that an effort is made to identify and record such effects.

After gathering the three kinds of evidence in the class of supplemental information, the evaluation worker should review the judgment of a program effectiveness, in terms of the stated objectives, with a view to formulating a revised judgment about the program. This revised judgment goes beyond effectiveness *per se* by explicitly taking into account supplemental learning (or lack of it), opinions and reactions of various parties, and whatever side effects may have been noted. This is not to say that the initial judgment is simply abandoned. Such a course would be imprudent. What needs to be done is to examine the evidence in the class of supplemental information to see whether there is any reason to cause one to modify the original judgments about the program and its effects. Even if initial judgments are not modified substantially, they may be qualified in ways which could prove valuable to program personnel administrators or others, associated with the program. For example, a program may be generally succeeding in its stated objectives but not be particularly well received by parents. Such information, incorporated into a judgment about the worth of the program, may be very useful for program improvement.

Costs

After completing this phase of the analysis, the matter of costs comes next. The estimation procedures recommended in chapter 7 should produce a wealth of information bearing on program costs. If the program has been compared to one or more alternatives in terms of costs, the evaluation worker will be in a reasonably strong position to make judgments about its worth.

In reviewing cost information, it is necessary to address the question of how well the program succeeded, given its expense. As noted in chapter 7, this judgment cannot be made in a vacuum. One has to have some notion, albeit crude, of the costs of alternative ways of meeting the educational need the program was intended to address. This may involve considerable guesswork if firm estimates are not available; it could, in fact, be virtually prohibitive to obtain. Note though, that in facing this larger set of issues, the evaluation worker is going beyond the stated objectives of course, program, or curriculum and is judging the program in terms of how well it fulfills a larger educational need. This judgment of worth is apt to take the evaluation worker into unfamiliar, and possibly uncomfortable, new territory. Yet it is critical that evaluation workers move to this higher level if they are to be more than technocrats.

A critical question which evaluators must address is whether there are less costly ways of meeting the educational need than the course, program, or curriculum under study. Such a judgment cannot be made hastily and will need to be highly qualified. After all, evaluation workers will have far less to go on about a decision alternative than they have about the program being evaluated; perforce, any judgments about alternative courses of action will need to be highly tentative. They should probably be regarded more as hypotheses than as conclusions. While no one advocates that judgments about educational enterprises be so highly qualified as to end up saying nothing, it must be recognized that the information base on which judgments are formulated may be so limited that little definitive can be said. On the other hand, when the available information permits a strong judgment, then it should be made. In the 1960s, for example, there was considerable enthusiasm about the use of computers in the classroom. Only later did educators realize that the costs involved in using computers in the instructional process were too high and the payoff too little (compared to conventional instruction) to justify their continued use. Careful analysis could have developed such a conclusion far earlier, and the conclusion could have been made with a high degree of confidence. It is rarely, of course, this simple. While one would like to make strong judgments, it may not be possible, given the limited knowledge base on which one has to build. Tentativeness—more often than not—will be the hallmark of the evaluation worker's judgments.

EVALUATIVE JUDGMENTS

An additional note about evaluative judgments is in order at this point. While no one deliberately sets out to be tentative in one's judgments or to overqualify them, the available evidence may not allow anything else. Few educational enterprises are such spectacular successes or dismal failures that unequivocal judgments can be made about them. The typical finding in research studies or instructional treatments is "no significant difference between treatments" on the outcome measures studied. It is quite likely the same finding will obtain in evaluation studies that include comparison with an alternative. This may be discouraging to program developers and teachers with a stake in a particular treatment; it should not be troublesome to the evaluation worker. The latter's task is to determine how well a program is working. Where it is working well and at reasonable cost, no attention needs to be paid; it can be devoted to where it is failing. Possible reasons why a program is not succeeding can then be identified, checked out, and suggestions for improvement made. As modifications are put into effect and further evaluations made, it should be possible to gradually but continually so improve courses, programs and curricula that they eventually do succeed. The goal of evaluation work must be the improvement of education either by identifying programs which are so bad they must be immediately eliminated; recognizing outright successes that should be continued; or—more likely—through the incremental improvement of existing programs. Educational evaluation, if properly done, should result in programs that are doomed to succeed!

There is little room in education for the mentality of the media—where things are judged as hits or flops. Most educational enterprises can safely be expected to fall somewhere in between. The evaluation worker must resist the temptation to reach for the extreme judgment; available evidence will hardly ever warrant it. An evaluation study may show that learners in a new course do not perform significantly better than learners in an older one: they may, however, have better attitudes towards school and do better in attendance. Rather than conclude that the new course is no better (than the old), one should recognize its benefits and seek to strengthen it—so that it will be an improvement on the old one in other ways as well. Such a commitment requires continuous evaluation rather than the one-shot try that currently characterizes much evaluation. Unfortunately, while many writers advocate ongoing evaluation of the kind described here, there is corresponding little commitment to actually doing it.

In judging the overall worth of an educational program, it has been recommended that the larger educational need the program is intended to meet serve as the major criterion. Neither the stated objectives, the operational program, nor even learner performance represent fully adequate bases for judgment. In order to determine if a program is pursuing worthless goals, there needs to be some basis for judgment. The educational need that the program is intended to fulfill seems to offer the most suitable basis. Any other is apt to be arbitrary and, perhaps, even capricious. The educational philosophy of the evaluation worker (or anyone else), for example, would seem highly inappropriate—and unscientific—as a standard for judgment, although it appears to be used more often than one would care to admit, especially by individuals who feel strongly that they can judge the adequacy of educational endeavors even without evidence. Exposing programs to personal standards for judgment is extremely hazardous, since programs will be judged on subjective grounds rather than on their own merits. Thus, an evaluation worker, personally convinced that open education is the solution to most of education's ills, will judge such programs highly, regardless of how bad or good they might actually be. One surely wishes to avoid such extremes.

If personal standards are not acceptable as a basis for judgment, the stated goals of the institution in which a program is located are not much better. While there is a certain surface plausibility in judging educational endeavors in terms of institutional goals, there is often such a large gap between program objectives and broad institutional goals that it is impossible to do so. Institutional goals are usually stated at such a high level of abstraction that they are virtually useless as criteria for judgment. Furthermore, such goals are often so ambiguous that they are open to a variety of interpretations, many of them quite personal. Most schools, for example, espouse citizenship as one of their goals. Unfortunately, there are as many definitions of good citizenship as there are people to define it. A similar case can be made for most such statements of institutional goals. They are, characteristically, vague and ambiguous statements representing aspirations and, as such, seem intended more to evoke allegiance to an institution than to serve as guides for action. For reasons such as these they usually cannot be used as criteria for judgment of operational programs.

Educational needs, on the other hand, have a much more practical quality. The improvement of reading proficiency, the training of qualified welders, capable and cultivated nurses are examples of educational needs which can serve as reasonably clear, specific guides for judging the adequacy of programs, courses, and curricula. Furthermore, such judgments can be competently made by reasonably proficient education workers. Neither an advanced degree in educational philosophy nor completion of a sequence of courses in multivariate statistics is needed to make evaluative judgments of the kind advocated here although, one hopes, such accomplishments would enhance the ability to make reasonable decisions.

POLITICAL CONSIDERATIONS

While educational considerations have been the chief concern throughout this book, it does not follow that they are the exclusive concern. Political factors and considerations can and do intrude on the evaluation process, and any evaluation worker who ignores them does so at some peril. Sometimes, evaluation studies are undertaken for political reasons—e.g., when an administrator hopes to gather evidence which can be used to justify an existing program so as to ward off critics. This is perfectly normal. People undertake all kinds of actions for all kinds of reasons. An evaluation worker may never fully know why he has been engaged to evaluate a particular program. It is even possible that clients may not be fully aware of their reasons for requesting that a particular program be evaluated. Why a program, course, or curriculum has been singled out for evaluation is not particularly relevant. What is important is that the evaluation study be conducted as fairly as possible.

While there are tales of clients specifying in advance of a study what the conclusions should be, this is not of primary concern here. Political pressure, even dishonesty, exists in a lot of places. To expect educational evaluation to be immune from this is naive and foolish. Evaluation workers can and should expect to be subjected to various pressures which are political in nature. What they do about them is what matters.

There are a number of courses of action open to evaluation workers subjected to political pressures. These can range from quiet (or not so quiet) withdrawal from the study to caving in and going along. Neither of these practices is recommended. Only as evaluation workers persist and do an honest job can their work be efficacious. Quitting or giving in is not likely to produce the kinds of results that evaluation workers aspire to achieve. It will probably be necessary to have a number of conversations with persons associated with the enterprise being evaluated. Much of this is intended to obtain information that is needed for the evaluation. This was discussed many times in previous chapters. In addition, it will be useful for workers to get ideas about the particular concerns program personnel and administrators have. How much pressure is on them? What would the likely effect of unfavorable judgments be? Are they committed to meeting the educational need that the program is addressing, or are they committed to the program *per se*? These are some of the major questions that need answers. They are not often directly talked about, but useful information bearing on them can usually be picked up while discussing various aspects of the evaluation.

If it appears that program personnel have a considerable stake in seeing that the results of an evaluation are favorable (a not uncommon situation), then it is important that evaluation worker and program personnel develop ways together which will be constructive and effective in dealing with information that is critical to a program. Two steps that have typically proved helpful are (1) early reporting, and (2) oral reports. Early reporting involves the preparation and submission of reports at various times during the course of an evaluation study. In research studies it is common practice to prepare progress reports for funding agencies, reporting on the work to date. Such reports are also useful in evaluation studies, since they serve to alert administrators and program personnel about what is being done and what is being learned about the enterprise being studied. Such early warning serves two purposes. First, it reduces if not eliminates any element of surprise about the findings of the study which, presented at a later time without preparation, could lead to attempts to discredit or dismiss the study. Second, it affords program personnel time to consider the findings, conclusions, and even recommendations and to decide what to do about them. Thus, when a formal report is presented, administrators and program personnel are prepared to deal with any criticisms or weakness in the program and state what they plan to do about them. In contrast, if unprepared, they will, more likely than not, end up disputing the findings. The former action is constructive, the latter nonproductive.

The second step that can be taken to deal witn information that is apt to be critical of a program is to transmit it orally. There is a certain starkness and finality to information presented in written form which can produce resistance on the part of the recipient. Orally presented information, on the other hand, can be discussed, clarified, examined, and generally dealt with insuch a way that its impact can be softened considerably. Such softening is not intended to result in a dismissal of negative findings but, rather, in an increased likelihood of their being accepted and in an increased willingness to do something about them. Oral presentations and discussions with program personnel may be among the most important aspects of an evaluation study, since it is here that the initial imparting of results will often take place, and the climate and context within which this takes place will determine whether program personnel move ahead in a constructive manner or dig in their heels and resist. The importance of oral communication has only recently begun to receive the attention it deserves. That the merging field of policy research recognizes the need for such communication is made abundantly clear by Castleton and Poty (1974, pp. 10–11):

> The typical and traditional way research findings are communicated is through publication. Papers read at professional conferences, articles, books, and even stenciled reports are the most widely used modes of communication.
>
> Yet, policy researchers must expect some resistance to their conclusions, resistance on the part of the policy maker that is emotional (due to commitments to other policies), cognitive (due to lack of information and training), and self-interested (the recommended policies may serve some groups less well than the obsolete ones do). Formal means of communications, such as those listed above, are particularly ineffective in overcoming such resistance. Frequently repeated, face-to-face exchanges seem very necessary. Presocialization (preparing for the report) and follow-up (after it is handed in) are essential. The report itself often is not really necessary; it serves more to fulfill contractual obligations and to provide an opportunity for and legitimization of interaction with the policy makers than to communicate with them.

Put differently, policy researchers must be willing to invest a significant amount of their time and energy in communicating. They must learn how the world looks to the policy makers, how best the policy makers will absorb the new ideas, which means of documentation and presentation will be most successful, and in what sequences the findings should be offered. A policy researcher must be able to interact effectively with politicians, bureaucrats, housewives, and minority leaders. Direct contact with policy makers, with the questions they raise, is useful and necessary to policy researchers; it clarifies in their mind the constraints policy maker face and must live with and must be shown how to overcome. Frequently the policy researcher alone has the authority and knowledge to deal with the policy maker's questions.

While one may take issue with the last sentence, the general point is well taken. As evaluation workers begin to recognize the pressures and constraints that administrative and program personnel work under and take these into account, they will increase their effectiveness markedly. Unfortunately, evaluation workers have not usually been noted for their sensitivity and tact. Oral presentation and discussion with program personnel and administrators may go a long way toward resolving, or better yet dissolving, what have long been regarded as major communication problems.

This is not to say that political problems and considerations will not intrude on an evaluation study. Adequate recognition of such problems, however, and honest and sensitive efforts to deal with them—usually in an anticipatory way—can lead to a satisfactory resolution, without any sacrifice in the integrity of a professional evaluation study.

SUMMARY

This chapter addressed two critical issues: the first, how to formulate judgments about the worth of an educational endeavor; the second, how to handle political factors that can intrude on an evaluation study. While suggestions were made, no settled prescription was made with regard to either issue.

With regard to judging the worth of an educational program, the necessity to go beyond program objectives and actual attainments in evaluation was stressed. Some guides were examined. The many ambiguities found in them suggested the central importance of the educational need that a particular undertaking was designed to meet. It was argued that the larger educational need might provide the soundest basis for judgments of value. The contribution of supplemental information in making judgments was also considered.

A consideration of political factors was even more disappointing.

That political factors can and do intrude on evaluation studies is an accepted fact and should be recognized as such: this was the thrust of our argument. While recognition of a problem is an essential first step, the proposals for solving it are modest. It was thought that early reports and oral presentation could be of some help. Unfortunately, this area has not been exposed to adequate investigation. It is hoped that greater attention will be devoted to it in the future.

REFERENCES

Beeby, C. 1938. *The Intermediate Schools of New Zealand*. Wellington: New Zealand Council for Educational Research.

Bloom, B. and Rakow, E. 1969. "Higher Mental Processes." In *Encyclopedia of Educational Research*, Edited by R. Abel. 4th ed. London: Macmillan.

Bogatz, G. and Ball, S. 1971. *The Second Year of Sesame Street: A Continuing Look*, vol. 2. Princeton: Educational Testing Service.

Castleman, N. and Poty, P. 1974. *Center for Policy Research: The First Five Years, 1968-1973*. New York: Center for Policy Research.

ADDITIONAL READINGS

Brickell, H. 1976. "The Influence of External Politics on the Role and Methodology of Evaluation." *Evaluation Comment* 5, no. 2: 1-6.

Popham, W.J. 1975. *Educational Evaluation*. Englewood Clifss, N.J.: Prentice-Hall.

Wolf, R. 1974. "Data Analysis and Reporting Considerations in Evaluation." In *Educational Evaluation: Current Applications*, edited by W.J. Popham. Berkeley: McCutchan.

13

REPORTING THE
RESULTS OF
EVALUATION STUDIES

INTRODUCTION

The importance of continuous oral communication with program personnel was stressed in the last chapter. It will be stressed again in this. Such communication, however, is no substitute for written reports. Written reports are necessary for at least three reasons. First, it is necessary for an organization to have a formal record of an evaluation of a course, program, or curriculum. Changes in personnel in an organization can and do occur. An official written report furnishes a base for official continuity. Second, written reports are often necessary to justify funding, meet legal or legislative requirements and, in general, satisfy a number of formal organizational demands. Third, an official report often furnishes a basis for the legitimation of various decisions about policy and practice. While such decisions will be made by professional personnel, administrators and governing boards, the formal written report is very often seen as a necessary basis for such decision making. No evaluation worker should conduct a formal evaluation study and not prepare a written report of his activities, findings, conclusions, judgments and recommendations.

Since formal written reports are routinely required in evaluation studies, it is necessary to consider what kinds of reports are necessary, the forms of such reports, how they might be prepared and disseminated, as well as what features of reporting should be followed and what ones should be avoided.

TYPES OF REPORTS

There are two general types of evaluation reports: progress reports and a final report. Progress reports usually include a relatively short summary of activities engaged in during a particular time period, a preview of upcoming activities, a statement of problems encountered and/or resolved and, possibly, a brief statement of preliminary findings. They are generally intended to keep administrators and program personnel informed about the progress of evaluation work. Frequently, information presented in a progress report will necessitate or result in a meeting between evaluation workers and administrators, program personnel, or both. The purpose of such meetings is usually to plan and coordinate activities so that both the program and the evaluation can proceed on schedule or without difficulty.

Progress reports can sometimes be used as a vehicle for soliciting needed information. For example, considerable time and effort in the early stages of an evaluation study is directed at the identification of the general and specific objectives of a program, course, or curriculum; if these are not already conveniently summarized. An early progress report can report the objectives as specified by program personnel and request comments and reactions. Similarly, other progress reports can report preliminary results and solicit ideas about explanations for particular findings. The chief purpose of the progress report, however, is to keep all concerned informed about the progress of an evaluation.

The final report is a rather different document since, in addition to reporting the results of the study, it will contain conclusions, judgments of the worth of the program, and recommendations about future action. As such, a final report of an evaluation study is to a certain extent a political document. Failure to recognize this fundamental point is likely to lead to considerable difficulty. For example, if the evaluation worker concludes that a particular course or program contributes nothing to meeting an educational need and recommends immediate termination, it may result in either loss of jobs or reassignment for some people. It could result in the abolition of one or more administrative positions that were established to oversee the program. With potentially so much at stake, the evaluation worker will need to exercise considerable care in the preparation of a final report and especially in the dissemination of its findings, conclusions and recommendations. Any failure to make sure that both the written final report and its presentation are handled with extreme delicacy could lead to rejection of part or all of the report. Since so much is at stake, it is vital that the evaluation worker take a number of steps to insure that the results of the evaluation effort will, at the very least, be given a fair hearing.

The steps required to insure a fair hearing for an evaluation effort begin long before the preparation of the final report. Initial contacts with administrative and program personnel should be used to define what the evaluation worker will and will not be doing. Agreements and understandings need to be reached about the scope of the evaluation study.

Distinctions between findings, conclusions, judgments, and recommendations need to be made clear to all involved. If administrative and program personnel do not want written recommendations as part of the final report, then *this* needs to be made clear. Parts of the final report can be transmitted orally, if this is desired. The important point is that such understandings and agreements be arrived at in concert and the sooner the better.

After initial contacts, it will be necessary for the evaluation worker to stay in touch with administrative and program personnel. Progress reports will help achieve this purpose. Face-to-face meetings to review progress and discuss other issues in connection with the evaluation are also essential. Such meetings are necessary to build and maintain a sense of trust, insure the cooperation necessary for the conduct of the study and, perhaps most important of all, minimize or even eliminate any element of surprise. Meetings are also necessary to review the work of the study and secure agreement on certain important points. It is critical, for example, that administrative and program personnel agree about the objectives of the enterprise being evaluated. Much of the initial work of the evaluation specialist will be directed towards identifying and specifying program objectives. This will be done on the basis of documents and discussion with various people. At some point, it will be necessary to secure agreemtnt that a particular set of objectives does indeed represent the educational intentions of an enterprise. Such agreement is necessary before serious evidence-gathering efforts can commence. If such agreement is not formally obtained, the evaluation worker runs the risk of having his efforts rejected on the basis that the objectives set forth in the report were not the ones the program sought to attain. This occurrence, unfortunately, is not rare. In fact it happens with unsatisfactorily high frequency. If one wishes to discredit an evaluation study because the results are not palatable, the quickest and surest way to do so is to impugn the program objectives as stated. Once they are disposed of, all else can be fairly easily dismissed. The evaluation worker will need to insure that agreements are reached at each stage of an evaluation study, that they are formally recorded and that administrative and program personnel are continuously informed about the conduct and progress of the study.

If continuous contact is maintained with administrative and program personnel and they are apprised of the progress of the study, possible problems about a final report will be considerably reduced. They will not be eliminated, however. The evaluation worker will need to take particular care about the organization, presentation, and discussion of results of an evaluation study.

Unfortunately, there is no ideal form for evaluation reports. In fact, there is not even a single form which is likely to satisfy the several audiences that will be its consumers. There are at least five forms an evaluation report can take. Each is appropriate for a somewhat different audience and for a rather different purpose. This is not to say that one will give different and even conflicting reports to different groups. Rather, it is that different groups have different informational needs, and a single reporting form is not likely to be satisfactory for all groups.

The most general form for reporting, and certainly the shortest, is the executive summary. It is normally between four and ten pages. It is tersely written and presents the major findings, conclusions, and recommendations of the study. It contains a minimum of supporting data and only the sketchiest description of the design and conduct of the study. It is written in nontechnical language and is intended for administrators and governing board members. It may be written in outline form and includes only as much reasoning and evidence as is absolutely necessary for a busy, and presumably, impatient reader who can give only the briefest time to reviewing an evaluation. While educational evaluation workers would typically wish that others were as interested in what they are doing as they are, the readers for whom executive summaries are intended are apt to be interested only in the results, conclusions, and recommendations and not care hardly at all for procedures, designs and analysis. The preparation of an executive summary requires considerable discipline and restraint.

In contrast to the executive summary, a full evaluation report is a more leisurely document. A full evaluation report will be the major source of inromation for most readers about what the program was about, what it set out to accomplish, how it actually operated and with what results. There will also be a separate section on conclusions and recommendations for future action, if this has been agreed upon earlier.

While the full evaluation report will normally be the major document produced from an evaluation, it will differ from a formal research report in a number of ways. Some of these differences are worth noting. First, an evaluation report should be written as simply as possible. Technical terms should be avoided wherever possible. Sentence structure should be simple; the writing direct. Sections of the report should be tried out on naive readers as soon as they have been written for a check on comprehensibility. Second, an evaluation report should generally try to avoid tabular presentations and, instead, rely on graphical displays as much as possible. Many persons may be apprehensive about numbers (this includes teachers and administrators), and inclusion of tabular presentations may get in the way of their reading of the report. The results of tests of statistical significance, F and t ratios as well as x^2 for example, are likely not to be understood or misunderstood. They may just as well not be reported bur rather presented expositorily in the text of the report. Third, as mentioned previously, there should be a clear distinction made between the results of the study and conclusions, judgments and recommendations. The more these sections of a report can be separated, the greater the likelihood that readers will not try to challenge the former. The device used by Beeby, reported in chapter 12, is an excellent way of separating the two. It can even be argued that readers be invited to draw their own conclusions, judgments and recommenations—should they wish to do so. That is, the evaluation worker's judgments, conclusions and recommendations are not the only ones that are possible. In contrast, the results and findings are less subject to challenge. They should represent what any qualified evaluation worker would have found, assuming the work was carried out with reasonable care and precision.

A third form of report, often used in connection with other forms, is the technical appendix. A technical appendix usually consists of a number of tables and the detailed results of statistical analyses. It often contains discussions of various technical issues encountered in the conduct of the study and data analysis, along with a description and rationale for how they were resolved. Such technical material is apt to be of little interest to most readers of the other reports but is included as part of the formal record for archival purposes and possibly for later reanalyses by others. In general, however, technical appendixes supply the detailed information which underlies many of the procedures used in the conduct of the study and the analysis of the data. Examples of exemplary technical appendixes can be found in the Sesame Street Evaluations (Bogatz and Ball 1971), the Equality of Educational Opportunity Survey (Coleman et al. 1966), the between schools analyses of the Equality of Educational Opportunity Survey (Mayeske et al. 1971) and the International Educational Achievement Studies (Peaker 1975).

An evaluation worker preparing a report of a study is continually confronted with the problems of deciding what findings and results to include in a summary, what to include in a main report and what material to relegate to a technical appendix. While no hard and fast rules can be given, it seems that only those findings which are absolutely vital to judging the overall worth of the program should be presented in an executive summary; while results and findings which, if omitted, would result in a serious gap, should be included in a main report. Whenever possible, detailed findings and results of data analyses should be placed in a technical appendix. There are two reasons for this. First, the inclusion of detailed quantitative material—in either an executive summary or main report—is apt to interrupt the flow of the narrative of a report. Such interruptions should be kept to a minimum. Second, the people for whom the report is intended are apt to have a rather limited technical background. Inclusion of technical material in either an executive summary or the main report will detract from the evaluation worker's main goal of effective communication. The technical appendix, on the other hand, may consist entirely of tabular material and extensive technical footnotes and commentary. An introductory section should inform the reader of the nature of the material included, and a note to the effect that assistance may be needed in reading and understanding the material should be included.

A fourth reporting form for an evaluation study would be a document written for teachers and other program personnel. Such a document would contain a brief summary of the study; possibly an extract from the executive summary; and a somewhat detailed presentation of findings bearing on the execution of the program and learner performance, along with recommendations about ways in which the program might be altered. The object of such a report is to bring those findings and issues— that are of direct and immediate concern to teachers—to their attention. It can serve as a basis for discussion and planning for improvement of the educational enterprise, especially if the document is presented in a sensitive and responsible way. This would involve, at a minimum, an oral presentation of the report to teachers by the evaluation worker and an invitation to review and discuss its contents. Such a presentation and discussion poses many potential problems. If the evaluation worker adopts the posture of an expert who is grading the efforts of teachers, resistance and rejection are apt to be the most likely response to such a presentation. This is perhaps one reason why such presentations do not occur with much frequency. On the other hand, if evaluation workers present their findings and recommendations in a modest and tentative manner and not as revealed truth, if they invite teachers to focus on how the course, program, or curriculum under study could be strengthened, then such meetings can be highly constructive affairs which can contribute to improvements in the educational enterprise. They must be handled with extreme delicacy, however. It would seem that the manner in which information is presented can have a far greater effect on the outcome of such meetings than the nature of the information presented.

Teachers can and do admit weaknesses in courses, programs, and curricula. They are most apt to do in an environment which is nonthreatening. As long as the goal of such meetings is program improvement and it is made clear to all that judgments about professional competence and personal effectiveness are not at issue, then it is likely that teachers will approach and participate in such meetings in a constructive manner. It may also be judicious to arrange to have no administrators present so as to further reduce the likelihood of any feelings of threat. If the conditions described here are met, the evaluation worker may find that such meetings are one of the most professionally rewarding aspects of his work, since it offers the prospect of a very direct contribution to the improvement of an educational enterprise.

A fifth form of report is one that is addressed to a lay audience. Parents and the general community not only have a right to know what is going on but need such information, if they are to make intelligent judgments about the job schools are doing. Periodic reporting is necessary if the groups that are called on to support educational institutions are to intelligently discharge their responsibilities. Reporting the results of an evaluation study to a lay audience is an extremely delicate undertaking, one in which the evaluation worker will need to work closely with administrative and program personnel and, most likely, public information specialists in the institution. Typically, reports to lay audiences will be prepared by someone *other than* the evaluation worker. A school district, for example, may publish a regular newsletter for the community: the editor and writers for such a publication will undoubtedly be in the best position to determine the general level at which reportorial articles should be written. The role of the evaluation worker would generally be confined to supplying the information for such reports and reviewing drafts for accuracy. The executive summary and the full final report will probably provide sufficient information about the results for developing reports to lay audiences. It is expected that the evaluation worker will need to meet with those who will actually be writing the report for the lay audience—to explain some of the technical aspects of the report and to identify important results that will be of particular interest to the intended audience. After that, the evaluation worker's major responsibility is to check for the accuracy of statements in the final report, whether it be a single article, a series of articles, or a separate publication. If a public presentation to a lay audience is scheduled, it is highly desirable that the evaluation worker be present to answer questions of a technical nature and to clarify various points and issues that might be poorly understood or misinterpreted.

THE PRESENTATION OF EVALUATION REPORTS

Just as there are no fixed rules for the forms of reporting the results of evaluation studies, there are no strictures either about the manner or timing of the presentation of such reports. Nor can one say very much about how many different forms of reporting should be used. All of these matters will have to be determined in consultatin with persons who are knowledgeable about the local educational scene. In general, an executive summary, a full final report, and a technical appendix will be required. The executive summary might be an abstract of the final report, and the technical appendix may be only an extra section of the final report. Local conditions and the magnitude of the program being evaluated will be important determiners of the extent of formal reporting. An individualized spelling program, undertaken in only a few classrooms in a single school, will require less reporting than a comprehensive mathematics program, carried out at a number of grade levels in an entire school district.

Some of the problems of timing in the presentation of written reports can be reduced if written and oral progress reports have kept all who are concerned with a program reasonably well informed. In addition, it is wise to submit drafts of sections of various reports to members of the various audiences for which they are intended for their review. There are several purposes for doing this. First, it will minimize, if not eliminate, any element or surprise for the intended readers. This should reduce the likelihood of later resistance or, at least, anticipate it. Second, having various persons review drafts of sections of an evaluation report permits the evaluation worker to find out if what has been written is clear and comprehensible. If it is, fine; if it is not, then it will have to be rewritten and reviewed again. An evaluation report must communicate. If it fails to do so for any significant number of people, it must be redone. Of course, the evaluation worker will have to be alert to distinguish between legitimate objections and objections based on other grounds, often unstated. For example, if a section of an evaluation report contains results that are clearly unflattering, they may be challenged by administrators and program personnel on various grounds, even clarity and comprehensibility. It is the responsibility of the evaluation worker to assess comments about the various sections of an evaluation report and decide what to do about them. A third reason for having various people read sections of an evaluation report in draft form is that the accuracy of statements about a program, course, or curriculum can be checked. The evaluation worker is not infallible, and honest mistakes may have been made in describing or reporting on a particular enterprise. By having those with the largest stake in a program read drafts of an evaluation report, any inaccuracies or mistakes are almost certain to be detected. The evaluation worker should be grateful for such exposure and take immediate steps to correct anything that is wrong. This will save the evaluation worker from embarrassment when the final report is officially submitted and (more important) reduce the likelihood that it will be challenged or discredited on the basis of technicalities.

The circulation of sections of drafts of evaluation reports is a practice that is strongly recommended for reasons presented above. It is not without some danger. Some of these dangers have been suggested. An evaluation report is not merely an educational document; it more often than not has political consequences. Jobs and positions may be at stake; financial considerations are involved; careers can be affected. Circulation of drafts of sections of an evaluation report telegraphs what is coming and affords interested groups the opportunity to mobilize forces for or against the study. This is not unusual, and the larger the enterprise is—in terms of money and personnel—the greater the political cross-currents are likely to be. If the evaluation worker recognizes this at the outset, he is less likely to be surprised by the reactions his report produce. But beyond that, it offers the evaluation worker an opportunity to gauge the kinds of reactions that are likely to be encountered later and the strength of those reactions. If reactions are positive, there is no problem. The question of importance is how one deals with negative and even hostile reactions.

There are a number of steps an evaluation worker can take to forestall negative criticism. The first and obvious one is to make sure that every finding likely to be challenged is reported fully and accurately and supported by the evidence. Drawing from reactions to initial drafts, the evaluation worker may choose to add material that will anticipate and counter some of the likely criticisms. A second step would be to play down those findings which arouse the strongest reactions *if such findings are not central to the study*. This strategy requires tact and fine judgment: peripheral issues should be played down. For example, if the teachers in a program have not given much time or effort to explaining the goals of a program to parents and other teachers but have remained somewhat isolated, some resentment may have been developed towards the program. There would probably be little to gain by making much of this point in a written report. Rather, the information should be transmitted orally to those concerned and appropriate action taken, especially if the rest of the program seems to be doing reasonably well.

Findings that are likely to be controversial must be handled with great care but that does *not* mean that they should be suppressed. In some cases, they may be given considerable prominence, if they are central to the evaluation of the program. In other cases, they may be omitted from the written report, if they are only peripheral. (They would, of course, need to be reported orally.) The actual disposition of various findings depends on their centrality to the evaluation of the program and the nature and extent of the anticipated reaction. No one argues that unflattering results should be suppressed; that would be unethical. The evaluation worker does, however, have some latitude in deciding *how* various kinds of information will be reported. The important consideration is to obtain a fair and full hearing for the full report of the evaluation. If the reporting of one finding or group of findings threatens this overall goal, the evaluation worker will have to consider carefully the way in which such material should be presented. Inclusion in a written report may result in a stiffening of resistance on the part of program personnel and even administrators; the presentation of the same material in oral form may elicit a more accepting response and (one hopes) willingness to change adverse policies and practices.

The above discussion applies primarily to the findings and results of an evaluation study. Judgments, conclusions and recommendations constitute a different matter. Judgments and conclusions are, to some extent, personal statements about an educational enterprise; the same holds recommendations about future action. While it is expected that such divisions will be intimately related to the results of the evaluation study, they also go considerably beyond them and will probably contain a fair dose of the evaluation worker's own views of the larger educational context in which the particular enterprise takes place, the educational needs to be met, and the weight to be accorded to the various classes of information. In properly preparing the reader of the evaluation report, the evaluation worker will point out the personal nature of the various judgments, conclusions and recommendations. It is important that the evaluation worker inform policy makers, administrators and teachers in advance about those judgments, conclusions and recommendations that may come as a surprise. Informing people of what to expect in the way of judgments, conclusions, and recommendations does not mean that one is obliged to modify them on the basis of informal reaction. The evaluation worker may choose to ignore initial reactions to this part of the report if he or she chooses to do so. The sole obligation is to inform about what is to come. If the evaluation worker decides to remove any judgments, conclusions, or recommendations from the final written report and transmits them orally, instead this is strictly the decision of the evaluation worker. One may choose to do this for strategic or other reasons but is under less obligation to do so than in the case of findings or results because of the more objective nature of the former.

EVALUATION AND ACTION

The relationship between the results of an evaluation and the subsequent action taken is extremely complex and unfortunately still only dimly understood. A number of evaluation workers have had the experience of conducting a study of a particular course, program, or curriculum and producing a report only to see that the decisions made about the enterprise that was studied are nearly opposite to what they recommended. Such events are, to say the least, frustrating; at times demoralizing; and, in some cases, a cause for cynicism among evaluation workers. What should be the relationship between the outcomes of an evaluation study and educational decision making?

As previously suggested, no definitive answers can be given to this question. Certain points are worth noting, however. First, decisions about educational ventures are the prerogative of governing boards and administrators. In some cases this power may be shared with teachers and other program personnel but, if this is done, it is done so because of a decision by a governing board or administration. The evaluation worker— especially if he or she is an outsider—has no decision-making authority with regard to educational policy or practice. Even if the evaluation worker is an employee of the institution, the evaluator is apt to have little or no authority in the area of decision policy or practice. Further, until philosophers become kings, no one is likely to advocate that evaluation workers be granted such powers. While they have considerable knowledge about the programs they are called upon to evaluate, this does not mean that they are in the very best position to decide about the future course of educational programs.

There are several reasons why decisions about educational programs may be at variance with recommendations of evaluation workers. This raises a second point about the relationship between the outcomes of an evaluation study and decision making. An evaluative judgment about a particular educational enterprise involves a weighting, either implicit or explicit, of various kinds of information. In the framework emphasized throughout this book, five classes of information have been repeatedly stressed. Synthesizing this information into an overall judgment of the worth of and educational enterprise involves a weighting process. This is the evaluation worker's prerogative and responsibility. It is also true that other individuals, using the same information base, can arrive at different conclusions and judgments and, furthermore, do so legitimately and reasonably. By applying a different set of weights to the same body of information, different conclusions can be drawn. A good example is when policy makers and administrators decide to terminate a successful but highly costly program. No one can say that such a decision is right or wrong. It reflects a different weighting of the same set of information.

The fact that other people, namely, governing boards and administrators, apply different weights to the same information is no reflection on the integrity or competence of the evaluation worker. In fact, it is the responsibility of the evaluator to point out that such differential weighting is not only possible but legitimate. The preface to the section on conclusions and recommendations should indicate this clearly. Thus, if the decisions that are eventually made do not accord with those that the evaluation worker advocates, this does not reflect on the high professional level of the evaluation study. It may have been an excellent study. Simply, the values of the decision makers, as reflected in the weighting of various classes of information, do not accord with those of the evaluation worker. Since decision makers have the ultimate responsibility for the management of an institution, they must have the authority to decide what will be done. The evaluation worker fulfills his professional function by conducting a study as best as can be done with the given resources and seeing to it that all relevant information, including conclusions and recommendations, are transmitted to the appropriate decision makers and program personnel.

Another reason for a difference between the evaluation worker's conclusions and the eventual decision with regard to future action may arise from the fact that decision makers deal with a larger set of considerations than does the evaluation worker. While the evaluation worker may be concerned with whether a particular educational program is effective in meeting a certain educational need, the decision maker is generally concerned with a set of different needs. Given limited resources, the decision maker must decide which ones will receive highest priority. Should a high school, for example, hire more guidance counselors or remedial reading teachers? Should an additional position be used to provide enrichment for gifted students or assistance for disadvantaged ones? These are policy questions which the evaluation worker is not likely to have much to say about. The task of decision must be left to others.

On some occasions, when decisions about a course, program, or curriculum run counter to what was recommended by an evaluation worker, the reason may be because there were segments of the community that were so opposed to it that continuation would have caused more problems than it would have resolved. This has happened on occasion where sex education programs have been introduced into communities with highly conservative segments, or when textbooks that contained material considered to be particularly offensive were adopted for use (only to be removed later on). Such events have sometimes taken evaluation workers by surprise.

It is difficult to generate much sympathy for evaluation workers in these cases. The framework for evaluation emphasized in this book has stressed the importance of gathering a wide range of information, bearing on an educational program. This includes not only performance data but other kinds as well. If evaluation workers have failed to gather critical information bearing directly on a program, then it is perhaps fitting that their recommendations are rejected. The evaluation worker must insure that as comprehensive a comprehensive body of information as possible is obtained in connection with the evaluation of a specific program. Nothing less will do.

The above discussion has considered only a few of the reasons why conclusions and recommendations in evaluation studies may differ radically from decisions taken about the future course of educational programs. There are many more. The relationship between evaluation and decision making is exceedingly complex, and considerable research will be needed to understand its nature. Evaluation workers who have discharged their professional responsibility at the very highest level cannot expect that their conclusions and recommendations will be accepted and acted on without modification. That there are limits to what the evaluation worker can know and do is important to recognize. As one professional on the educational scene, the evaluation worker can contribute significantly to the educational enterprise. But it is also important to recognize that the evaluation worker can not know or do everything.

REFERENCES

Coleman, J., et al. 1966. *Equality of Educational Opportunity.* Washington: U.S. Government Printing Office.

Mayeske, G., et al. 1969. *A Study of Our Nation's Schools.* Washington: U.S. Government Printing Office.

Peaker, G. 1975. *An Empirical Study of Education in Twenty-One Countries: A Technical Report.* New York: Halstead Press (John Wiley).

Walker, D. 1976. *The Iea Six Subject Survey: An Empirical Study of Education in Twenty-One Countries.* New York: Halstead Press (John Wiley).

ADDITIONAL READINGS

Popham, W.J. 1975. *Educational Evaluation.* Englewood Cliffs, N.J.: Prentice-Hall.

Wolf, R. 1974. "Data Analysis and Reporting Considerations in Evaluation." On *Educational Evaluation: Current Applications,* edited by W.J. Popham. Berkeley: McCutchan.

INDEX

ABOUT THE AUTHOR

RICHARD M. WOLF is Professor of Psychology and Education at Teachers College, Columbia University in New York. Previously, he taught at the University of Southern California and the University of Chicago.

Dr. Wolf has published widely in the areas of evaluation and measurement. His previous books are *Achievement in America* (1977) and *Crucial Issues in Testing* (1974), the latter co-authored with Ralph W. Tyler. His articles have appeared in the *Journal of Educational Measurement, International Review of Education, Comparative Education Review, Psychology in the Schools* and *World Book Encyclopedia*. In 1975, he was a Fulbright Lecturer in New Zealand.

Dr. Wolf holds a B.A. degree from Antioch College, and Ed. M. from the University of Buffalo and a Ph.D. from the University of Chicago.

RELATED TITLES
Published by
Praeger Special Studies

*COST-BENEFIT ANALYSIS: New and Expanded Edition

E.J. Mishan

NEW METHODS IN SOCIAL SCIENCE RESEARCH: Policy Sciences
and Futures Research

T. Harrell Allen

*SOCIAL AUDITING: Evaluating the Impact of Corporate Programs

David H. Blake
William C. Frederick
Mildred S. Myers

*Also available in paperback.